HEART OF A DOG ■ ALE[...]

Adapted from a 1925 story by M[...]ll Bulgakov which remained unpublished in the USSR until 1986, *Heart of a Dog* tells of a 'scientific' experiment to turn a dog into a man. An allegory questioning Lenin and foreseeing Stalin, this dramatisation by director-playwright Chervinsky caused a sensation in Moscow in 1987. Its British premiere was staged at Essex University in 1988.

STARS IN THE MORNING SKY ■ ALEXANDER GALIN

Based on a true-life 'purge' of Moscow's prostitutes during the 1980 Olympic Games, *Stars in the Morning Sky* was first seen in Britain in 1988 in its original production by the Maly Theatre, Leningrad. 'Galin uses the brutal detail of these women's lives to smash complacent assumptions about the condition of Soviet society.' (*Guardian*)

A MAN WITH CONNECTIONS ■ ALEXANDER GELMAN

Dealing with a marital and professional crisis in the life of a construction-site supervisor, '*A Man with Connections* is rather like a cross between Arthur Miller and Alan Ayckbourn.' (*Guardian*) Still running at the Moscow Art Theatre, the play was first staged in Britain at the Traverse Theatre Edinburgh in 1988 and then in London at the Royal Court in early 1989.

FORGET HEROSTRATUS! ■ GRIGORY GORIN

Written and staged in the pre-Glasnost era, *Forget Herostratus!* shows Gorin disguising a political message in a classical allegory – in this case the burning of the Temple of Diana and the trial of its perpetrator – provoking comparisons with Hitler, the Reichstag fire and the then prevailing Soviet judiciary system. It was first performed in Britain on Radio 3 in November 1986.

THREE GIRLS IN BLUE ■ LUDMILA PETRUSHEVSKAYA

Often compared with both Chekhov and Gogol, Petrushevskaya, the USSR's leading woman playwright, is known for the humanity and truth to life of her characters. *Three Girls in Blue* follows the realistically confused doings of its three women protagonists and is full of insight into their apparently inconsequential lives. The British premiere was on Radio 3 in April 1988.

In the same series

STARS IN THE MORNING SKY

■ FIVE NEW PLAYS FROM THE SOVIET UNION

HEART OF A DOG ■ ALEXANDER CHERVINSKY
Translated by MICHAEL GLENNY

STARS IN THE MORNING SKY ■ ALEXANDER GALIN
Translated by MICHAEL GLENNY and CATHY PORTER

A MAN WITH CONNECTIONS ■ ALEXANDER GELMAN
Translated by STEPHEN MULRINE

FORGET HEROSTRATUS! ■ GRIGORY GORIN
Translated by MICHAEL GLENNY

THREE GIRLS IN BLUE ■ LUDMILA PETRUSHEVSKAYA
Translated by LIANE AUKIN and MICHAEL GLENNY

INTRODUCED BY ■ MICHAEL GLENNY

NICK HERN BOOKS
■ A Division of Walker Books Limited

A Nick Hern Book

Stars in the Morning Sky first published in 1989 as an original
paperback by Nick Hern Books, a division of Walker Books
Limited, 87 Vauxhall Walk, London SE11 5HJ

Heart of a Dog © 1989 by VAAP
Copyright in this translation © 1989 by Michael Glenny

Stars in the Morning Sky © 1989 by VAAP
Copyright in this translation © 1989 by Michael Glenny and
Cathy Porter

A Man with Connections © 1989 by VAAP
Copyright in this translation © 1989 by Stephen Mulrine

Forget Herostratus! © 1989 by VAAP
Copyright in this translation © 1989 by Michael Glenny

Three Girls in Blue © 1989 by VAAP
Copyright in this translation © 1989 by Liane Aukin and Michael
Glenny

Introduction copyright © 1989 by Michael Glenny
Set in ITC New Baskerville by Book Ens, Saffron Walden, Essex
and printed by Billings of Worcester

British Library Cataloguing in Publication Data
Stars in the morning sky: new Soviet play
   1. Drama in Russian, 1945–   . Anthologies. English
   texts
   891.72′44′08

   ISBN 1-85459-020-0

Contents

Introduction

In the little more than seventy years of its existence, the Soviet
Union has had a bumpy ride on history's switchback. Erupting in
1917, during the bloodiest conflict in recorded time, the Russian
revolution that was meant to create a radically new kind of state
was immediately followed by four years of civil war and famine.
Having barely recovered, Soviet society was again shaken to its
foundations by Stalin's twin coercive drives to collectivise the
countryside and industrialise the towns, which also demanded
their human sacrifice of several million lives. No sooner had that
wave of death and upheaval subsided than another, in the form of
Stalin's purges (begun in 1936, waning and then waxing in ferocity
until the dictator's death in 1953), reduced the Soviet population
by at least a further 14 million lives – to say nothing of the
officially admitted 12 million Soviet casualties in World War II, a
figure now thought to be a serious underestimate.

In between, there have been periods – comparatively brief –
when the socio-political upheavals of Soviet life have 'levelled out'
in calmer spells of relative liberalism and an absence of harsh
pressure from above. Such were the period of the 1920s, the
'Khrushchev Thaw' of the decade from 1955 to 1964, and the
present era, beginning in 1985, characterised by Gorbachov's even
more ideologically relaxed policy of *glasnost'*, which means
'freedom of speech', or more broadly 'openness'.

When the heavy hands of the censor and the ideologue have
been lifted from Russian culture, it has been like the release of
oxygen from an iron cylinder. These times of relief, when Soviet
society has breathed more freely, have always been marked by an
upsurge in literary and artistic creativity – and nowhere more so
than in the theatre. At the time of writing (1988) we are witnessing
the greatest outburst of untrammelled expression in dramatic
literature and originality in stage productions since the 1920s. The
present collection of five recent Soviet plays – all of which have
had an airing, however brief, on Western stages and airwaves – is
a first glimpse of the sudden, exhilarating renaissance of a great
tradition of writing for the theatre, which had clearly never died
but had survived the bad times in silence.

The somewhat grim note struck in the opening paragraph is intended as a reminder that Soviet authors and their audiences have not had a lot to laugh about over recent decades. To this must be added the influence of a strong tradition, stemming from the very origins of Russian dramatic literature in the 18th century, which has treated the stage more as a forum than a place of merely frivolous entertainment, and which – while catching and holding audiences with the devices of intrigue, irony, ridicule, suspense, even melodrama – has a fundamentally moral, didactic purpose.

What is more, all the authors in this collection have lived through the years when the officially promulgated – and *enforced* – Soviet literary doctrine was the set of guidelines known as 'Socialist Realism', which demanded an ultimately up-beat treatment of what the Communist Party regarded as proper issues. Every play had to culminate in the inevitable triumph of the 'positive hero', who personified the Party's social ideal, and whose single-minded earnestness was barely allowed the relief of a smile, let alone a joke, unless it were a shaft of heavy ridicule aimed at the villains, who symbolised whatever 'evils' were the target of the Party's current propaganda campaign. Most of the present crop of plays represent their authors' ways of throwing off this kind of ideological straitjacket.

The 'realism' element has tended to persist in the work of many of today's Soviet playwrights, but it is now an authentic realism rather than mere scenic naturalism. In the play by Petrushevskaya, for instance, there is more than a whiff of the lavatory, let alone the kitchen sink; but in a Soviet context these genuinely down-to-earth preoccupations are, paradoxically, like a gust of fresh air. In most other significant respects, too, these plays briskly overturn that now discredited doctrine of 'Socialist Realism' and stand it on its head. Propaganda is out; conventional 'heroes' have gone; moral ambiguity now rules; and the result is infinitely more realistic and true to real-life experience than the phony situations and inauthentic, schematised characterisation which made past Soviet plays into little more than contrived, politically-slanted lantern-lectures.

Until recently, Soviet playwrights were under orders to present audiences with a picture of their society which could be summed up as: 'Wholesome bread-and-butter today, and, if we all do as nanny tells us, there will be jam tomorrow'. *Glasnost'* has meant that this kind of whitewashing is largely a thing of the past, as is the once-obligatory up-beat ending. Catharsis has taken the place of false optimism. Three out of the five plays in this collection mount a frontal assault on some particularly virulent manifestations of hypocrisy, double standards and moral corruption in present-day Soviet society, an assault dictated not by the Party but by the artistic conscience of three exceptionally talented individuals – Alexander Galin, Ludmila Petrushevskaya and Alexander Gelman – who have chosen widely diverse topics and treated them in appropriately different ways. On the other hand, Gorin's play, which was written in pre-*glasnost'* days towards the end of the Brezhnev era, looks outward and employs a historical parallel to point to a more universal menace; while Chervinsky's highly skilled adaptation of a story by Bulgakov (himself one of Soviet Russia's most brilliant playwrights) ventures on a satire that cuts very close to the bone, for its target is Lenin himself – hitherto a no-go area for criticism or humour, however oblique.

Stars in the Morning Sky by Alexander Galin, has been chosen to lend its title to the whole book because it happens to express so well the motif that underlies the collection: the appearance of bright points of light in the sky after a night that has been little else but dark and overcast. Born in 1946, the author has other plays to his credit.

Galin tends to approach his subject-matter from a slightly odd, unexpected angle and has a gift for investing the most unpromising relationships with a dimension that can only be described as poetic, as for instance in *Retro*, a comedy of everyday life about a retired, widowed miner with a nest-egg and a much-coveted flat in Moscow, who is being wooed by several middle-aged ladies in search of accommodation. His female characters, although some of them may be rather comic or absurd, are created with a remarkable degree of sensitivity and empathy, and in *Stars in the Morning Sky* they not only predominate in the cast (rare enough in itself), they are the *raison d'être* of the play. Its most startling feature, which has helped to ensure full houses in the Soviet Union, is that Galin has chosen to deal openly with the issue of prostitution – until very recently an utterly tabu subject in that country, never allowed to be so much as hinted at in print, still less on the stage or screen. What is more, it is not treated from the male viewpoint or with the moralistic, condemnatory attitude of Soviet officialdom, but rather from the angle of the women themselves.

The play is based on a real-life situation: before and during the 1980 Moscow Olympics, when thousands of foreigners came to the USSR for the Games, the police rounded up all the capital's prostitutes from their haunts on the streets, in cafés, restaurants, bars and railway-stations, and deported them to makeshift accommodation in places located in a radius of at least 100 kilometres from the centre of the city, in order that they should not 'spoil the picture' for the visitors from abroad. In a negative way – the entire *removal* of an awkward human element – it was a classic case of the government sweeping one of its most visible 'black spots' under the carpet, by resort to an age-old Russian method: the creation of a 'Potemkin village', a false façade of propriety and exemplary social hygiene.

Alexander Gelman's *A Man with Connections* is another of the new wave of plays in which Soviet playwrights have suddenly been enabled to write about social reality as *they* see it and not in accordance with dogma and ideology. In this play, Gelman makes a telling frontal assault on a part of the Soviet system which, as he sees it, breeds hypocrisy, cheating and double standards and corrupts the personality of anyone professionally obliged to try and make the system work. This and other new plays, different though they may be in form and subject-matter, are part of an upsurge of new writing for the stage which in the Soviet context is revolutionary. As well as bearing the inimitable stamp of credibility that is the mark of writing based on an author's own experience and convictions, these plays have also, at a stroke, overturned the deadening formula inherited from Stalin: instead of the individual being the villain who is betraying the system and preventing it from functioning properly, it is the appallingly flawed system itself that is shown up as the force crushing and dehumanising the individual.

Born in 1939, Alexander Gelman is one of today's most performed playwrights in the Soviet Union. Several of his earlier plays were located in factories or other workplaces. They managed to pass the now-abolished theatre censorship and get performed because they outwardly corresponded to an officially approved genre: the 'production drama', in which a group of honest workers, usually spearheaded by a keen young (or wise old) Party member, succeed in 'unmasking' an inefficient or corrupt manager and having him ousted in the final scene. Gelman's plays in this mode were, however, deceptive: being built not around simplistic Communist Party slogans but on plausibly real clashes of personality; they were psychologically authentic and at the same time subversive of stereotyped, dogmatic attitudes.

Apparently true to type, *A Man with Connections* concerns a senior manager in Soviet industry who is in trouble, in this case a departmental head in a civil engineering and construction enterprise, but there any resemblance to the cliché-ridden 'production dramas' of the past stops. This play, in fact, could have been consciously written as a grim, upside-down parody of that discredited genre: most importantly, the action takes place between a man and his wife in their own home and not in the usual public arena such as the boardroom, the factory floor or a building site; here there is no chorus of honest, indignant workers; no *deus ex machina* from the Party or the ministry descends in the last act to dispense justice and put everything to rights. The play is much more of a tragedy in the classic sense of a man destroyed by his very qualities – or what pass for qualities in the creaking, inefficient, often corrupt world of Soviet industry. It is also a truly classic piece in that it observes the Aristotelian unities of time, place and action, while the only departure from the two-character dialogue are a few brief but heart-stopping lines from a voice on the telephone – the modern equivalent of the Messenger in ancient Greek tragedy.

While our theatre managers love two-handers because they are cheap to produce, they are relatively rare in Soviet playwriting. In the USSR – a country in which every theatre is made up of a large, permanent, salaried company of actors – managements and actors alike are keen to have plays with big casts, which keep as many as possible of the company's members engaged in performance. Two-handers also present a unique challenge to an author's professional skills, and *A Man with Connections* shows Gelman as a master of the genre. Appalled but fascinated, we are drawn into a merciless duel between a pair of all-too-seasoned antagonists – a long-married couple – in which the moral and psychological advantage slithers from one partner to the other as the struggle sways this way and that, the tension slackens and then rises again as each contestant in turn pulls out stone after stone from the satchel of the past to sling at the other. One doesn't have to be a sovietologist to appreciate the play at this, its most basic and universal level; it belongs in the same league as Albee's *Who's Afraid of Virginia Woolf?* But some clues to the specifics of the Soviet context can help us to appreciate it to the full.

Gelman's ultimate target is the mechanism of the Soviet economy, with its dreadful inflexibility, clumsiness and inefficiency which, combined with a rigidly hierarchical 'command' system of management, regularly fails to produce the goods (significant exceptions to this are those branches of the economy that are geared to ultimately non-economic aims and are inherently susceptible to command-type management: the armaments industry and the space race). Being the kind of writer that he is, Gelman is not particularly interested in whether or not Soviet industry produces enough missiles or concrete or machine-tools or nuts and bolts: he is interested in people, and he has singled out an industrial manager as a particularly glaring example of the – literally – inhuman pressures with which the system bears down upon the people working in it, people who, in fact, constitute a large proportion of the total Soviet population and who are treated by that system (in Lenin's revealingly mechanistic phrase) like 'little screws and cogwheels'.

The only means by which this lumbering, Heath Robinson mechanism manages to function at all, even with such inadequate results, is through the desperate efforts of managers at all levels, who deploy an astounding array of under-the-counter deals, 'old boy' arrangements, barter, 'fixing', fudging, bribery and coercion. And because most of this has to be done on or beyond the fringes of legality (Soviet law prescribes very severe penalties for 'economic crimes', up to and including the death penalty), to be a manager in Soviet industry is one of the most stressful occupations in the world. It is only made tolerable by the often considerable chances open to them of feathering their own nests, and by the fact that because they are *all* in it, most managers are themselves too compromised to risk betraying their colleagues. Anyone who tries blowing the whistle is likely to get destroyed, too, in the ensuing crash. It is precisely this nerve-racking kind of situation that has so eroded the human qualities and powers of judgment of Andrei Golubev, the central character of Gelman's play, as to cause him to make the rash blunder which finally brings down Nemesis upon him as a man: it cripples his son for life and destroys his marriage. But it doesn't end his career: a skilled survivor in his particular world of distorted values, he 'manages' even this crisis so well that he actually gets promoted.

At a guess, Ludmila Petrushevskaya is in her early fifties. The guesswork (based on one or two rather unflattering photographs) is necessary because this writer is very reticent, not only about her age but about her life-story in general; only a few trickles of biographical fact have here and there seeped into print. Although brought up in an orphanage in Siberia, her intellectual endowment must have been formidable, because she was able to study journalism at Moscow University (the Oxbridge of Soviet higher education), where the entry standards are high and fiercely competitive. She came to playwriting relatively late, having started with short stories which for a long time no editor wanted to publish. She writes her plays with great speed and without drafts. *Three Girls in Blue*, for instance, was written in the amazingly short space of four days, little more than the time needed – in between her other work and domestic commitments – to knock out the words on a typewriter. One of the most positive results of this method, which it is to be hoped comes through, even if only partially, in translation, is the exhilarating freshness and immediacy of Petrushevskaya's dialogue.

It would be hard to name another modern Soviet playwright who is quite as bold and unorthodox as Petrushevskaya. In fact it has mainly been her failure to observe the accepted Soviet conventions ('positive' characters; optimistic endings; a general tone of uplift) that caused the initial difficulties she experienced in getting her plays accepted by the somewhat cliquish and hidebound pundits of Moscow's theatrical 'establishment'. In their opinion, Petrushevskaya's plays hold out no hope for their characters; her vision of the world is disenchanted and more than a touch sombre. In one sense this may be true; she is a painfully honest writer, and there is not a lot to be enchanted about in the reality of Soviet life, especially for that half of the population who belong to what many observers, both Soviet and foreign, see as even more of an underclass than in the West: women. Yet Petrushevskaya, for one, does not wholly share that judgment on her work. She regards many of her plays (including *Three Girls in Blue*) as comedies.

Even if they are comedies, their humour is heavily laced with bitterness and absurdity. In this, she is in good company; Chekhov always stubbornly insisted that his plays were comedies. Petrushevskaya also belongs within another significant Russian literary tradition that has largely been in abeyance in the decades since the revolution: the stance first made famous by Gogol, who characterised his own work as 'laughter through tears'.

The late Alexei Arbuzov, who, if anyone, was Petrushevskaya's mentor in the craft of playwriting, said of her work that it offered us '. . . a messy and confused world' – in other words, the *real* world. Ill-tempered bickering in a run-down *dacha* near Moscow; little tragedies acted out in Moscow flats; lonely, crotchety old women; bemused grown-ups; cruel children; weariness, edginess, a lack of purpose: *mutatis mutandis*, we can probably recognise much of it from our own experience. Like most of Petrushevskaya's plays, *Three Girls in Blue* has little detectable plot; rather, it captures those times when, although things happen, we find ourselves drifting or reacting to events or to other people rather than living. Underneath the muddled surface, though, there is a plot – of the kind in which life obliges us to play a role, and one that is seldom to our liking. This is conveyed all the more convincingly because Petrushevskaya's characters are drawn in such a way that we are never quite sure whether she sympathises with them, fears them or despises them. At least, this ambiguity is true where her women are concerned; it is rare to find an adult male character in her plays who is anything but a manipulative slob.

All this may sound as if reading *Three Girls in Blue* or seeing a performance of it is an experience to be avoided. But it is the sign of great writers – and I think that epithet must be applied to Ludmila Petrushevskaya – that their words grip us even when the subject-matter is uncomfortable, disturbing, even grim, and we are drawn onward by a fascinated compulsion to know what happens next, to find out how – or whether – the characters are going to survive the tangles in which the author has enmeshed them. This is precisely the effect exerted by her plays, and by none of them more strongly than *Three Girls in Blue*.

With Grigory Gorin's *Forget Herostratus!* we are transported to a different era – two and a half centuries before the birth of Christ. It also belongs to a different genre of playwriting, that of the structured narrative plot, which takes a historical event as its starting point but is then developed by the author according to the logic of characters who are entirely of his own creation, in order to point a moral for our own times.

Gorin, born in 1940, is a versatile man. Having published many short stories, he is also a popular and successful playwright, the author of several screenplays, and – which makes him unique in the Moscow literary scene – the host of the only regular chat-show on Soviet television. While *Forget Herostratus!* treats of a subject where there is little scope for hilarity, it is full of irony, rather à la Bernard Shaw, and in Gorin's other work for the stage his humour and sense of the absurd make him one of those scarce creatures in the Soviet theatre, an author who can write really funny plays.

During the two somewhat grey decades from the mid-sixties to the mid-eighties, Gorin turned to the device often chosen by other humorists at times when to be too direct in aiming their barbed comments would invite serious trouble: he assumed the persona of fantasists and satirists of past times and other countries. In this he was following in the footsteps of an earlier Soviet playwright, Yevgeny Schwartz, who managed the brilliant feat of adapting some of the fairy stories of Hans Christian

Andersen and others into subtly pointed comments on the
tyrannies and absurdities of dictators of his own time – most
notably of Stalin. It is no coincidence that Grigory Gorin recently
wrote the screenplay for a Soviet film based on the most famous
and most trenchant of Schwartz's political satires in fairytale guise,
The Dragon. (The film has been retitled *To Kill a Dragon*, and is
regularly filling the biggest cinema in Moscow; it is greatly to be
hoped that it will be released outside the USSR.) The results of
Gorin's own use of this device for the stage are three plays based
on classics of satire from Flemish, German and English literature:
Till Eulenspiegel, Baron Münchhausen and the Tales of Dean
Swift.

To suggest that *Forget Herostratus!* evokes echoes of George
Bernard Shaw (one thinks of *Androcles and the Lion* or *Caesar and
Cleopatra*) in no way implies that Gorin is an imitator; as his other
plays prove, the wit and irony that we may be tempted to label
'Shavian' is entirely Gorin's own and is, what's more, a rare
commodity in Soviet Russian literature, which has never been
very long on laughs. The choice of a distant historical setting
enables the canny Soviet playwright to make jokes and point to
the follies and weaknesses of politicians which, had they been
located in the present day, would have immediately provoked the
censor's blue pencil – and this despite the fact that Gorin is not
even concerned with Soviet politics but with the rise of Hitler.

The thought which prompted Gorin to write this play was the
possible analogy between two historic acts of arson which,
although almost exactly 2,000 years apart in time, might have
shared a certain similarity of motivation: the destruction by fire of
one of the seven wonders of the ancient world, the great
Artemisium or Temple of Diana at Ephesus – and the burning of
the Berlin Reichstag, which helped to pave the way for Hitler's
seizure of power. Building on what little of fact or legend is
known about Herostratus, the destoyer of the Artemisium, who is
said to have been an insignificant man obsessed by a desire to
become famous by hook or by crook (in which he certainly
succeeded), Gorin sees in him a parallel with Hitler, whom he
thus postulates as also being someone with such a massive
inferiority complex that his means of compensating for it had to
be correspondingly gigantic.

His more serious aim in the play, however, is rather similar to
that which prompted Brecht to write *The Resistible Rise of Arturo Ui*,
namely to show that the rise to power of a man who began as
little more than a petty crook driven by megalomania was made
possible by the stupidity, greed, laziness and weakness of those

who should have – and could have – stopped him in his tracks when he was still only one of several small-time, ranting demagogues on the fringe of German politics.

Gorin's treatment of this theme differs from that of Brecht in that Herostratus *is* stopped before his sinister political ambitions can come to fruition. The really interesting aspect of the play, seen in the context of Soviet ideology, is the nature of the character who eliminates this threat by killing Herostratus – namely Cleon, the chief magistrate of Ephesus. Cleon derives his authority and moral strength from the fact, emphasised by Gorin, that thanks to its Greek political traditions (although the city is under Persian rule) the judiciary of Ephesus is independent of the executive power of the Persian governor. In other words, Gorin is saying that justice and good government are only effectively secured by that cornerstone of civil liberties, the separation of powers. That may be an unexciting truism in a democratic country; but it is a concept that has been scorned and specifically rejected by the political theorists and rulers of the Soviet Union from Lenin onwards.

Although *Forget Herostratus!* was both written and performed in the latter years of the Brezhnev era, Gorin's admirable and grossly heterodox political message, which is the crux of his play, was obviously so cleverly wrapped up in parable and in historical disguise that the censor failed to spot it – a classic and successful case of the nimbly intelligent writer using the age-old methods of Aesop to evade and defeat a seemingly all-powerful apparatus of dogma and political repression. Furthermore, this can now be uttered aloud, because the separation of the Soviet judiciary from the executive power is one of the main proposals for the reform of the USSR's legal and political structures that is being put forward by Gorbachov. All this – and an ingenious, talented, highly entertaining play too!

It may be paradoxical that the opening piece in this collection of modern Soviet plays is not only an adaptation of a novel dating from 1925, but of a novel written by an author who was arguably Soviet Russia's greatest playwright – Mikhail Bulgakov. For nearly forty years the original of *Heart of a Dog* was kept in a locked box hidden (literally) under Bulgakov's widow's bed: in late 1969, under an oath of secrecy, Yelena Sergeyevna Bulgakova lent me the typescript of the novel with strict instructions to read it that night and to return it next morning. Having passed this test satisfactorily, I was then allowed to smuggle a carbon copy out of the USSR (under my shirt), whereupon I translated it and the

English version was published in London and New York twenty years before its publication in the author's homeland. (That translation is now due to be reissued by Collins-Harvill).

Even before Bulgakov's *Heart of a Dog* was finally published in a Russian literary journal in 1986, it was seized upon in proof by no fewer than two playwrights and adapted for the stage. The two different versions then started to run simultaneously in two Moscow theatres located less than a mile apart; at the time of writing in late 1988, they were still playing to full houses. Having seen the two productions I had no difficulty in selecting the play written by Alexander Chervinsky, which I found to be closer to Bulgakov's original in both spirit and letter. I have little doubt that if that short satirical novel had not been officially suppressed as soon as it was written, Bulgakov himself would have turned it into a play: written with all the instincts of a born playwright (it dates from the year in which he was engaged in the immensely successful adaptation of his own novel *The White Guard* into the play *The Days of the Turbins*), the story, the characters and the dialogue are naturally dramatic and these qualities have been seized upon and cleverly exploited by Chervinsky.

Heart of a Dog was banned from the outset because its satire, though indirect and skilfully wrapped up in metaphor, was an attack on Marxism, on the Bolshevik revolution and – oh, sacrilege! – on Lenin, its theorist, leader and driving force. Superficially the story is a science-fiction romp, full of absurdities and laughs; but behind this comic mask, Bulgakov was making a basic critique of the very fundamentals of Marxism-Leninism (as Soviet ideology later came to be called). His first and most damaging objection to Marxism was to question its claim to be 'scientific', in the sense that in physics and chemistry the known, empirically tested laws of these natural sciences enable a specific action to produce a predictable effect or reaction. In questioning whether a theory of social organisation such as Marxism can be called 'scientific' in that sense, he also challenged the implied assumption of Lenin and the Bolsheviks that they could apply to Marxism the same axiom that justifies researchers in the natural sciences: namely that experimentation is always justified by the benefits that will result from increased knowledge. In other words Bulgakov argued that to use human beings as guinea-pigs to test some hitherto unproven theory about society is morally impermissible and ultimately self-defeating.

In calling his scientist 'Professor Preobrazhensky', Bulgakov was using word-play to make his point clear: the name derives from the Russian word *preobrazhenie*, which means 'transformation'. The professor's aim, through the techniques of transplanting certain vital glands, is to 'transform' his patients. The analogy with Lenin was clear: by means of the instant, drastic and invasive surgery of revolution, involving the removal of 'glands' which determined the nature of the old 'body politic' and the implantation of new ones taken from a theoretically 'superior' system, the coarse, lazy and ignorant human material that typified the population under the old regime could be transformed, by a stroke of the knife, into the enlightened, conscientious citizens needed for the new 'superior' society envisaged by the ardent practitioners of the 'science' of Marxism.

The difference between real life and the events on stage is that 'Professor Preobrazhensky' realised his mistake and reversed it, whereas in reality no such doubts ever caused the makers of the Bolshevik revolution to have second thoughts. There is even a grimly prophetic touch in the behaviour of Sharikov, the dog-turned-man. As soon as he is given some power as a minor official, he starts ruthlessly destroying his 'enemies' – cats. Considering that Bulgakov's original novel was written in the mid twenties, when Stalin was not yet in power, this episode now seems like an uncannily prescient metaphor for Stalin's murderous purges of his 'enemies' once he felt himself firmly in the saddle by the mid-1930s.

Even this splendidly absurd comedy thus has more links with the other plays in this collection than it might seem to have at first sight, apart from the common factor of their emergence on the Soviet stage under a liberalising, reforming government. In their very different ways all of them tackle the important, underlying issues of their time, but thanks to the talent of their authors, they do it in essentially theatrical terms which grip us, move us and amuse us while planting thoughts in our minds that are both disturbing and stimulating.

Michael Glenny
December 1988

HEART OF A DOG ■ ALEXANDER CHERVINSKY

Translated by MICHAEL GLENNY

Adapted from a 1925 story by Mikhail Bulgakov which remained unpublished in the USSR until 1986, *Heart of a Dog* tells of a 'scientific' experiment to turn a dog into a man. An allegory questioning Lenin and foreseeing Stalin, this dramatisation by director-playwright Chervinsky caused a sensation in Moscow in 1987. Its British premiere was staged at Essex University in 1988.

Characters

DOG, alias SHARIK, alias POLYGRAPH POLYGRAPHOVICH
  SHARIKOV
PHILIP PHILIPOVICH PREOBRAZHENSKY, professor of
  neuro-surgery
IVAN ARNOLDOVICH BORMENTAL, surgeon
ZINA, housemaid/nurse/receptionist to Professor
  Preobrazhensky
FYODOR, porter in Professor Preobrazhensky's block of flats
SHVONDER, chairman of the House Committee
PESTRUKHIN, secretary of the House Committee
VOZNESENSKAYA, member of the House Committee

FIRST OGPU MAN ⎫
SECOND OGPU MAN ⎬ officers of the State Political Police
THIRD OGPU MAN ⎭

DARYA PETROVNA, the Professor's Cook
REPORTER ⎫
YOUNG MAN ⎬ journalists
FAT JOURNALIST ⎭

GENTLEMAN WITH MONOCLE
PATIENT
ARMY OFFICER
DETECTIVE
THIN GIRL
OLD WOMAN
FIRST POLICEMAN
SECOND POLICEMAN

Heart of a Dog was first performed in this translation by Essex University Theatre on 16 June 1988. The cast was as follows:

DOG alias SHARIK, alias POLYGRAPH POLYGRAPHOVICH SHARIKOV	Geoff Costley
PHILIP PHILIPOVICH PREOBRAZHENSKY	Leslie Bell
IVAN ARNOLDOVICH BORMENTAL	Neil Cox
ZINA ⎱ THIN GIRL ⎰	Rachel King
FYODOR	Richard Watkins
SHVONDER	Andy Watts
VOZNESENSKAYA	Sarah Tuck
OGPU MAN	Stephen Powell
DARYA PETROVNA	Liz King
OLD WOMAN	Suzanne Lynch
JOURNALIST	Adam Baron
POLICEMAN	Nick Timmings
FOREIGN GENTLEMAN WITH MONOCLE ⎱ DETECTIVE ⎰ PATIENT WITH GREEN HAIR	Ben Holmes

Artistic Director   Faynia Williams
Costumes by Gemma Best
Lighting by Dorian Kelly
Sound by Andy Holyer

Scene One

Offstage a beautiful soprano voice is singing one of Amneris's arias from
Aida. *Howling wind and snowstorm. A large poster, flapping in the wind
on a hoarding, announces in large letters: 'Professor Preobrazhensky's
Life-giving Ray. Ensures Eternal Youth and Immortality'. The large front
door of a house has been boarded up.*

> A DOG *crawls out from under the advertisement hoarding at the
> same time as* Prof. PHILIP PHILIPOVICH
> PREOBRAZHENSKY *enters – fur-coated, fur-hatted, and muffled
> up against the blizzard.*

DOG. Ooow-owowowow . . . ooow-ow-oow-owow! I'm dying! . . .
There's a snowstorm moaning a requiem over me and I'm
howling with it . . . what else can I do? I'm a goner . . .
Owowow-ooow-ow-oow! That bastard in a dirty white cap,
the cook at the canteen, threw out a saucepanful of boiling
water and scalded my left side. Clumsy oaf – and him a
proletarian, too.

P.P.P. How can people be so careless. God, how that must hurt!

DOG. Hard-faced bugger, he was. Scalded me right through to
the bone. I'm really done for this time.

P.P.P. Tomorrow the skin will develop ulcers.

DOG. And how am I supposed to cure them? In summer you
can go and roll in Sokolniki Park, where there's a special
grass that does you good, and people drop plenty of greasy
food-wrappings for you to lick. But where can you go in
winter?

P.P.P. *(looking at* DOG's *wounds).* Have people been kicking you
and throwing bricks at you?

DOG. 'Course they have. People are like that – kick a dog when
he's down and too weak to bite back. But the worst was that
boiling water – it took all my fur off.

P.P.P. With the whole of your left flank bare and unprotected,
you'll catch pneumonia.

DOG. If you get pneumonia, the only thing you can do is lie up under the steps leading to a doorway, but then who's going to run around the dustbins looking for food for me? I can only crawl on my belly till I'm so weak that anyone could finish me off with a whack of their stick. And then the dustmen'll pick me up by the legs and sling me on the dust-cart. I despise dustmen – they handle so much muck, they get to be worse than pigs . . . Cooks are different – some of them are all right. For instance, there was that Vlas from Prechistenka Street. He's dead now, God rest his soul. I don't know how many dogs' lives he must have saved. He was a great character, a gentleman's cook – used to work for Count Tolstoy's family. Even used to throw you a bone now and again, I was told.

P.P.P. Oh, the human race! (*Exit.*)

DOG (*howls after* P.P.P). Oooow-ow-oow-ooo! Where's he gone? Thought he might be going to give me a bite to eat. . . .

Enter THIN GIRL. *The howling snowstorm spins her round, blows up her skirt to above her knees.*

THIN GIRL. Here, doggy! Good doggy! Here Sharik, Sharik . . . Why are you whimpering so, you poor little thing? Has someone hurt you?

DOG. Who are you calling 'Sharik'? Sharik? That's not my name. I haven't even *got* a name – I'm just a stray who's been nearly scalded to death.

THIN GIRL. Oh God, this weather . . . and my stomach aches so. It's all that endless boiled salt beef they give us in the canteen. And then they use the stock for soup, so that's salty too. When will it all end? (*Runs off.*)

DOG. Poor kid – she hates the stuff, wrinkles up her nose, but she eats it. Can't afford to go to a decent restaurant on her pay, so she eats at the canteen, where it's 40 kopeks for a two-course meal, and it's only worth 15 'cos the manager pockets the other 25 kopeks. Anyway, it's not the right sort of food for her. She's got TB in her right lung, she's having her period, her legs are cold, and the wind whistles up her crutch because she wears those thin lacy little knickers – just to please her lover. If she tried to wear flannel ones he'd throw her out for looking a frump. He's made good now, he's chairman of something-or-other, and all he makes in graft goes on women and champagne. He went hungry as a kid, so now he says: 'So what? Hell, you can't take it with you!' I feel sorry for her, poor girl . . . But I feel a lot sorrier for myself. At least she has a warm home to go to, but where can I go? Ooow-ow-ow-ooow!

Enter P.P.P., *who goes straight over to the* DOG.

DOG. What's that? What's that in his right-hand pocket? It smells of minced horsemeat with garlic and peppercorns!

P.P.P. *takes out of his pocket something long and thin wrapped in greaseproof paper.*

DOG. Sausage!! Bet he doesn't give me any. Oh, master! I'm dying. A dog has the soul of a slave, we'll sell ourselves to anyone who'll feed us . . . What d'you want a lousy horsemeat sausage for? . . . Bet he doesn't give me any.

P.P.P. *(breaking off a piece of sausage).* Here, Sharik, here boy!

DOG. He calls me Sharik too! But what do I care? You can call me anything you like! *(Sinks his teeth into the sausage and gobbles it down.)* Let me lick your hand, master! Let me kiss your boots!

P.P.P. That's enough for now. *(Strokes* DOG *and feels his neck.)* No collar. A stray. Excellent. You're just what I need.

DOG. You can kick me if you like, I won't say a word.

P.P.P. Good dog – follow me.

DOG. I'll follow you to the ends of the earth! . . . Hey, what's that? A cat! Clear off, you! He didn't buy a sausage just to give to any riff-raff! Go on, clear off! Grrrr! . . . That's right – you stay up that tree.

P.P.P. *breaks off another piece of sausage.*

DOG. Funny man, he's using it to make me come along with him. Don't worry, I'm not going anywhere. I'll follow you wherever you go.

P.P.P. This way.

DOG. Obukhov Street, eh? And very nice too. Posh. Yes, the likes of him wouldn't eat rotten salt beef, and if anybody tried to serve him any he'd kick up a row and write to the newspapers about it.

A REPORTER, *freezing in a thin summer coat, emerges from a doorway.*

REPORTER. Excuse me, I'm from the press.

DOG. Talk of the devil!

P.P.P. Out of my way, sir.

DOG (*threatens* REPORTER). Grrr!

REPORTER. Look, I'm freezing to death! I'll only take a minute or two of your time. Just one little interview about the role of Russia's brilliant inventors in the national economy.

P.P.P. Go for him, Sharik!

DOG. Clear off, you! (*Savagely:*) Grrrr! Owowow! Grrrrr!

REPORTER *vanishes.*

P.P.P. Good doggy! Come on, this way.

DOG. This way? Anywhere for you, master . . . You can tell he eats well, doesn't steal and isn't afraid of anyone. That's because he always has a full stomach.

P.P.P. This way, please.

DOG. With pleasure . . . Er, sorry, no . . . There's a porter in there, I know him of old. . . .

A large, imposing front door opens as if by magic. In the light of the hallway stands FYODOR, *a uniformed porter.*

DOG. They're even worse than janitors, nastier than cats. Hate the lot of 'em. Murderers in gold braid and peaked caps.

P.P.P. (*to* DOG). Don't be afraid, in you go.

FYODOR. Good evening, professor.

P.P.P. Good evening, Fyodor.

DOG. My God! What must this man be? He can bring a dog off the streets into a cooperative apartment house? And look at that villain in the peaked cap – doesn't say a word! He doesn't look very happy about it, but that's as it should be. He really respects this gentleman, my new master. And to think how many times he's poked his broom in my face before now!

P.P.P. Come on, come on.

DOG. Don't worry. I'll go wherever you go.

P.P.P. Were there any letters for me, Fyodor?

FYODOR. No, sir. But those newspapermen were here again.

P.P.P. Did you tell them to go to hell?

FYODOR. Yes, sir.

P.P.P. All of them?

FYODOR. All of them, sir. (*Leans towards* P.P.P., *confidentially:*) The House Committee has made No. 3 take in more tenants by compulsory order.

P.P.P. (*horrified*). Wha-at!

FYODOR. (*putting his finger to his lips*). That's right, sir, though I shouldn't be telling you – four of them.

P.P.P. My God, what must it be like in that flat now? And what about the owner?

FYODOR. He's going to divide two of his rooms by putting up partitions.

P.P.P. What is the place coming to?

FYODOR. Extra tenants are to be put into all the flats except yours. There was a House Committee meeting this afternoon.

P.P.P. What next? God Almighty! . . . Come on, doggy.

DOG. I'm coming. My side is starting to hurt, so I can't move too fast. Allow me to lick your boot.

P.P.P. This way.

> P.P.P. *rings the bell of his handsome front door. The* DOG *tries to read the brass plate bearing the words* 'Professor P. P. Preobrazhensky'.

DOG (*reads with difficulty*). Poodle – P, Rusk – R, Offal – O . . . P – R –) . . . Surely he can't be a proletarian?!

Scene Two

The front door opens noiselessly to reveal ZINA *in the doorway, dressed in black dress, white apron and white lace cap. She looks at the* DOG *and his master in surprise and some distaste.*

P.P.P. Zina, meet Mr. Sharik.

The hall is lit by an electric light with an opal-glass shade in the form of a tulip. A full-length mirror reflects the scruffy, wounded figure of the DOG. Beside the mirror is a terrifying stag's head crowned with many-branched antlers hung with coats, beneath it a row of galoshes on a low stand.

ZINA. Wherever did you find that *creature*, Philip Philipovich?

ZINA helps P.P.P. to take off his coat of dark brown fox-fur and hangs it up.

ZINA. My God, he's covered in lice!

P.P.P. Nonsense! Where are the lice?

His fur coat removed, P.P.P. is revealed as wearing a black suit, with a gold watch-chain across his stomach.

Hold still, don't wriggle so, you little fool. H'mm . . . that's not lice . . . Will you keep still, damn you! . . . He's been scalded. Who was the brute who scalded you?

DOG. That bloody cook!

P.P.P. Zina, into the examination-room with him at once and bring me my white coat.

Exit P.P.P.

ZINA. Stay there, Sharik, I'm going to wipe your paws.

Exit ZINA. Left alone, the DOG at once cocks his hind leg against the wicker-work umbrella-stand, then sniffs at P.P.P.'s fur coat and at the galoshes. ZINA re-enters; she is no longer dressed as a housemaid but wears a white coat and a nurse's cap.

ZINA. Here, doggy, doggy! (*She advances towards the dog, with hands outstretched to catch him.*)

DOG. Oh, no you don't! I see your game now! Him and his sausage. It was a trick to entice me into a dog's hospital. They'll make me drink castor oil and snip all the fur off my flank with scissors. You won't catch me, though!!

The DOG eludes ZINA, crouches and jumps at the door, which he hits with his uninjured flank. With a yelp, he starts to dash around the hallway, knocking over the umbrella-stand and other objects.

ZINA. Come here!

Enter P.P.P., *also wearing a white coat. With him is Dr.*
BORMENTAL, *similarly dressed, hiding a bottle of brown liquid and
a cotton-wool pad behind his back.*

BORMENTAL (*cheerfully*). Stand still, you silly dog! Zina, get hold
of him by the scruff of his neck.

ZINA. God, he's as slippery as an eel!

P.P.P. Now, now – what's all this?

The DOG *lunges at* BORMENTAL *and bites him on the knee.*
BORMENTAL *shouts in pain, but manages to clamp the cotton-wool
pad over the* DOG's *muzzle. The* DOG *struggles furiously and
succeeds in smashing the tulip-shaped lamp, plunging the scene into
darkness. In the dark, the* DOG *can be heard howling plaintively:*

DOG. Goodbye, Moscow! I'm going to the dogs' heaven. Why did
you do this to me? It's all over . . . I'm dying . . . I'm dead.
. . .

A beautiful soprano voice is heard singing an aria from Aida.

Scene Three

Brilliant lighting suddenly reveals the operating theatre of Prof. P.P.P.'s
*private clinic, complete with articulated operating table and, behind it, a
sinister-looking apparatus that resembles a very large version of a magic
lantern. A glass-fronted cabinet contains rows of disgusting-looking objects
preserved in sealed jars of alcohol. A branch of a tree protrudes from one
wall; on it sits a large stuffed* OWL, *whose eyes can light up; the bird is
also capable of speech. The* DOG *is lying on the floor; it opens one eye
languidly, looks around, and examines its bandaged flank.*

DOG. So they caught me before I could get away, the crafty
buggers. What was that filthy-smelling stuff they held to my
nose? But they seem to have done a good job on my scalded
side.

Opens both eyes and sees Dr. BORMENTAL *dabbing the dog-bite on
his knee with iodine.*

DOG. That was my doing. I'll be in trouble now.

The OWL's *eyes flash on and off a few times.*

P.P.P. Why did you bite the nice doctor?

DOG (*whimpers repentantly*). Owowowow!

BORMENTAL (*smiling*). Silly dog! It doesn't hurt at all. Nothing whatever to worry about. But tell me, Philip Philipovich, how did you persuade such a neurotic dog to come home with you?

P.P.P. By kindness, Ivan Arnoldovich. The only possible way to treat any living creature is by kindness.

DOG. No, he's definitely *not* a vet and this is not a dog's hospital.

P.P.P. You will never succeed with terror or cruelty, no matter what may be the animal's stage of development. I have always insisted on that principle, and always will. Terror completely paralyses the nervous system . . . Zina! . . . so none of the animal's reactions will be normal.

Enter ZINA.

P.P.P. Zina, I bought a rouble's-worth of Polish sausage for this four-legged villain. I think it's in the kitchen. Please be so kind as to feed him.

ZINA. Polish sausage! Good God! You could have bought him a pound of off-cuts and end-pieces for twenty kopecks. I wouldn't mind the Polish sausage myself. (*Exit.*)

DOG. And hurry up! . . . As soon as I've had something to eat, I'm going to sort out that owl. . . .

ZINA *brings the sausage on a plate and the* DOG *devours it whole.*

P.P.P. Ivan Arnoldovich, we must now proceed with the greatest care. We need a *good* corpse. As soon as a suitable one dies, out with his heart, brain and testicles, into the nutritive fluid and straight to me.

DOG. Lord, am I in luck. Why on earth did he choose me? He only had to crook his little finger and he could have had a pedigree Great Dane.

BORMENTAL. Don't worry, Philip Philipovich, the pathologist has promised me.

DOG. Perhaps I'm dreaming. I'll wake up and it'll all vanish. No warmth, no food. And it's back to the alleyways, the freezing pavements, bad-tempered people, hanging around outside the canteen . . . God, that would be unbearable after this.

Door-bell rings.

P.P.P. Patients. Right, I'll see the first one.

Exeunt ZINA *and* BORMENTAL.

Sharik, come here.

P.P.P. *sits down behind his desk and immediately assumes an air of extreme dignity and importance. The* DOG, *politely retiring to a corner, cocks his hind leg, returns to his master and lies down at his feet.*

P.P.P. Barbarian. You must be trained out of that.

Enter ZINA *and* FYODOR, *flustered and worried.*

ZINA. It's not a patient, professor.

P.P.P. Then why did you let him in? Send him out!

FYODOR. He says he has an official order to see you.

FYODOR *hands* P.P.P. *a piece of paper, which* P.P.P. *reads and explodes in fury.*

P.P.P. *(calming down).* All right, send him in.

Enter YOUNG MAN *with notebook.*

YOUNG MAN. Please forgive me, professor, for taking up your valuable time, but my newspaper wants some facts and an explanation.

P.P.P. I am not obliged to explain anything to anyone.

DOG. Got that? No explanations! Grrr!

YOUNG MAN. What are you working on at the moment?

P.P.P. I do not intend to publish anything until my research is completed.

YOUNG MAN. Is it true you have invented a ray that can renew and prolong life?

P.P.P. You must realise – I have not yet fully researched this project. It is possible that the ray might improve and increase the vital functions.

YOUNG MAN. To what degree? *(Starts scribbling in his notebook.)*

P.P.P. *(shouts).* By a thousand times!

YOUNG MAN. Is it true that you can give their youth back to your patients?

P.P.P. (*shouts*). Not only that! Perpetual youth!

YOUNG MAN. So have you discovered the secret of immortality?

P.P.P. Yes!

YOUNG MAN. That will mean a complete revolution in animal husbandry.

P.P.P. Absolutely!! Now, what else do you want?

YOUNG MAN. A photo of you, please.

P.P.P. What? My photograph? In your newspaper? I can see from your face that you're going to write some absolute tripe about me.

YOUNG MAN. Professor, you have a duty to keep the Moscow proletariat informed. . . .

P.P.P. I have no such duty! And now be kind enough to get out of here this instant and stop preventing me from working!! Fyodor! Fyodor! (*Enter* FYODOR.) Show him out, please!

YOUNG MAN. I shall make a complaint. . . .

DOG. May I bite him?

FYODOR. Get out before you find yourself in trouble. (*Grabs* YOUNG MAN *by the arm and frog-marches him out.*)

P.P.P. (*mops his brow*). Next!

Enter ZINA.

ZINA. The next one's not a patient either. He says he has an appointment.

P.P.P. If he's not a patient, who gave him an appointment?

DOG. No, it's not a dream. He needs me. He's brought me here for a purpose. The professor has taste – he wouldn't pick up any old fleabag. . . .

The OWL's *eyes flash.*

OWL. You fool.

DOG. Grrrr! . . . I'll fix that owl. . . .

Enter GENTLEMAN WITH MONOCLE, *who hands his visiting card to the professor.*

P.P.P. *(reading the visiting card)*. Well, sir, what can I do for you?

GENTLEMAN *(with a foreign accent)*. Will the professor permit me to smoke a cigar?

P.P.P. He will.

GENTLEMAN. And may I sit down?

P.P.P. You may.

GENTLEMAN. I fully realise that the professor is extremely busy.

P.P.P. Indeed I am.

GENTLEMAN. Time is money, as the saying goes. My cigar does not disturb the professor?

P.P.P. It does not.

GENTLEMAN. So – the professor has discovered a ray that gives new life. Am I correct?

P.P.P. New life? Nonsense. That's all an invention of a pack of unscrupulous journalists.

GENTLEMAN. Modesty is the supreme ornament of all truly great scientists. Your work on this ray is already known in cities abroad. The whole world is speaking the name of Professor Preobrazhensky.

DOG *(enquiringly)*. Grrr?

GENTLEMAN. The whole world is following the professor's work with panting breath. But we all know very well how difficult is the situation for scientists in Soviet Russia. *Entre nous soit dit* . . . I trust we are quite alone in here?

DOG. No, you aren't.

GENTLEMAN. Alas, they do not well appreciate scientific labours in this country. And that is why I wish to talk with the professor. A certain foreign state offers the professor financial aids for his laboratory work – completely, er . . . without ropes . . . , er . . . strings, strings! Why should you throw your pearl before swines, as it says in the holy writing? This foreign state know the professor is obliged to work also in private practice in order to earn money for the experimentation, by giving back their youths to revolting lechers and fading ladies. This state also know how the professor was hard in the years 1917 to 1920, during the (*Giggles.*) he, he, he! . . . revolution. All that I say is naturally strictest secret.

DOG. Owowow!

GENTLEMAN. In a word – the professor will inform the foreign state in the results of his work, and for that it will finance the professor. First it is interesting to acquaint myself with the plans and drawings of the apparatus. (*Takes a large wad of colourful banknotes from his pocket.*) Some little trifle, for example 5000 rouble, as deposit, the professor may receive this moment. Even no receipt is necessary. . . .

P.P.P. (*exploding with fury, shouts*). Get out!! Out!! Out!! Get out!!!!

The GENTLEMAN WITH MONOCLE *vanishes. Enter, in alarm,* BORMENTAL *and* ZINA, *the latter carrying a pair of galoshes.*

BORMENTAL. His galoshes. . . .

ZINA. He left in such a hurry, he forget them.

P.P.P. Throw them out!

ZINA. But what if he comes back for them?

P.P.P. Hand them in to the Committee! Let them deal with that spy's galoshes!

Exeunt ZINA *and* BORMENTAL *with the galoshes. Still extremely angry and disturbed,* P.P.P. *grabs the telephone receiver.*

P.P.P. Get me that place, what's it called . . . yes, the Lubyanka. I'm afraid I don't know the number . . . Oh, *you* know it by heart? Good . . . Thank you . . . Hallo, this is Professor Preobrazhensky. I'm not sure which of your departments to notify, but a suspicious character in galoshes has been to see me . . . Was he foreign? Yes, of course . . . Why? Because he smoked a cigar and was extremely polite, so he couldn't have been a Russian . . . Oh, yes, and he had a foreign accent. . . .

A click in the receiver brings the conversation to a sudden end.
Enter ZINA.

P.P.P. Did you give the galoshes to the House Committee?

ZINA. They came on their own.

P.P.P. What, the galoshes?

ZINA. No, the House Committee.

Enter SHVONDER, VOZNESENSKAYA *and* PESTRUKHIN, *the very personification of the Dictatorship of the Proletariat.*

P.P.P. What can I do for you, gentlemen?

VOZNESENSKAYA. *(dressed in trousers, leather jacket and peaked cap, she looks very like a young man).* Firstly, we're not gentlemen.

P.P.P. Oh, forgive me . . . comrades.

VOZNESENSKAYA. No, I mean we're not all *men.*

P.P.P. Are you a man or a woman?

SHVONDER. What's the difference, comrade?

P.P.P. You mean . . . you don't know?

VOZNESENSKAYA: I'm a woman.

VOZNESENSKAYA *blushes furiously. The youngest of the three,* PESTRUKHIN, *a blonde youth in a grey persian-lamb fur hat, also blushes scarlet.*

P.P.P. In that case you, madam, may leave your cap on, but I would ask you two gentlemen to remove your headgear.

The two men look perplexed. P.P.P. *himself takes off* PESTRUKHIN's *fur hat.*

SHVONDER. We've come to you because. . . .

P.P.P. Before we go any further, who are 'we'?

SHVONDER *(barely restraining his annoyance).* We are the new House Committee of this building. My name's Shvonder, this is Voznesenskaya and he's comrade Pestrukhin. So we. . . .

P.P.P. Are you the new tenants who were compulsorily installed in No. 3?

SHVONDER. That's us.

P.P.P. *(in despair).* Oh my God, this is the end!

SHVONDER. Why are you laughing, professor?

P.P.P. Laughing?! You think I'm laughing? I'm in total despair. What will happen to the central heating now?

VOZNESENSKAYA. Are you trying to be funny with us, professor?

P.P.P. Why have you come to see me? Tell me quickly. I'm just about to have my lunch.

SHVONDER. We, as the newly appointed House Committee, have come to see you after a general meeting of the tenants – which you didn't attend – when the occupancy-quotient of your living-space was tabled. . . .

P.P.P. Occupancy-quotient? Living-space? Tabled? Kindly try talking Russian instead of double-dutch.

SHVONDER. You're going to give up at least one room, because we're putting some more people into your flat, so. . . .

P.P.P. Stop. Say no more. I've got the message. You know, of course, that under the decree of 1st August of this year, my apartment is exempt from billetting, requisitioning or installation of further tenants.

SHVONDER. Yes, we know. But the meeting came to the conclusion that, taken all round and not beating about the bush but weighing it up, you are occupying an unacceptably excessive area of living-space. Totally excessive. You, an unmarried citizen without spouse, offspring or elderly dependent relatives, are living alone in seven rooms.

P.P.P. I live and work here, alone, in seven rooms and I would like to have one more room. I need it for a library.

The trio is struck dumb.

PESTRUKHIN. Another room? That makes, er . . . eight! That's piling it on a bit, isn't it?

VOZNESENSKAYA. It's unbelievable!

P.P.P. I have a consulting-room, which, please note, is also my library; a dining-room; my study – that makes three; an examination-room – four; an operating-theatre – five; my bedroom – six; the maid's room – seven. End of conversation, I think. May I go and have my lunch now?

PESTRUKHIN. Excuse me, but. . . .

SHVONDER. Excuse me, but it was your dining-room we came to see you about. The meeting passed a resolution asking you, as a contribution to socialist labour discipline, to voluntarily give up your dining-room. No one in Moscow has a dining-room any more.

VOZNESENSKAYA. Not even Isadora Duncan.

Something appears to happen to P.P.P. *which causes his face to go purple.*

SHVONDER. And your examination-room, too. You can easily carry out examinations in your study.

P.P.P. And where am I supposed to eat?

ALL THREE (*in chorus*). In the bedroom.

P.P.P. (*in a voice of suppressed emotion*). So I am to eat in my bedroom, operate in the maid's room and examine my patients in the dining-room . . . It is quite likely, I suppose, that Isadora Duncan follows that method . . . *But I am not Isadora Duncan!* . . . I shall continue to dine in the dining-room and operate in the operating-theatre. Tell that to your next general meeting.

SHVONDER. In that case, professor, in view of your totally unreasonable and obstinate opposition to the committee's proposal, I have no alternative but to institute proceedings for lodging of a complaint against you in the appropriate quarters of higher authority.

P.P.P. Aha. I see. (*His voice takes on a suspiciously polite tone.*) Would you be so very kind as to wait one moment? I won't keep you for long, I assure you.

DOG. What a man! Just like me. He'll knock them sideways in a moment, I can tell . . . Ooh, that long streak of piss – what wouldn't I give to sink my teeth into the back of his knee just about his boot-top . . . grrrr!

P.P.P. *picks up the telephone receiver.*

P.P.P. Hello . . . Central Committee . . . I'd like to speak to Ivan Alexandrovich, please . . . it's Professor Preobrazhensky . . . Ivan Alexandrovich? Good afternoon – so glad I was able to reach you . . . Yes, thanks, I'm very well . . . Ivan Alexandrovich, I'm afraid your operation is cancelled . . . Yes, along with all my other operations. I am having to give up working in Moscow, and in fact in Russia altogether . . . Yes, I've had an interesting offer from abroad . . . And now the last straw: three people have come to see me, including a female transvestite dressed as a man and two men armed with revolvers, who are terrorising me in my own apartment with the aim of taking part of it away from me. . . .

SHVONDER. Look here, professor. . . .

P.P.P. In other words they are threatening me with force to make me give up my examination-room, which will oblige me to operate in an unsuitable room in which I previously dissected rabbits and dogfish. I'm sorry, but in the interests of my patients, modern surgical practice will simply not allow me to work under those conditions. I am therefore terminating my practice, shutting up the apartment and going abroad. I shall give the keys to Shvonder, the leader of this gang of armed extortionists. He can do my operations. Perhaps you'd like me to book you in as his first patient? . . . But what am I to do? (*The trio freezes in silent horror.*) I don't like it any more than you do . . . What? . . . Oh no, Ivan Alexandrovich! I simply can't agree to that. No, my patience has finally snapped. This is the second time since August . . . What? . . . H'mm . . . But only on one condition: I don't care how you arrange it, but I want an absolutely cast-iron directive which will ensure that neither Shvonder nor anyone else can so much as knock on my front door – ever again . . . Of course. As far as they are concerned, I am dead and this apartment is a sealed vault . . . Well, that's another matter . . . Very good. I'll put him on the line now. Wait a moment. (*In a silky voice, to* SHVONDER:) Someone would like to speak to you.

SHVONDER. You twisted everything we said, professor. . . .

P.P.P. Kindly refrain from using such expressions.

SHVONDER (*nervous, confused; into the receiver*). Hullo. Yes . . . Chairman of the Housing Committee . . . We were acting strictly according to the rules . . . The professor already has special status. We know about his work . . . We were going to leave him five whole rooms . . . All right, if that's how it is . . . All right. . . .

Crimson in the face, SHVONDER *replaces the receiver.*

DOG. What a man, eh?! He can beat me as much as he likes now – I'm not leaving this place.

PESTRUKHIN *and* VOZNESENSKAYA *stare glumly at the crestfallen* SHVONDER.

VOZNESENSKAYA. If only I'd had a chance to talk to that Ivan Alexandrovich, I'd have shown him. . . .

P.P.P. I can always call him up again. Would you like to talk to him here and now?

VOZNESENSKAYA. You're being sarcastic, aren't you, professor? And enjoying it. No, we're going in a moment. But as head of the cultural department of this housing community, I want to offer you the chance (*produces several garishly-coloured magazines from inside her jacket*) – the chance of buying several of these magazines. Fifty kopecks each. The proceeds go to the starving and oppressed children of Germany.

P.P.P. No, I won't have any, thank you.

The trio registers total amazement.

VOZNESENSKAYA. Why . . . why not?

P.P.P. Because I don't want to.

VOZNESENSKAYA. Don't you feel sorry for the starving and oppressed children of Germany?

P.P.P. I feel *very* sorry for them.

VOZNESENSKAYA. Yet you can't spare fifty kopecks?

P.P.P. Yes, I could.

VOZNESENSKAYA. Then . . . why?

P.P.P. Because I don't want to.

Silence.

VOZNESENSKAYA. You know, professor, if you weren't famous all over the world and if certain people in high places weren't protecting you in the most disgraceful fashion – (PESTRUKHIN, *alarmed, tugs at the hem of her jacket, but she pushes him away*) – people with whom we shall most certainly have this out . . . you ought to be arrested. . . .

P.P.P. (*with curiosity*). On what charge?

VOZNESENSKAYA. Because you hate the proletariat.

P.P.P. (*losing patience; shouts*). Yes – I do not like the proletariat!

In the total silence that follows this remark, a deep bass motor-car horn is heard offstage, followed by the downstairs front door slamming, the rhythmic clump of three pairs of hobnailed boots on the staircase and a ring at the front door of the apartment. Enter THREE OGPU MEN *in tunics, breeches, boots and peaked caps.*

FIRST OGPU. OGPU! State Political Police!

VOZNESENSKAYA (*overjoyed*). Greetings, comrade!

FIRST OGPU. Who is this, Philip Philipovich?

P.P.P. I don't know. They just burst in without being invited.

VOZNESENSKAYA. We are the House Committee of this building.

FIRST OGPU. All right, you can act as official witnesses. Where are the galoshes, Philip Philipovich?

P.P.P. Here they are.

SECOND OGPU. We are taking these galoshes as evidence in the presence of the official witnesses.

SECOND OGPU *takes the galoshes, wraps them in newspaper and carries them off.*

SHVONDER. Comrades, as chairman of the House Committee, I. . .

FIRST OGPU (*ignoring* SHVONDER). Philip Philipovich, could you describe your visitor's appearance?

P.P.P. Oh, God knows . . . Unpleasant face . . . what you'd call degenerate . . . brilliantined hair parted in the middle . . . spats . . . smokes cigars. . . .

THIRD OGPU. Did he have one glass eye?

P.P.P. No. Both eyes kept swivelling from side to side.

FIRST OGPU (*to* THIRD OGPU). Is it him?

THIRD OGPU. I doubt it. He doesn't give money without a receipt. This one's a bigger fish.

P.P.P. Who *was* this scoundrel?

FIRST OGPU. A con-man. But we must ask you to keep today's events absolutely secret. Rest assured, Philip Philipovich, you won't be bothered any more, either at home or in your clinic. Steps will be taken. You and your work are absolutely safe. I'm putting a man on your door round the clock. We are here to protect you from any undesirable visitors.

P.P.P. I suppose you couldn't have your man shoot any reporters, could you?

THIRD OGPU *doubles up with laughter.*

FIRST OGPU (*also laughing*). Impossible, I'm afraid. Goodbye, Philip Philipovich.

P.P.P. Thank you, gentlemen. (*Presses a bell, which rings somewhere offstage.*)

Enter ZINA.

P.P.P. You may serve lunch now, Zina.

Exeunt OGPU MEN, SHVONDER, VOZNESENSKAYA *and* PESTRUKHIN.

Scene Four

The terrifying operating-table has been replaced by a dining-table. As heavy and solid as the vault over a rich man's grave, it is covered by a snow-white tablecloth; upon it are two placesettings, two starched table-napkins folded into the shape of a mitre, and three bottles filled with dark liquids. P.P.P. *and* BORMENTAL *are seated at the table. The* DOG *is sitting at the feet of his benefactor.* ZINA, *having shed her white coat and re-assumed her saucy maid's uniform, brings in a covered silver entrée dish, in which something can be heard sizzling.*

P.P.P. Doctor Bormental, I beg you to try this delicious morsel! If you tell me you don't like it, I'm your enemy for life!

P.P.P. *offers* BORMENTAL *a tit-bit and pours out two glasses of wine. His eyes gleam with gastronomic anticipation.*

BORMENTAL. It is delicious – incomparable!

P.P.P. There you are! (*On the end of a fork he offers another tit-bit to the* DOG, *who snaps it up with the speed and skill of a conjuror.*)

ZINA. If you feed that dog in the dining-room, you'll never be able to get him out of here again.

P.P.P. It doesn't matter, just for once. The poor thing's starving. Kindly note, Ivan Arnoldovich, that the only people who start their meal with cold hors d'oeuvres and soup are the few remaining landlords and capitalists who haven't yet been strung up by the Bolsheviks. Any self-respecting person starts off with a hot first course. Eating, Ivan Arnoldovich, is an art.

Most people simply don't know how to eat. One must not only know *what* to eat but *when* and *where*. And how to talk when you're eating. There are proper topics of conversation to accompany sturgeon, and others to go with roast beef.

DOG. What's happened to me? It's a funny feeling – I'm not staring at the food any more. Can I really be *full*? Don't say it's going to be like this every day from now on!!!

P.P.P. And that is how it should be every day.

P.P.P. gets up from the table, passes through the hall to the front door and opens it to reveal SECOND OGPU MAN, *dressed in his para-military-style uniform, who is standing guard on the landing.*

P.P.P. How are you going to eat out here?

SECOND OGPU. Don't worry, professor, we're taking it in turns. I'll be relieved soon. No one disturbing you, I hope?

P.P.P. I must say you've organised it extremely well. (*Returns to the table.*) And my advice to you, Ivan Arnoldovich, is not to talk about either politics or medicine at table. And don't read the newspapers before lunch. I have conducted some research on it in my clinic. Patients who have been reading newspapers in the waiting-room exhibit an impaired knee-jerk reflex and loss of appetite. I advised them . . . (*The sound of a mixed choir, somewhat deadened by the ceiling, is heard coming from above.*)

P.P.P. Zina, my dear, what is the meaning of that . . . er, singing?

ZINA. It's a general meeting of the tenants, Philip Philipovich, called by the House Committee.

P.P.P. Not again! Oh well, at least we know what will happen. First it's community singing every evening, then the pipes will freeze in the lavatories, next the central heating boiler will burst . . . and so on. And what a splendid house it used to be!

BORMENTAL. You take too gloomy a view of things. The situation has greatly improved recently.

P.P.P. My dear fellow, I cannot tolerate unfounded hypotheses. I am a man of facts, hard facts. I'm well known for it in the medical world, not only in Russia but all over the world. If I say something, it means that it is based on some fact from which I have drawn a logical conclusion. And in this case the fact is the following: the galoshes-rack in this house.

BORMENTAL. Really? That's interesting. . . .

P.P.P. I have been living in this house since 1903. And for all that
time, there has not been a single instance – I will underline
that in red pencil: 'Not a single instance' *until now* of the
disappearance from the main downstairs hallway of every
galosh without exception, three walking-sticks, an overcoat
and the porter's samovar. I will not even mention the fiasco
of the central heating. Indeed, I will concede that perhaps
central heating is no longer necessary when there has been a
revolution. But I am *impelled* to ask: why should one be
forced to keep one's galoshes under lock and key? Why has
the carpet been removed from the main staircase? Did Karl
Marx forbid us to have stair-carpets? Can you point out a
single passage in the complete works of Karl Marx where it
says that porches must be boarded up and tenants must go
all round the house and come in by the back door? What
good does it do to anyone? Why can't the proletariat leave its
galoshes downstairs, instead of wearing them to clump up the
uncarpeted stairs and cover the marble steps in filth?

BORMENTAL (*timidly*). But the proletariat *has* no galoshes, Philip
Philipovich. . . .

P.P.P. Oh yes it has! And those galoshes are *mine*! My very own
galoshes! And who do you suppose pinched them? Did I?
Impossible. One can't steal one's own property. Was it the
bourgeois Vassily Pavlovich who lives upstairs? (*Points upwards
to the ceiling.*) The mere suggestion is absurd. And who the
devil removed the flowers from the landings? Why is the
electricity, which if I remember rightly has not failed for
twenty years, now cut off regularly once a month for an
indefinite period?

BORMENTAL. It's the economic dislocation caused by the civil
war, Philip Philipovich.

P.P.P. No! No, my dear Ivan Arnoldovich, kindly refrain from
using that expression. What is this 'economic dislocation' that
everyone is so fond of blaming? Is it a witch, who flies
around on a broomstick smashing the bulbs in all the street
lamps? It simply doesn't exist! What lies behind that bogus
phrase? (P.P.P. *angrily addresses this question to the* OWL, *but
answers it himself*:) I'll tell you what it really means: if instead
of operating on my patients I start singing in a choir, then
economic dislocation will start in my household. If when I go

to the lavatory I start pissing on the floor instead of into the bowl, and if you and Zina start doing the same thing, then dislocation starts in the lavatory. (*Warming to his subject,* P.P.P. *becomes louder and more oratorical until by the end of his remarks he sounds like an Old Testament prophet.*) Ergo, 'dislocation' is in people's heads and not in water-closets. When people shout: 'Beat dislocation!', what they really mean is that everyone needs to give themselves a good kick up the backside. And then when they have kicked all these delusions and excuses out of themselves and they start cleaning out sheds, mending burst pipes, sweeping the streets, planting potatoes and producing goods that other people need – which is what they should have been doing all along – then 'economic dislocation' will vanish of its own accord.

DOG (*enthusiastically*). That's right! You tell 'em! Ow-oow-owow! Grrrr!

P.P.P. What's the matter with you?!

DOG. Hurrrr-ah! He could make a fortune at political meetings. Still, you can see he's not short of a rouble or two already.

P.P.P. You call it 'economic dislocation'! And I tell you that nothing will change in this house until you make those people shut up and stop singing! As soon as they cease giving their concerts, the situation will immediately and automatically start improving.

DOG. Owow-oow-ow?

BORMENTAL. (*jokingly*). That's counter-revolutionary propaganda, Philip Philipovich!

P.P.P. There's nothing counter-revolutionary whatever in what I'm saying! Nothing but plain common sense based on a certain amount of experience. We shall do nothing today. *Aida* is on at the Bolshoi tonight. I haven't heard *Aida* for ages, and I'm very fond of it. . . .

BORMENTAL. How will you find the time, Philip Philipovich?

P.P.P. You can always find time if you're never in a hurry. Of course, if I started going to meetings and singing like a nightingale instead of getting on with my proper job, I'd never find time to go anywhere. I'm a great believer in the division of labour. Let them sing at the Bolshoi, and I will operate. That's the way it should be. And then there won't be any 'economic dislocation'. Sharik, come here.

DOG. I'm full, master – I can't eat any more.

But the DOG *crawls to* P.P.P. *all the same.* P.P.P. *goes to the glass-fronted cabinet, where human brains and other more obscene objects are floating in liquid-filled glass jars; from a shelf he takes a gleaming new dog-collar and fastens it around the* DOG's *neck. Exeunt* P.P.P. *and* BORMENTAL, *leaving the* DOG *alone.*

DOG. A collar . . . That means – it's for good! A collar to a dog is like a briefcase to a civil servant. I have a master! A master in dark brown fox-fur with millions of snowflakes gleaming on the collar, a master who smells of tangerines, petrol, cigars, eau-de-cologne and expensive suits. His voice resounds through the house like a cavalry-trumpet! I've drawn the winning prize in the dogs' lottery!

OWL (*lighting up its eyes*). You creep.

DOG. Creep nothing! I live here now. They've combed out all my fleas.

OWL. Arse-licker.

DOG. He loves me! He spoils me! I could chew up his trousers or his shoes and he'd forgive me, because he's a good man – he's a magician, a wizard and a sorcerer out of dogs' fairy-tales! And my flank has healed! (*Tears off his bandage.*) Oh, my new life! Oh, master! Oh how I'll love him! . . . Now for that sodding owl. . . .

The DOG *jumps up, pulls the* OWL *off its branch on the wall and starts to tear it open; two electric wires and the stuffing, made of strips of red rag, burst out of the* OWL's *stomach.*

Enter ZINA, *who clasps her hands in horror, then sits down, puts the* DOG's *head on her knees and starts to scratch him behind his ear. The soprano voice bursts into an aria from* Aida. *Enter* P.P.P.

P.P.P. Why did you tear that poor owl to pieces, you villain? (*Puts on a white coat.*)

ZINA. I purposely didn't clear up the mess so that you could see what your new pet has done. Smack him across the muzzle, Philip Philipovich, to teach him not to be so destructive. (*Puts on a white coat.*)

P.P.P. Why did you bite Doctor Bormental? (*Points to the torn remnants of the* OWL.) And why did you have to pull all the stuffing out of poor old Professor Mechnikov? (*Dons a white surgeon's cap.*)

ZINA (*in a sugary voice*). You should give him a good whipping, or else he'll be thoroughly spoiled. (*Puts on a nurse's cap.*)

P.P.P. You must never whip any creature, remember that once and for all. (ZINA *helps him to put on a rubber apron and rubber gloves.*)

ZINA. He's already eaten us out of house and home in less than a week. I wonder he doesn't burst. (*Opens out the operating-table.*)

P.P.P. Remember, one can only ever make animals or humans do what you want by kindness and subtle suggestion.

ZINA *switches on a brilliant light. Enter* BORMENTAL *and* FYODOR *the porter, both dragging a large trunk.*

ZINA (*pushing a glass-topped, wheeled table, laden with surgical instruments, towards the operating-table*). Lord, what a shaggy dog the professor's found this time.

FYODOR. And fat, too.

DOG. What's he up to? Why has he put on a white cap? My flank has healed up, after all . . . I'm getting out of here!

BORMENTAL. The corpse, Philip Philipovich.

P.P.P. When did he die?

BORMENTAL. Three hours ago.

P.P.P. (*putting on a surgical mask and flexing his rubber-encased fingers*). Excellent.

DOG. But where could I go? I'm a gentleman's dog now, a civilised creature, I've tasted the good life. I can't go back to the backyards and the gutter.

P.P.P. Whatever you do, don't alarm or excite the dog.

DOG. Anyway, what is freedom? It's a mirage, a fiction, a politician's catchword.

P.P.P. On to the table with him.

DOG. You can take me if you like, but you ought to be ashamed of yourselves. Four against one. It's disgraceful! Shame on you.

The DOG *tries to run away, but only slides on the slippery parquet, and is caught and held fast by* ZINA, BORMENTAL *and* FYODOR.

Scene Five

The operating theatre. Brilliant light. The DOG *has been strapped to the operating table and chloroformed by Dr.* BORMENTAL. P.P.P., BORMENTAL *and* ZINA *are all wearing white gowns and masks.* FYODOR *stands by the door.*

P.P.P. Lock all the doors, don't answer the telephone and don't let anybody in, Fyodor.

FYODOR. Very good, professor. (*Exit hastily.*)

ZINA (*covers the* DOG *with a sheet*). Can I go now, please? (*Without waiting for an answer, she runs off.*)

P.P.P. Pity, really – I shall miss him. I'd grown used to having him around . . . Ivan Arnoldovich, when you have opened up the dog's skull and I go into the brain, I beg you to give me the cerebellum from the corpse's brain *instantly*. You will then connect it up to the apparatus without a second's delay. Is he asleep?

BORMENTAL. Yes, he's sound asleep now.

P.P.P. Then let's begin.

BORMENTAL *takes a gleaming surgical saw from the glass-topped instrument table, bends over the* DOG's *head and starts sawing. The muffled sound of singing by the House Committee choir comes up through the floor.*

BORMENTAL. Ready.

P.P.P. Careful now, Ivan Arnoldovich, this is the most vital moment.

All the lights go out.

P.P.P. (*roars*). God damn and blast them!! A power failure at a moment like this! Zina – quickly!

The sound of the invisible choir swells. ZINA *runs in with a hurricane-lamp. Holding it over the operating table, she turns her head away in order not to see the operation.*

FIRST OGPU *(enters with hurricane-lamp).* Are you all right, professor? Can you manage like this?

P.P.P. Scissors?

BORMENTAL *clatters the instruments on the glass-topped table as he fumbles for the surgical scissors.* FIRST OGPU *comes over and holds his lamp over the instrument table.*

FIRST OGPU. There they are.

P.P.P. Forceps!

BORMENTAL. His pulse is weakening.

P.P.P. So what are you waiting for? Inject adrenalin!

BORMENTAL *(fumbling among the instruments for a syringe).* Where the hell is the syringe?

P.P.P. *(angrily).* Oh, don't bother! He's probably dead already. How can anyone possibly operate under these circumstances? Give me the corpse's brain!

FIRST OGPU *goes over to the trunk, takes out of it a boot, a half-empty bottle of port, then a human head. He hands the head to* BORMENTAL, *who quickly saws it open, then hands it to* P.P.P. *The* FAT JOURNALIST *appears in the doorway, carrying a hurricane-lamp.*

FAT JOURNALIST. The door wasn't shut, professor. I'm from the *Industrial Post.* Please say a few words to our readers about your work.

P.P.P. *(to* BORMENTAL). Is he dead?

BORMENTAL. Pulse no more than a thread.

A PATIENT *appears in the doorway holding a hurricane-lamp – he is an old man with green hair and an uncontrollable twitch in his right leg.*

PATIENT. Please forgive me for coming in without ringing, professor, but I had to come and tell you how thrilled and delighted I am with your treatment. You're a magician, a sorcerer! I'm young again! Every night I dream of hordes of young girls!

FAT JOURNALIST (*setting up a camera on a tripod*). Just a few words about the application of your invention to Soviet industry, please, professor.

PATIENT. *Parole d'honneur*, professor, the last time I felt like this was 25 years ago – in Paris!

P.P.P. (*to* BORMENTAL). Clamp. Scalpel. Clamp.

FAT JOURNALIST. Is it true, professor, that your invention guarantees a colossal rate of growth in all living tissue? (*A flash of magnesium powder as he photographs* P.P.P. *at work.*)

P.P.P. Clamp. Scalpel. Is he dead?

BORMENTAL. Still alive – just.

FAT JOURNALIST. So, professor – what exactly is your invention?

FIRST OGPU. Professor Preobrazhensky has invented a vitalising ray that can accelerate growth and stimulate new growth. The device works by electricity.

FAT JOURNALIST. That's very interesting. What would you like to tell our readers?

FIRST OGPU. The professor sends all your readers warmest proletarian greetings.

FAT JOURNALIST. Thank you very, very much indeed!

P.P.P. (*to* BORMENTAL). You can suture him up now. Poor dog. He's not still breathing, is he?

BORMENTAL. Yes, he is.

PATIENT. You're a magician, professor. I'm young again!

Enter DARYA PETROVNA. *In one hand she holds an old-fashioned oil-lamp, in the other a roast turkey on a dish.*

PATIENT (*to* DARYA PETROVNA). *Ah, madame* – you are quite ravishing!

DARYA P. I'm the cook. The turkey's ready, Philip Philipovich. Do you want your lunch now? If you leave it much longer the bird will be all dry. What shall I do with it?

FIRST OGPU. Bring it here. (*Takes the turkey and puts it on the glass-topped instrument table. To* PATIENT.) What's happened to your hair?

PATIENT. That charlatan! Gave me this dye and said it would turn my hair brown – and look at it! Oh professor, if only you could rejuvenate my hair as well!

FIRST OGPU. We'll be able to do everything in time. You can all go now.

FAT JOURNALIST. Thank you!

Exeunt FAT JOURNALIST, DARYA PETROVNA *and* PATIENT.

Scene Six

By the light of a candle held by ZINA, BORMENTAL *is finishing his suturing.*

BORMENTAL. He's sewn up now, Philip Philipovich.

P.P.P. Is he really going to survive, I wonder? No, no, he's bound to die. Pity. He was a nice dog, affectionate and good tempered.

The electric lighting suddenly comes on again.

P.P.P. Switch on the apparatus at once!

BORMENTAL *swtiches on the apparatus, from which comes the sudden sound of the soprano singing an aria from* Aida. ZINA *blows out the candle, looks at the* DOG, *sobs and runs off.*

FIRST OGPU. Keep working and don't worry – I'll see to it that no one disturbs you.

Exit FIRST OGPU MAN *on tiptoe.*

P.P.P. *(taking off his cap, apron and white coat).* Take down my notes, please, Ivan Arnoldovich.

BORMENTAL *takes off his rubber gloves and fetches notebook and pen.*

P.P.P. Write as follows: Subject – laboratory dog. Male. Breed – mongrel. Name – Sharik.

BORMENTAL. He moved!

P.P.P. Don't say he's coming round! . . . Continue: Fur, thick and chestnut-brown. The animal has been the subject of the world's first operation to transplant the brain, heart and testicles of a human male who died three hours before the operation. Indications leading to the operation: the need for experimental evidence on transplanting the vital organs and the effect thereon of the ray.

BORMENTAL. Philip Philipovich – he's scratching himself.

P.P.P. Nice doggy, good doggy. . . .

DOG. Oowoooo . . . Aaaaah . . . Ooowaa. . . .

P.P.P. Emitted a groan similar to the cry of a human infant. Pulse normal.

BORMENTAL. Look – his fur is falling off.

P.P.P. Continue: The first observable effect of the ray – localised loss of hair. Poor dog.

DOG. Srehctub!

P.P.P. (*undoing the straps holding the* DOG *to the operating-table*). Continue: Barked, but abnormally.

BORMENTAL. His tail has fallen off!

P.P.P. Continue: (*Dictates:*) Loss of hair becoming general. Diagnosis not determined. Visible lengthening of the limbs and extremities and growth of the cranium . . . Completely unexpected effect!

The DOG *sits up on the operating-table, scratches himself, picks up his disconnected tail in his hand and wags it.*

DOG (*cheerfully*). Srehctub! Srehctub!

BORMENTAL. He's talking!

P.P.P. Calm yourself, Ivan Arnoldovich. We are scientists. Write down whatever you hear him say. He clearly barked the word 'Srehctub'.

DOG. Pohs-srehctub! Pohs-srehctub!

BORMENTAL (*writing*). Pohs-srehctub. If you read it backwards, Philip Philipovich, you get the words 'Butchers-shop'.

P.P.P. (*stroking the* DOG's *head*). Well done! Well done!

DOG (*to* BORMENTAL). Fuck off, you! (*Licks* P.P.P.'s *hand.*)

BORMENTAL. He's talking. (*Claps his hands in excitement.*)

The DOG *catches sight of the turkey and licks his chops.*

P.P.P. Eat, Sharik, eat! . . . Yes, you may, you may.

DOG (*gratefully*). Stop pushing, you bastard. Srehctub! (*Starts to eat the turkey.*)

P.P.P. Splendid. Continue the notes: Loss of body-hair now total, except for the head, the chin, the chest and pubic region. Lower limbs and skull continue to grow. The muzzle has virtually disappeared, to be replaced by a flat nose and mouth.

P.P.P. *covers the dog with a sheet.*

DOG. Pohs-srehctub!

Wrapped in the sheet, the DOG *jumps off the operating-table, rubs himself against* P.P.P's *leg, runs around* BORMENTAL, *then picks up the bottle standing beside the trunk and drinks the entire contents from the mouth of the bottle.*

P.P.P. Quickly, my dear Ivan Arnoldovich! Continue the notes: The transplants combined with irradiation have produced an unexpected result – humanisation. The subject's degree of verbal comprehension must now be tested.

DOG. Pohs-srehctub. Daddy.

P.P.P. My God! Here, boy!

The DOG *nuzzles* P.P.P.

BORMENTAL (*excitedly*). He's talking!

P.P.P. (*tenderly*). The habitus is that of a human male in process of formation. Hair: silky. Appetite appears good. Growth continuing rapidly.

DOG (*looking into* P.P.P.'s *eyes*). Srehctub! No queue-barging, you sodding bastards!

BORMENTAL. *What* did he say? Really, Sharik!

P.P.P. Who was that corpse, Ivan Arnoldovich?

From inside the trunk BORMENTAL *produces a human arm, the hand of which holds an identity card gripped by the fingers.*

BORMENTAL (*pointing to a tattoo on the arm*). He seems to have been called Klim. (*Wrenches the identity card from the fingers with difficulty, opens it and reads it:*) Klim Grigorievich Chugunkin.

Aged 25. Criminal record: Two acquittals and one conviction. On the first two occasions he was saved by his proletarian origin, the third time he was given a suspended sentence of 15 years. Cause of death: knife-blow to the heart in a bar in the Taganka district . . . Philip Philipovich, I congratulate you – this is a historic moment! Without using Faust's retort you have created a homunculus! Professor Preobrazhensky – you have created human life! Using only the surgeon's knife you have brought a new unit of the human race into the world!

P.P.P. (*rubbing his hands*). Now, now, Ivan Arnoldovich – I must say I wasn't expecting anything like this. Zina! Bring some clothes and dress him.

Enter ZINA with jacket and trousers. The DOG gambols around her.

ZINA. Oh, stop it . . . Stand still, Sharik! . . . He's just like a child.

DOG. Srehctub! Srehctub! Stupid bitch!

Squealing with delight, the DOG snatches the jacket, away from ZINA with his teeth and gallops around the room.

ZINA. Here – give that back!

BORMENTAL *and* ZINA *rush to catch the* DOG, *who suddenly drops the jacket, twists his head round and circles around backwards as he tries to bite something on his back.*
DOG. Bugger off! I'll get you!

P.P.P. It's a flea. We must give him a bath.

All try and help the DOG catch the flea. Exit ZINA, to return with DARYA PETROVNA, carrying a large basin, and FYODOR, carrying an enamel jug of hot water. The DOG is led away behind a screen, where DARYA PETROVNA and FYODOR can be heard washing and dressing him.

Scene Seven

The erstwhile DOG, now apparently fully human, is seated on a chair, wearing ill-fitting jacket and trousers. P.P.P. sits at the piano; Dr. BORMENTAL stands beside him, observing the NEW MAN's reactions: the two scientists are conducting a test to determine whether the NEW MAN can reproduce the tones of the diatonic scale.

P.P.P. *strikes middle 'C' on the piano.*

BORMENTAL *(sings).* Do-o-o-o!

P.P.P. *strikes 'D'.*

BORMENTAL *(sings).* Re-e-e-e!

NEW MAN *(thoughtfully).* Fucking bourgeoisie. . . .

Enter from the hall FIRST OGPU MAN, *holding a newspaper. He quietly asks* P.P.P.:

FIRST OGPU. How is the work going?

P.P.P. *puts his finger to his lips and strikes 'E'.*

BORMENTAL. Mi-mi-i-i!

NEW MAN *yawns, politely covering his mouth with his hand.*

P.P.P. *strikes 'F'.*

BORMENTAL. Fa-a-a-a!

FIRST OGPU. They're writing about us in the papers, professor. Listen: 'Rumours about Martians having landed in Obukhov Street are entirely without foundation. The rumours were put about by street-traders in the Sukharevka flea-market. Seven traders have been arrested for spreading rumours.' I won't disturb you any more.

FIRST OGPU MAN puts the newspaper on an armchair; exit on tiptoe. P.P.P. strikes 'G' on the piano, followed by 'A', 'B' and 'C'.

BORMENTAL. So-ol! . . . La-a-a! . . . Ti-i-i! . . . Do-o-oooo!

NEW MAN *(leaps up).* I'll kill you, you mother-fucker!

NEW MAN dashes off into the hall. Scuffling sounds are heard around the flat; doors slam; ZINA and DARYA PETROVNA scream, and the NEW MAN gives a howl.

P.P.P.
BORMENTAL } *(in chorus).* The cat! My God – the cat!

P.P.P. and BORMENTAL run off. FIRST OGPU MAN looks in and runs off again. All gather outside the locked frosted-glass bathroom door. Behind it, shadowy figures can be seen leaping about.

ZINA. He's locked himself in the bathroom!

P.P.P. Patience and kindness! Patience and kindness! Ivan Arnoldovich, for god's sake go and calm the patients in the waiting-room.

FIRST OGPU. Open up this minute!

NEW MAN. I'll kill you!

The glass in the transom above the door suddenly shatters as a CAT *flies through it, lands on its feet and runs off like a bullet. From the bathroom comes the sound of a powerful stream of water flowing from a bath-tap. An* OLD WOMAN *puts her head round the door from the hall.*

OLD WOMAN. Oh, Lord Jesus!

P.P.P. What do you want?

OLD WOMAN. I want to see the talking dog.

FIRST OGPU (*banging on the bathroom door*). Open up!

P.P.P. (*to* OLD WOMAN). Get out of here this second!

OLD WOMAN (*amazed and distressed; staggers back*). You're very sharp today, professor. (*Exit.*)

Enter BORMENTAL.

BORMENTAL (*to* P.P.P.). There are 17 patients in the waiting-room.

P.P.P. Send them all home. I'm not seeing anyone today. (*Raps on the bathroom door with his knuckles.*) Come on, old boy, please come out at once!

Exit BORMENTAL.

NEW MAN. Owoow-owowow!

P.P.P. What the hell is he saying? (*Loudly:*) I can't hear you – turn off the water!

ZINA. Look – there he is!

The NEW MAN's *face appears in the transom. Two fresh, bleeding scratches have appeared on either side of his nose.*

P.P.P. Why won't you come out? Turn off the water!

NEW MAN (*miserably*). Owoow-owowooo

FIRST OGPU (*pointing to water beginning to seep under the bathroom door*). Water. . . .

NEW MAN. Bow-wow-wow!

P.P.P. (*barely restraining himself*). Open the door!

NEW MAN. The bloody thing won't open!

ZINA. Oh my God, he's pushed the little safety-lock!

P.P.P. (*loudly, trying to make himself heard above the noise of the water*). There's . . . a . . . little . . . knob . . . just . . . under . . . the . . . door-handle! Push . . . it . . . *up*!

ZINA. No – push it *down*! *Down*!

The NEW MAN *disappears for a second or two, then reappears in the transom.*

NEW MAN (*terrified*). Can't see a fucking thing!

P.P.P. Then switch on the light!

NEW MAN. That bloody cat smashed the light-bulb. I'd just got hold of him by the hind legs when I turned the tap on by mistake, and now I can't find it.

Enter FYODOR *with a step-ladder, which he positions beside the bathroom door. He climbs up the ladder and peers into the bathroom through the transom.*

FYODOR. Should I open the door? The water-pressure will be terrific.

ZINA. Doesn't matter – that door's *got* to be opened.

P.P.P. (*to* ZINA). You're right. (*To* FYODOR:) Go ahead, Fyodor – open it.

FYODOR *climbs through the transom and opens the door. A tidal wave floods out of the bathroom. The tap is turned off.*

FIRST OGPU. I'll see to it that no one disturbs you.

Exit FIRST OPGU MAN, *trying to avoid the streams of water. Exit* ZINA.

P.P.P. (*through bathroom doorway, to* NEW MAN). Well – where are you?

FYODOR. He's afraid to come out.

NEW MAN. Will you beat me, dad?

P.P.P. You idiot.

Enter ZINA *and* DARYA PETROVNA *with buckets, mops and*

floor-cloths. They tuck up their skirts, FYODOR *and the* NEW MAN *roll up their trousers, and the four start mopping up the water with cloths and mops, squeezing it out into the buckets. Through the half-open door into the hall,* BORMENTAL *is heard talking to a* PATIENT.

BORMENTAL. I'm afraid there will be no surgery hours today. The professor is unwell. Please keep away from the door – a pipe has burst.

PATIENT. But when *can* he see me?

BORMENTAL. Zina, my dear, it's running out on to the staircase!

ZINA. These cloths are so sodden, they can't soak it up fast enough!

P.P.P. The flat's ruined. . . .

PATIENT. When will he do my operation?

BORMENTAL (*patiently*). A pipe has burst. . . .

PATIENT. I could always come in my galoshes.

The NEW MAN *rolls up the carpet into a tube, kneels down in the puddle and uses the rolled-up carpet to push the water back into the bathroom.*

NEW MAN (*calmly*). Bloody brute. Fucking anti-Soviet bourgeois. . . .

P.P.P. Who are you talking about?

NEW MAN. The sodding cat, of course.

BORMENTAL. How much longer are you going to go on chasing cats? You ought to be ashamed of yourself. It's disgraceful. You're no better than a savage.

NEW MAN. Who, me? I'm no savage. I just can't bear having that brute in the flat, that's all. So I wanted to teach him a lesson!

BORMENTAL. *You're* the one who needs to be taught a lesson. Just look at you. Go and get changed!

NEW MAN (*rubbing the scratches on his face with a dirty hand*). Nearly had my eye out, he did. It's a counter-revolutionary bourgeois plot . . . (*Exit.*)

FYODOR. We've mopped it all up now, Philip Philipovich.

P.P.P. (*giving* FYODOR *a handsome tip*). I'm most grateful, Fyodor. There's something for your trouble.

FYODOR. Thank you very much, sir. Glad to oblige.

P.P.P. You're soaking wet. Go and have a glass of Darya Petrovna's vodka in the kitchen.

FYODOR. Thank you very much, sir . . . Er, I'm sorry, Philip Philipovich, there was one more thing . . . don't know how to put it, seeing as you've had all *this* trouble . . . I hardly like to ask, really . . . but there was this window broken in No. 7 on the first floor, you see . . . the fact is, that er . . . new young fellow of yours was throwing stones at it, and. . . .

P.P.P. Was he throwing stones at a cat?

FYODOR. Well, yes . . . but he smashed the window and hit the tenant, Vassily Petrovich, instead. And he's threatening to sue you.

P.P.P. The devil he is. What for?

FYODOR. Your, er . . . young man put his arm round Vassily Petrovich's cook. They had a bit of a barney, and she complained. . . .

VOICE OF NEW MAN. She's only a cook, but the way she goes on – you'd think she was a bloody commissar.

P.P.P. How much?

FYODOR. A hundred and fifty.

P.P.P. *hands money to* FYODOR.

VOICE OF NEW MAN. You're not going to give that rogue a hundred and fifty, are you? 'Specially when he's been carrying on with that cook himself. . . .

BORMENTAL. Shut up! How dare you!

FYODOR. Well, if that isn't the bloody limit! The cheek of him. I'd like to fetch him one round the ear-'ole.

P.P.P. (*sadly*). Now, Fyodor – really. . . .

FYODOR. Beg pardon, Philip Philipovich, but I feel sorry for you, what with all this. . . .

The electric light goes out, and the sound of the House Committee choir comes through the walls.

FYODOR. 'Ere we go again. . . .

Scene Eight

When the lights come on again, the dining-table has been set for lunch. The NEW MAN *enters, dips his finger into a sauce-boat of mayonnaise and uses it to polish the toes of his patent-leather shoes. He settles himself in* P.P.P.'s *armchair and opens a newspaper, clearly imitating* P.P.P.'s *habitual actions. Enter* P.P.P., *who chases the* NEW MAN *out of the chair.*

P.P.P. What is that revolting object? I'm referring to your tie.

NEW MAN (*moving over into another armchair, without relinquishing the newspaper*). It's a very smart tie.

P.P.P. And those shoes. Surely Dr. Bormental didn't choose them, did he?

NEW MAN. I told him to get patent-leather ones. Why should I be any worse than other people? Walk down Kuznetsky Most and take a look – everyone's wearing patent-leather shoes.

P.P.P. Take off that nauseating thing from your neck. This is not a circus . . . And I don't want to hear any more swearing out of you. And don't spit on the floor. If you must spit, use the spittoon over there. And kindly improve your aim when you piss. And cease talking to Zina. She complains that you are always lurking around dark corners waiting to pounce on her. You're not in a public bar now.

NEW MAN (*sighs*). Being a bit hard on me, aren't you, dad? Why all the rules and regulations?

P.P.P. And what do you mean by calling me 'dad'? I will not have this familiarity. You will address me by my name and patronymic – I am Philip Philipovich to you.

NEW MAN. Look, what is all this? Don't spit, don't smoke – it's like being in a tramcar. Why don't you just leave me alone? I didn't ask to have the operation done, did I? You pick up an animal, split his skull open – and now you don't like what you've done. I don't suppose I ever gave you my permission to do the operation. Nor my parents didn't, either. I reckon I could sue you!

P.P.P. Are you permitting yourself to express dissatisfaction that you were turned into a human being? Perhaps you would prefer to revert to scavenging among the dustbins again?

NEW MAN (*hiding behind the newspaper*). Why do you have to sneer like that? 'Scavenging among the dustbins'! I earned my crust and I survived – which is more than you'd have done if you had to live like that. And what if I'd died on you when I was on the operating-table? What have you got to say to that, comrade?

P.P.P. (*with long-suffering patience*). I am *not* your comrade.

NEW MAN. Oh no, of course not, how silly of me . . . we know our place, don't we . . . How could *we* be your comrades?! The very idea! We never studied at university, did we? We've never lived in a fifteen-room flat, have we? But all that's got to change now. Since the revolution everyone has the right. . . .

The NEW MAN *suddenly clicks his teeth and thrusts his nose under his armpit.*

P.P.P. Catch fleas with your fingers! Your fingers, I say! Though I can't understand why you've got any fleas.

NEW MAN. I don't breed them on purpose, do I? Obviously, fleas like me. (*Feels under his armpit with his fingers and pulls out a tuft of ginger hair, which he flicks into the air.*) Look, dad, I wanted to ask you something. . . .

P.P.P. What?

NEW MAN. Papers. I need papers, Philip Philipovich.

P.P.P. What sort of papers?

NEW MAN. Firstly, the House Committee. . . .

P.P.P. What has the House Committee got to do with it?

NEW MAN. Well, when they meet me on the stairs, they ask me – politely, mind you – when I'm going to be properly registered and get a residence permit.

P.P.P. I forbade you to loiter on the staircase!

NEW MAN. What d'you mean – 'loiter'? That sounds a bit rude, doesn't it? I want to be free like everyone else! I've got as much right to use the stairs as you have.

The NEW MAN *stamps his patent-leathered foot on the parquet.*

P.P.P. (*hastily drinks a glass of water*). It's not a question of what I *sound* like. It's a complicated matter . . . So what else did your *dear friends* in the House Committee have to say to you?

NEW MAN. You don't have to be sarcastic about them. Their job is to look after my interests. Listen to this. (*Reads from newspaper.*) 'There is no doubt that this person is his illegitimate, as it was called in rotten bourgeois society, son. So that is how our bourgeois pseudo-scientists amuse themselves. He can occupy his seven rooms until the shining sword of proletarian justice glints over his head like a red ray of the approaching communist sunrise. Signed: Shvonder.' He's the one who's looking after our interests.

P.P.P. The scoundrel! Zina! (*Fastidiously takes the newspaper in two fingers.*)

Enter ZINA.

Zina! (*Holding out the newspaper.*) Kindly put this in the stove!

Exit ZINA *with newspaper.*

And exactly *whose* interests is he looking after?

NEW MAN. That's obvious – the working elements.

P.P.P. And on what grounds are you classed among the 'working element'?

NEW MAN. That's obvious too – 'cos I'm not a bourgeois, am I?

P.P.P. All right. What does he propose to do to defend your revolutionary interests?

NEW MAN. He's going to register me for a residence permit. Who ever heard of anyone living in Moscow without a residence permit?

P.P.P. Listen: how am I going to get you a permit? Don't forget that you are a . . . a laboratory creature. You have neither first name nor surname!

NEW MAN. I can always choose a name for myself. I read a name written in a newspaper article just now, and – bingo! That's me.

P.P.P. What would you like to call yourself?

NEW MAN (*straightening his tie*). Polygraph Polygraphovich.

P.P.P. Don't play the fool. I'm asking you seriously.

NEW MAN. I am serious. I can't call myself after my mother, can I? She was a bitch and I'm her son . . . well, you see the problem. And all I ever hear from you is 'fool, idiot, blockhead'. Is it true that only professors are allowed to swear in Russia?

P.P.P. Excuse me. My nerves are in shreds . . . It was just that the name you chose sounded rather strange. Where on earth did you dig it up?

NEW MAN. The House Committee suggested it. They found the name on a calendar.

P.P.P. No such name can possibly exist in any calendar.

NEW MAN (*giggles*). I thought it was pretty weird, too! (*Takes down a calendar from the wall.*) There you are – it's hanging in your own room.

P.P.P. Where? (*Glances at the calendar.*) Zina!

Enter ZINA.

Put this in the stove too!

Exit ZINA *with the calendar.*

P.P.P. Well, what surname have you chosen?

NEW MAN. I'm prepared to take the surname I've inherited.

P.P.P. What do you mean – 'inherited'?

NEW MAN. Sharikov.

Sound of voices in the hall. The NEW MAN *gets up and opens the door into the hall, where* FIRST OGPU MAN *is standing and arguing with three men.*

NEW MAN (*to* FIRST OGPU). Let them in.

Scene Nine

Enter SHVONDER *and two* JOURNALISTS, *one of whom sets up a camera on a tripod, while the other gets out a notebook and pen.*

SHVONDER (*handing* P.P.P. *a sheet of paper*). Sign here please, professor: 'I hereby certify that the Bearer really is Polygraph Polygraphovich, who was conceived in my apartment.'

P.P.P. Good God! You don't really expect me to sign this, do you? I'll be the laughing-stock of the medical world. He was never 'conceived'. . . .

SHVONDER (*with cool* schadenfreude). You were doing an experiment, professor. And you conceived citizen Sharikov!

SHARIKOV (*picking a bone out of the soup-tureen*). That's the simple truth.

P.P.P. (*to* SHARIKOV). Kindly don't interfere. You're quite wrong to say it's 'the simple truth'. It's not simple at all.

SHARIKOV. Why shouldn't I interfere? It's me you're talking about.

SHVONDER. Citizen Sharikov is absolutely right. He is entitled to participate in a discussion of his personal affairs. This concerns his documentation. A citizen's personal documentation is of paramount importance. If he is not in possession of correct and appropriate documents, issued by the competent authority, the state does not consider him to be a valid unit of population. Put it another way – he doesn't exist.

FIRST JOURNALIST *ignites a magnesium flash and photographs the group.*

P.P.P. (*to* JOURNALISTS). Get out!!!

Exeunt JOURNALISTS.

(*To* SHVONDER:) I object in principle to these idiotic documents.

SHVONDER. And I cannot permit an undocumented tenant to reside in this house. Who knows what complications it might cause? Suppose a war against the imperialists suddenly broke out?

SHARIKOV. I'm not going to join the army and fight, that's for sure!

SHVONDER. Your remark, citizen Sharikov, betrays an unacceptably low level of political awareness. You will be legally obliged to register for military service pending the call-up of your age-group.

SHARIKOV. I'll register all right, but I'm buggered if I'm going to fight.

P.P.P. (*with* schadenfreude). There – you see?!!

P.P.P. *signs the document.* SHVONDER *appears embarrassed.*

SHARIKOV. I was severely wounded during the operation. You should see what they did to me.

Shows scar on his head, the cat's scratches on his face and starts to unbuckle his belt and undo his fly.

SHVONDER (*embarrassed*). All right, that's enough. (*Slight pause while a thought comes into his head. Frowns:*) Are you by any chance an anarchist or an anti-collectivist individualist?

SHARIKOV. I'm none of those, whatever they are, but I ought to be registered as medically unfit. (*Starts to gnaw the bone, first dipping it in the mayonnaise.*)

SHVONDER (*nonplussed*). Well, that doesn't matter for the moment . . . What does matter, though, is that we will transmit the professor's certificate to the police and they will issue you with the proper identity document and residence permit.

P.P.P. (*inspired by a sudden brainwave; to* SHVONDER). Look here . . . Do you by any chance . . . You don't happen to have a spare room, do you? I would gladly pay the rent of it for. . . .

SHVONDER (*vengefully*). No, professor, I very much regret to inform you that *no* rooms are available. And aren't likely to be either.

Exit SHVONDER, *colliding with* BORMENTAL *in the doorway.*

Scene Ten

Enter ZINA.

ZINA. Luncheon is served, gentlemen.

BORMENTAL (*to* SHARIKOV, *sharply*). Kindly put on a napkin!

SHARIKOV (*picks up the sauce-boat and dips the bone into the mayonnaise*). Oh, stop nagging, will you?

BORMENTAL. Put it on! (*Sits down at table.*)

P.P.P. Thank you, Ivan Arnoldovich. I find it so tedious always having to correct his manners. I've been feeling more tired over these last few weeks than I have felt for the past fourteen years. (*Sits down at table.*)

BORMENTAL (*to* SHARIKOV). I will not allow you to start your meal until you have put on your napkin. Zina, take the mayonnaise away from Sharikov.

SHARIKOV. Why should she take it away from me? I'll put that thing on right away.

Shielding the mayonnaise from ZINA *with his left hand, he uses his right hand to stuff a table-napkin into his collar.*

BORMENTAL. And now please sit down and eat with a knife and fork.

SHARIKOV (*sighs*). Can I have a glass of vodka?

BORMENTAL. Haven't you had enough already? You've been hitting the vodka rather hard lately.

SHARIKOV. Do you grudge me the vodka?

P.P.P. Don't be such an idiot!! You are. . . .

BORMENTAL. Let me deal with this, Philip Philipovich. That, Sharikov, is utter nonsense. You don't know what you're talking about. Naturally I don't grudge you the vodka; it's not my vodka, it belongs to Philip Philipovich. The point is that it's extremely bad for you. That's my first objection. The second is that even without vodka you behave disgracefully.

SHARIKOV *sighs again and pours himself a glass of vodka.*

BORMENTAL. You should offer it to others – first to Philip Philipovich, then to me; finally you may pour some for yourself.

SHARIKOV's *mouth is twisted into a slight, sarcastic smile. He pours vodka into two more glasses.*

SHARIKOV. It's getting to be like the army here: napkin here, tie there, don't speak without saying 'excuse me' or 'please' or 'thank you'. There's so much 'please' and 'thank you', you never get time to say what you mean. Why d'you have to make life so complicated? Anyone might think we were back under the tsarist regime . . . (*Raises his glass.*) Well, here's how . . . (SHARIKOV *tosses back his glassful, frowns and sniffs a piece of bread; his eyes fill with tears.*)

BORMENTAL (*to* P.P.P.). Can't be helped, I suppose – Klim Chugunkin. (*To* SHARIKOV). Well, what shall we do this evening?

SHARIKOV. Why don't we go to the circus? That's best of all.

P.P.P. You can go to the circus every day of the week – and you usually do. If I were you I'd go to the theatre for a change.

SHARIKOV. I won't go to the theatre.

BORMENTAL. Why don't you like the theatre?

SHARIKOV (*peers through his empty glass as though it were an opera-glass*). It's a load of rubbish . . . talk, talk, talk . . . nothing but bourgeois propaganda, if you ask me. . . .

P.P.P. *leans back in his chair and roars with laughter.*

BORMENTAL. You ought to read a book now and then, Sharikov, and then you would. . . .

SHARIKOV. I have been reading a book. . . .

Swiftly and cunningly SHARIKOV *pours himself half a glass of vodka.*

P.P.P. Zina, my dear, please remove the vodka. We don't need it any more.

ZINA *takes the vodka decanter and exits.*

What are you reading? I gave you *Robinson Crusoe*.

SHARIKOV. No, not that. I'm reading . . . what d'you call it? . . . Engels' correspondence with . . . whatsisname . . . that other German . . . yes, that villain Kautsky.

BORMENTAL *freezes with a forkful of food halfway to his mouth;* P.P.P. *spills his wine.* SHARIKOV *seizes the moment to toss down his vodka.*

P.P.P. And what is your opinion of it?

SHARIKOV. I'm against it.

P.P.P. Against whom? Engels or Kautsky?

SHARIKOV. Both of 'em.

P.P.P. Ye gods!

SHARIKOV. They write too much . . . this congress, that congress, Germans . . . gives you a headache. Anyway, this Engels says you should take everything away from some people and share it out fairly. . . .

BORMENTAL. And how does he propose to do this?

SHARIKOV (*made talkative by the vodka*). I haven't got to that bit yet, but I can tell you. It's easy. You take it away from people who live in seven rooms and own forty pairs of trousers, and

you give it to the people who have to find their food by
scrounging in dustbins.

P.P.P. Was your remark about the seven rooms a reference to me,
by any chance?

SHARIKOV *does not reply.*

Well, I'm not against sharing things out. Ivan Arnoldovich –
how many patients did we have to turn away yesterday?

BORMENTAL. Thirty-nine.

P.P.P. That makes 390 roubles in lost fees. Now let's share out
that loss between the three of us – we won't count Zina and
Darya Petrovna. So your share is 130 roubles, Sharikov.
Hand it over, please.

SHARIKOV *(frightened)*. You can't mean it! What for?

P.P.P. *(finally losing patience; shouts)*. For the flooded bathroom, the
smashed transom, the ruined carpets and the cat!!

BORMENTAL *(alarmed for P.P.P.)*. Philip Philipovich. . . .

P.P.P. No, let me finish. This is intolerable! Who killed Madame
Popova's cat? Who?!!

BORMENTAL. The day before yesterday, Sharikov, you bit a lady
on the staircase.

SHARIKOV. She slapped me on the face.

BORMENTAL. Yes – because you put your arms around her and
tweaked her nipples. You really are the. . . .

P.P.P. *(interrupting, loudly)*. You are the lowest form of life! A
creature in the formative stage and correspondingly weak in
intellect, you, in the presence of people with a university
education, behave with a vulgar familiarity that is intolerable.
You offer advice to Engels on the redistribution of property
. . . and at the same time you've eaten all my toothpaste
because you like the taste of peppermint. . . .

BORMENTAL. The day before yesterday. . . .

P.P.P. Now get this into your thick head: you need to shut up,
listen to what people are saying to you and learn to become
at least a halfway decent member of a socialist society. What
scoundrel gave you that book?

SHARIKOV (*dazed by the attack from both sides*). According to you, everyone's a scoundrel. If you want to know, Shvonder gave it to me. He's not a scoundrel . . . He said it would help me to get educated.

P.P.P. (*his voice rising from a shout to a squeak*). I see now what sort of an *education* you've been getting! Zina!!

BORMENTAL (*shouts*). Zina!

SHARIKOV (*roars*). Zina!

Enter ZINA.

P.P.P. (*all self-control lost*). In my consulting-room! (*To* SHARIKOV:) Is it in the consulting-room?

SHARIKOV (*obediently*). Yes. A green book. From the library.

P.P.P. (*to* ZINA). A green book! Engels' corespondence with whatsisname . . . Into the stove with it this instant!

Exit ZINA.

On my word of honour, I would gladly string up that Shvonder on the nearest tree!

Awkward silence. SHARIKOV *produces a crumpled cigarette from his pocket and lights it, trying hard to ensure that the smoke is not blown towards* P.P.P.

Ivan Arnoldovich, do me a favour and take him to the circus. Only for God's sake – look in the programme first and make sure there are no cats.

SHARIKOV. Who'd let a bloody cat into the circus?

P.P.P. (*ambiguously*). They let all sorts in there. What are the acts in the circus tonight?

BORMENTAL (*looking in the newspaper*). Elephants, and someone called the Ultimate in Human Dexterity.

SHARIKOV. Elephants are all right. They're decent, useful animals.

P.P.P. (*wearily*). Fortunately they are also a great deal bigger than you. You can go . . . (*To* BORMENTAL:) Listen, Ivan Arnoldovich – don't get into any conversations in the bar at the circus. And whatever you do, don't give Sharikov any vodka. In fact – I know it's an imposition to ask this – stay away from the bar altogether.

BORMENTAL. Very well, Philip Philipovich. Come on, Sharikov.

Exeunt BORMENTAL *and* SHARIKOV. P.P.P. *switches on the green-shaded lamp on his desk and starts to pace up and down the room, his brow creased in deep thought. Finally he puts out his cigar, goes over to the glass-fronted cabinet, takes out one of the sealed glass jars and studies it under the light. The object floating in the clear liquid is the brain that belonged to* SHARIKOV *in his primal, canine incarnation.*

Scene Eleven

From offstage come sounds of clattering utensils, breaking glass and shouting. Enter DARYA PETROVNA *in nightdress and* ZINA *clutching an unbuttoned cardigan across her bosom. In her muscular grasp* DARYA PETROVNA *is dragging the drunken* SHARIKOV *by the scruff of his neck; he is wearing a leather jacket several sizes too big for him and dirty, scuffed leather trousers. A furious* BORMENTAL *in his shirtsleeves brings up the rear of the party.*

DARYA PETROVNA (*shaking* SHARIKOV *as though he were a sack of potatoes*). There, professor – take a look at him, our young lodger, Telegraph Telegraphovich. I've been married, but Zina is an innocent girl. It was a good thing I woke up.

SHARIKOV (*furious*). I was just having a drink to celebrate, because I got a job today!

P.P.P. Oh, for God's sake . . . Darya Petrovna, please accept my apologies.

BORMENTAL *rolls up his shirtsleeves and advances threateningly on* SHARIKOV.

SHARIKOV. I got a job today, I tell you!

P.P.P. Ivan Arnoldovich – don't!

BORMENTAL *grips* SHARIKOV *around the throat.* P.P.P. *tries feebly to pull* SHARIKOV *free of the surgeon's powerful grasp.*

SHARIKOV. You can't fight over me! Help!

BORMENTAL (*his fingers still around* SHARIKOV's *throat*). Repeat after me: forgive me. . . .

SHARIKOV (*hoarsely*). All right, I will. . . .

P.P.P. Doctor Bormental, I implore you!

BORMENTAL. . . . Forgive me, dear, kind Darya Petrovna and dear, good Zinaida. . . .

ZINA. Prokofievna. . . .

SHARIKOV (*gasping for breath*). Forgive me, dear, kind Darya Petrovna and dear, good Zinaida Prokofievna. . . .

BORMENTAL. For behaving in such a disgusting manner. . . .

SHARIKOV. For behaving in such a disgusting manner. . . .

BORMENTAL. When I was drunk. . . .

SHARIKOV. When I was dr . . . (*Gurgles.*)

DARYA PETROVNA. Let go, you're strangling him!

BORMENTAL. And I will behave myself from now on. Got it?

SHARIKOV. . . . Behave myself from now on . . . But I *have* got a job! So as you wouldn't call me an idle layabout any longer. Look, there's a stifficate to prove it.

Gives a paper to P.P.P.

P.P.P. Mr. Sharikov, yesterday you brought here two drunken friends of yours, after which a malachite ashtray and my beaver-fur hat disappeared from the hall. Who were they? Who are those villains?

SHARIKOV. I don't know them personally. Only they're not villains, they're good and. . . .

P.P.P. And what's more they stole twenty roubles! How on earth did they manage it? They were both blind drunk!

SHARIKOV (*hiccupping*). They didn't take the money. Anyway, I'm not the only person living here. It could've been . . . (*Hiccups and belches.*) Oh God, I feel terrible. . . .

P.P.P. Aha – I suppose Dr. Bormental pinched the twenty roubles?

SHARIKOV. Anyway, it wasn't me . . . Oh, I feel sick . . . Maybe Zina took it.

BORMENTAL *again grips him by the throat.*

SHARIKOV (*gasping*). Hey, . . . leggo. . . .

ZINA. What?! How dare you!! (*Bursts into noisy tears.*)

BORMENTAL. Zina, don't . . . No one imagines you did it. . . .

P.P.P. Oh Zina, don't be such a silly girl. . . .

SHARIKOV (*trying to pull free*). Aaaah! Oooooh! . . . Christ, I feel really terrible. . . .

BORMENTAL (*realising what is about to happen*). Somebody get a bucket, for God's sake!

BORMENTAL *drags* SHARIKOV *behind a screen, whence come groans and sounds of vomiting. Exeunt* ZINA *and* DARYA PETROVNA.

SHARIKOV (*groaning, gasping, spluttering*). But I got a job, I tell you!

P.P.P. (*looks at the paper that* SHARIKOV *gave him*). 'This is to certify that the Bearer, Polygraph Polygraphovich Sharikov, is in the employ of the Cleansing Department of Moscow City Council as foreman of the sub-division for the elimination of stray animals – in brackets – cats.' I see . . . And who fixed you up with this job? No, don't tell me – I can guess.

SHARIKOV (*emerging from behind the screen*). Well, yes – it was Shvonder.

FIRST OGPU MAN *enters from the hall.*

FIRST OGPU. I hope you're not being disturbed, professor?

P.P.P. Yes, I am! By Shvonder. I suppose you couldn't shoot Shvonder, could you?

FIRST OGPU MAN *smiles, shakes his head and exits.*

P.P.P. (*to* SHARIKOV). Why are you giving off such a disgusting smell?

SHARIKOV (*sniffing himself*). It's because of my job. We were strangling cats all day yesterday.

BORMENTAL *again approaches* SHARIKOV *with menacing intent.*

SHARIKOV. Keep away, Bormental.

P.P.P. Don't Ivan Arnoldovich. (*To* SHARIKOV.) And what do you do with these cats?

SHARIKOV. They go to make fur coats. The factory dyes them and sells them as squirrel. Keep your hands off me, Bormental.

BORMENTAL. You will kindly address me as 'Ivan Arnoldovich'!

SHARIKOV. All right – but only if you call me 'Polygraph Polygraphovich'.

P.P.P. No! In my apartment I forbid anyone to call you that! If you think calling you 'Sharikov' is too familiar, we will call you 'Mister Sharikov'.

SHARIKOV. I'm not a mister. All the misters are in Paris.

P.P.P. This is Shvonder's doing! No, there will be no one but misters in this apartment as long as I am in it! I shall put an advertisement in the 'Accommodation Wanted' column of the newspaper today, and I promise you I will find you a room of your own.

SHARIKOV (*by now quite sober*). Oh, no. I'm not such a fool as to leave this place.

P.P.P. What?!

BORMENTAL *clenches his fists and advances.*

SHARIKOV. Don't, Mr. Bormental. Look . . . (*Takes another piece of paper out of his pocket.*) Look at this. I am a member of this tenancy association, and Preobrazhensky, the responsible tenant of this apartment, No. 5, is legally obliged to provide me with separate living-space amounting in area to not less than 45 square feet. Kindly take notice of *that*!

P.P.P. I swear I will personally shoot that Shvonder!

BORMENTAL (*in a warning tone*). Philip Philipovich, *seien Sie vorsichtig*!

P.P.P. This is too much. For pulling this trick, I will henceforth deprive you of all food in this apartment. You may have your 45 square feet. But that revolting scrap of paper does not oblige me to feed you.

SHARIKOV (*frightened*). I can't stay here without food. Where am I going to eat?

P.P.P.
BORMENTAL } (*in chorus*). In that case – behave yourself!

SHARIKOV. But what have I done wrong? I've got a job – and I've got married!

Scene Twelve

Enter, looking around in nervous embarrassment, the THIN GIRL *in a threadbare overcoat.*

SHARIKOV. She and I got hitched at the register office. She's our typist at the city Cleansing Department. She's going to live with me. Bormental will have to move out of your consulting-room. He has a flat of his own.

P.P.P. My dear young lady, please be so kind as to join me in my study for a moment.

SHARIKOV (*suspiciously*). I'm going with her.

BORMENTAL (*with steely politeness*). Excuse me, but you are not. The professor wishes to have a private talk with the lady. We will stay here.

> P.P.P. *escorts the* THIN GIRL *out.* SHARIKOV *paces nervously about the room.* BORMENTAL *watches* SHARIKOV *closely. Then his grimace of revulsion changes to a look of pity; he goes over to the cabinet, takes out a dog's collar and lead, and shakes the collar.*

BORMENTAL. Walkies! Sharik – walkies!

> SHARIKOV *gives a yelp and a whine, rushes over to his tormentor, seizes the lead in his teeth and, shaking his head from side to side, prances towards the door.* BORMENTAL *tickles his stomach. In irrepressible joy,* SHARIKOV *leaps around him. From offstage come sounds of the* THIN GIRL's *muffled sobs.* SHARIKOV *comes to his senses, spits out the lead, picks a cigarette-end out of an ashtray and lights up. Enter* P.P.P. *and the* THIN GIRL *who is pressing a wet, crumpled handkerchief to her mouth.*

THIN GIRL (*sobbing*). He said . . . he was wounded in the fighting.

P.P.P. (*relentlessly*). He's lying. I feel sincerely sorry for you, but you really can't go around marrying the first man you meet just because he happens to work in your office. That's no way to behave . . . Look, allow me. . . . (*Takes money out of his wallet.*)

THIN GIRL. I'm being poisoned! . . . They give us nothing but salt beef in our canteen, salt beef every day . . . It's making me ill! And he threatened to get me the sack if I didn't . . . He said he'd been an officer in the Red Army, that we'd live together in a posh flat, and eat pineapple every day . . . I'm really good-hearted, he said, the only thing I hate is cats. And I gave him a ring to show we were properly married.

P.P.P. (*to* SHARIKOV). So you're good-hearted, are you?

SHARIKOV. Yes, I am.

P.P.P. (*to* THIN GIRL). You'll get over it. You're still so young . . . There, take the money . . . regard it as a loan, if you like.

THIN GIRL (*takes the money and powders her nose. To* SHARIKOV). Beast!

P.P.P. (*to* SHARIKOV). Kindly explain to this lady why you have that scar on your head.

SHARIKOV (*in desperation*). I was wounded, fighting against the Whites in the civil war!

P.P.P. Stop that rubbish. Give her back her ring.

SHARIKOV *obediently takes off the ring and hands it to the* THIN GIRL.

BORMENTAL. Don't be afraid of him.

SHARIKOV (*to* THIN GIRL). Right, you haven't heard the last of me. Tomorrow I'll see to it that you get the sack.

BORMENTAL. Don't worry, I won't let him. (*Gives* SHARIKOV *such a look that the latter staggers backwards and hits the back of his head against the cabinet.*) What is her name? Her surname?

SHARIKOV *is terrified by* BORMENTAL's *threatening attitude.*

SHARIKOV. Vasnetsova.

BORMENTAL (*gripping* SHARIKOV *firmly by the lapels of his jacket*). Every day I shall personally enquire at the city's Cleansing Department to make sure that citizeness Vasnetsova has not been dismissed. And if I find out that you have had her sacked, I shall personally shoot you. Take care, Sharikov – I mean what I say!

SHARIKOV (*quietly*). You aren't the only one who's got a revolver. . . .

Suddenly, seizing his moment, SHARIKOV *makes a dash for the door and exits.* BORMENTAL *comforts the* THIN GIRL *and escorts her off. Exhausted,* P.P.P. *sinks into an armchair. The muffled choir of the House Committee is heard singing. The electric light flickers, but does not go out.*

Scene Thirteen

P.P.P. rises from his armchair. He goes over to the cabinet, and from one of its compartments he takes a bottle of brandy and two glasses. Enter BORMENTAL. P.P.P. pours out two glasses of brandy. They sit down in silence.

BORMENTAL *(after draining his glass of brandy)*. Philip Philipovich . . . I will never forget how I came to you as a half-starved student and you took me under your wing in the department . . . To me, you arc far more than a professor, a scientist . . . My respect for you in boundless.

P.P.P. My dear fellow, I know I sometimes bark at you when we are operating. You must forgive an old man's quick temper . . . If someone were to tie me up now and give me fifty lashes, I swear to God I would pay them fifty roubles . . . You see, my life's work . . . has been a concern to improve the human race. And *now* look what has happened . . . I acted as any scientist would, yet. . . .

BORMENTAL. You are a great scientist! But you can't go on like this! I wouldn't presume to give you advice, but look at yourself – you're worn to a shred. You can't work when you're in this state.

P.P.P. Yes, it's absolutely impossible.

BORMENTAL. Look, Philip Philipovich: if you like, I am prepared to put arsenic into his food – entirely on my own responsibility. After all, in the final analysis he's nothing more than one of your laboratory animals.

P.P.P. No, I won't let you do it. I'm sixty years old, and I am therefore entitled to give *you* some advice: never undertake a criminal act, no matter who it may be aimed at and no matter what apparent good may result from it. Live to a peaceful old age with clean hands.

BORMENTAL. I know it could go wrong, but I am profoundly convinced that there is no other solution . . . Philip Philipovich, you're a person with a world-wide reputation . . . for heaven's sake, they would never touch you!

P.P.P. All the more reason for not letting you do it.

BORMENTAL. But why?

P.P.P. Precisely because you do not have a world-wide reputation.

BORMENTAL. What has that got to do with it?

P.P.P. To leave a colleague in the lurch if there were to be a
catastrophe and hide behind my reputation as a scientist?
No, I'm sorry . . . I'm a graduate of Moscow University; I'm
not Sharikov.

P.P.P. *proudly pulls back his shoulders and sits up straight. The
baritone honk of a car horn is heard offstage. Enter the* THREE
OGPU MEN; *they salute as an* ARMY OFFICER *enters behind
them. The* ARMY OFFICER *clicks his heels politely and puts his
helmet on the table. Exeunt the* THREE OGPU MEN.

P.P.P. (*to* ARMY OFFICER). Have your pains started again, my
dear fellow?

OFFICER (*sitting down*). No, thank you, professor. I'm not here as
your patient; I've come on another matter. H'mm . . . Philip
Philipovich, since I have the greatest respect for you, I
decided to warn you . . . (*Produces a piece of paper from his
pocket.*) It's a good thing I was told about this in time . . .
(*Hands the paper to* P.P.P.)

P.P.P. (*as he reads the paper, his expression changes*). ' . . . also
threatening to kill the chairman of the House Committee,
from which it is evident that he is in possession of a firearm.
He also makes counter-revolutionary speeches. He even
ordered his servant, Zinaida Prokofievna Bunina, to burn a
volume of Friedrich Engels' works in the stove. Dr.
Bormental is secretly and illegally living, without a residence
permit, in the professor's apartment. Signed: P. P. Sharikov,
Foreman, Sub-Division for Destruction of Vagrant Feline
Quadrupeds, Moscow City Cleansing Department. Witnessed
by: Shvonder, Chairman, House Committee, and Pestrukhin,
Secretary.' . . . Will you allow me to keep this? Or perhaps
you need it in order that the law may take its course?

OFFICER (*offended*). Come now, professor – you really take too
suspicious a view of us. I came to give it to you.

P.P.P. Please forgive me. I really didn't mean to offend you. You
cannot imagine what a strain this has been. . . .

OFFICER. Indeed, I can well imagine it! Even so, it would be
interesting to take a look at him. He has made you a legend
all over Moscow.

P.P.P. waves his hand in despair. Enter THREE OGPU MEN, *who stand to attention.*

OFFICER. I must say, though – he sounds an absolute little shit.

The ARMY OFFICER *stands up, puts on his helmet, clicks his heels, salutes and exits. The* THREE OGPU MEN *salute him and follow him out. From offstage comes a sudden clattering, the smashing of glass and a canine howl from* SHARIKOV.

P.P.P. *(sighs deeply). Finita la commedia* . . . Ivan Arnoldovich, would you say that in your opinion I know something about the anatomy and physiology of, let's say, the human brain?

BORMENTAL. Why on earth do you ask such a question?

P.P.P. Because I, too, believe that I know a little more about it than do a lot of people in Moscow.

BORMENTAL. Or in London! Or in Oxford! Or even in Cambridge!

P.P.P. So this is my prognosis: no one will ever succeed in making a human being out of him. And you may quote me. Tell anybody who asks that Preobrazhensky said: '*Finita la commedia!*' As you are my friend, however, I will let you into a secret: 'That stupid old ass Preobrazhensky bungled this operation as badly as if he'd been a third-year medical student.' *(Pause.)* We did make a certain discovery, but you know what that was – namely that irradiating the patient with my machine turned a perfectly nice dog into a piece of pseudo-human scum so revolting that it makes your hair stand on end.

BORMENTAL. My God, I'm just beginning to realise what Sharikov might turn into. And if Shvonder really gets to work on him. . . .

P.P.P. Shvonder! It's Shvonder who's the biggest fool of us all. Sharikov is a much more dangerous threat to him than to me. Right now Shvonder is trying to turn Sharikov on to me, not realising that if someone else in their turn were to turn Sharikov on to Shvonder himself, there'd quickly be nothing left of Shvonder but the bones and the beak.

BORMENTAL. Just think how many cats Sharikov has destroyed already!

P.P.P. The cats are only a temporary phase. In a month or two, when his canine instincts have completely atrophied, he will stop chasing them. No – the whole horror is that he no longer has the heart of a dog: he has the heart of a man. And one of the most repulsive specimens to be found in all nature.

BORMENTAL. Of course! Klim Chugunkin! Three convictions, an alcoholic, a thief, a hooligan and a swine! . . . But what if we had given him the brain of, say, Spinoza?

P.P.P. My dear fellow, you could implant the brain of Spinoza or anyone else you like and turn a dog into a creature at the highest stage of development, provided the wretched animal didn't die under the knife. But what the hell for, I'd like to know? Why create him artificially, when some washer-woman could give birth to him at any time? After all, in 1879 a certain *hausfrau* in Ulm gave birth to Albert Einstein . . . No, doctor, the human race itself takes care of this matter, and in the normal process of evolution it creates dozens of outstanding geniuses who will astound the world. My discovery isn't worth a bent kopeck . . . Theoretically it is interesting. But practically? No, I'm afraid the only place for our Sharikov is in the dustbin. *Finita la commedia!*

SHARIKOV *runs on, his face covered in blood.*

SHARIKOV (*clutching his bleeding face*). Help! Help!

P.P.P. (*very calmly*). Is it the cat again?

SHARIKOV. No, it's a razor! I borrowed Bormental's razor. . . .

BORMENTAL. I've told you a hundred times. . . .

SHARIKOV. I just wanted to shave! Ow, it hurts! Oh, oh help!

P.P.P. Collect all your belongings – trousers, overcoat, whatever you need, then get out of this apartment and don't come back.

SHARIKOV. What?! Ooowowooh! Fuck you. . . .

P.P.P. (*in a monotone*). I want you out of here in half an hour.

SHARIKOV (*viciously*). What's this, then? I've got my rights. I'm staying here in my 45 square feet and there's fuck-all you can do about it.

P.P.P. Get out of this apartment.

BORMENTAL. Don't exhaust yourself, Philip Philipovich. (*Fetches the dog's collar and lead from the glass-fronted cabinet.*) Sharik! Sharik! Here, boy! Good boy! Walkies! Walkies!

SHARIKOV freezes, bares his teeth, then suddenly cocks a snook at BORMENTAL, turns and makes the same gestures at P.P.P. He swings back to face BORMENTAL, pulls a revolver out of his pocket and points it at him. In a flash SHARIKOV is lying on his back on the floor with BORMENTAL sitting on his chest and smothering him with a cushion. The telephone-bell starts ringing insistently. P.P.P. cuts the telephone cord with a scalpel. The ringing stops. P.P.P. goes over to the glass-fronted cabinet and takes down the sealed jar in which the DOG's brain is floating in clear liquid.

P.P.P. Zina! Darya Petrovna!

Enter ZINA and DARYA PETROVNA. Three of them pick up the limp body of SHARIKOV, while ZINA opens out the operating-table, the lights go out. DARYA PETROVNA and ZINA light candles while P.P.P. and BORMENTAL don their surgical gear.

Scene Fourteen

The lights come on again to illuminate P.P.P.'s dining-room. P.P.P. and BORMENTAL are seated at table, which is laid with snow-white linen, gleaming silver and crystal. ZINA, in housemaid's uniform, brings in a covered silver entrée dish, beneath which something is sizzling. Enter FIRST OGPU MAN, who smiles and announces to P.P.P.:

FIRST OGPU. A detective officer, professor, and two policemen.

P.P.P. Be a good fellow and show them in.

Enter SECOND and THIRD OGPU MEN, TWO POLICEMEN, SHVONDER, DETECTIVE, VOZNESENSKAYA, PESTRUKHIN, FYODOR and DARYA PETROVNA.

DETECTIVE (*embarrassed*). Excuse me, professor. Rather awkward, this. We have a warrant to search your premises and, depending on what we find, to make certain arrests.

P.P.P. Whom do you intend to arrest? And on what charge?

DETECTIVE. The charge against Professor Preobrazhensky and Dr. Bormental is of having murdered one Polygraph Sharikov, employee of the Moscow City Cleansing

Department, and against citizeness Zinaida Bunina and citizeness Darya Ivanova of being accessories before the fact to the said murder.

ZINA bursts into tears. Everyone looks at her.

P.P.P. I'm afraid I don't understand. Who is this Sharikov? Ah, yes, of course – I suppose you mean the dog on which I performed an operation.

DETECTIVE. Look, professor, you are not charged with murdering a *dog*. . . .

SHVONDER. But you are charged with killing him when he was a *man*! That's what it's all about!

P.P.P. A man? He talked, but that doesn't mean he was human. Anyway, that's not important. The dog Sharik is alive and well and no one has killed him.

DETECTIVE. In that case, professor, you must produce him. He disappeared ten days ago, and the information we have received is – forgive me – very disturbing.

P.P.P. Doctor Bormental, please show Sharik to this gentleman.

BORMENTAL. Sharik! Walkies!

In bounds the DOG; he jumps up, seizes his lead and collar in his teeth and starts to race around the table. Having calmed down, he sits in an armchair and crosses his legs. One of the POLICEMEN crosses himself.

DETECTIVE. How did this creature come to work in the Moscow City Cleansing Department?

P.P.P. I had nothing to do with it. If I'm not mistaken, it was Mr. Shvonder who recommended him for the job.

DETECTIVE. I am baffled. (*To* FIRST POLICEMAN.) Is that him?

FIRST POLICEMAN. That's him all right, sir.

SECOND POLICEMAN. Yes, that's him.

FYODOR. That's him, the brute . . . except that he's all covered in fur now.

SHVONDER. But he *could* talk!!

P.P.P. He can still talk, only less and less all the time, so seize
   your chance now or he will soon be completely silent –
   except for barking, whining and growling.

DETECTIVE. But why?

P.P.P. Science has not yet discovered the means of turning
   animals into people. I tried but failed, as you see. He can still
   talk a little, but he has already begun to revert to his primary,
   canine nature.

DOG (*loudly*). Stop swearing! (*Stands up.*) All done by kindness!

   The DETECTIVE *drops his briefcase and faints. He is caught by*
   FYODOR *and* FIRST POLICEMAN. *General confusion.*

P.P.P. Zina, get him some smelling-salts. (*Exit* ZINA.)

BORMENTAL. I shall personally fling Shvonder down the stairs if
   he ever shows himself in Professor Preobrazhensky's
   apartment again.

SHVONDER. I protest at that remark and I demand to have it
   entered in the minutes. (*Stares at* PESTRUKHIN, *who spreads
   his hands helplessly, meaning: 'There are no minutes!'.*)

FIRST OGPU. Meanwhile, comrades, you are all free to go.

   FIRST POLICEMAN *and* FYODOR *carry out the unconscious*
   DETECTIVE, *followed by all others except* P.P.P. *and* FIRST
   OGPU MAN, *who stays behind to ask:*

FIRST OGPU. How is your work getting on now, professor?

   P.P.P. *does not hear him, but hums a tune thoughtfully. From a shelf
   in the glass-fronted cabinet he takes down a jar containing a human
   brain.*

FIRST OGPU. I'll see to it that no one disturbs you.

   Exit FIRST OGPU MAN, *closing the door firmly behind him. The*
   DOG *lies down at his master's feet.*

Curtain

STARS IN THE MORNING SKY ■ ALEXANDER GALIN

Translated by MICHAEL GLENNY and CATHY PORTER

Based on a true-life 'purge' of Moscow's prostitutes during the 1980 Olympic Games, *Stars in the Morning Sky* was first seen in Britain in 1988 in its original production by the Maly Theatre, Leningrad. 'Galin uses the brutal detail of these women's lives to smash complacent assumptions about the condition of Soviet society.' (*Guardian*)

Characters

VALENTINA
LAURA
ANNA
MARIA
NIKOLAI
ALEXANDER
KLARA

Stars in the Morning Sky was first staged in Britain in a Russian-language production by the Maly Theatre, Leningrad at the Glasgow Mayfest on 9 May 1988 and at the Riverside Studios, London, on 18 May 1988. The cast was as follows:

VALENTINA	Galina Filimonova
NIKOLAI	Sergei Kozyrev
MARIA	Natalya Akimova
LARA	Irena Seleznyova
KLARA	Marina Gridasova
ANNA	Tatiana Shestakova
ALEXANDER	Vladimir Osipchuk

Staged by Lev Dodin
Co-director Tatiana Shestakova
Set Designer and Technical Director Alexei Porai-Koshitz

ACT ONE

The roof of the shack is in holes. The walls are cracked. A strong wind slowly blows open the creaking door, momentarily revealing a distant road in the hills. Then the gloom descends again. Dusty sunbeams penetrate the cracks in the walls, brightening the boarded-up windows and the rows of rusty iron bedsteads. Enter VALENTINA. She fastens the door shut and puts a suitcase on a bed. LAURA stands by the entrance holding her valise and gazing into the distance.

LAURA. What can I tell you about myself? Life's full of surprises
. . . Who said that? Was it Voltaire? My ancestors were
aristocrats . . . Mummy's family were scientists. Daddy was
very handsome – half gypsy, half Yugoslav. So Mummy, an
upper-class girl, ran off with a juggler . . ! .

VALENTINA. What's your name again? I've forgotten.

LAURA. I'm called Laura.

VALENTINA. Laura!

LAURA. My granddad called me Larissa . . . Friends call me
Laura.

VALENTINA. Who might they be?

LAURA. People I'm close to. . . .

VALENTINA. So your 'friends' call you Laura, do they? What's
your father's name?

LAURA. Father was called Florian.

VALENTINA. Laura and Florian! How sweet! You're a real little
prairie flower! Even your smell . . . I don't know about your
'friends', but the bees certainly go for it. There's a whole hive
of them over there. . . .

LAURA. It's Dior. Have some.

VALENTINA. All right, I will! All I ever attract is the flies. Here's
one now, lovely as a bride. (*Brushes away a fly.*) Do you live
with your parents, Laura?

LAURA. I *told* you – you don't listen. Mother ran off with a juggler. I was born on tour, and packed off to my grandmother's.

VALENTINA (*watching the fly*). Tell me about her.

LAURA. She lived with Granddad – he was a professor of medicine.

VALENTINA (*catching the fly in her hand, and bringing it to her ear*). Listen to it buzzing – it wants to go free! Was your mother an actress?

LAURA. She was in the circus! First she helped the juggler, then the animal-tamer.

Silence. She chokes back tears.

VALENTINA (*smiling*). Then what?

Silence.

VALENTINA. Was she eaten up?

LAURA. Mummy was savaged by a tigress. Daddy jumped off a cliff. He loved her so much.

She gets out cigarettes and a lighter.

VALENTINA (*sharply*). Put that away!

LAURA. Why, what's the matter?

VALENTINA. Put it away, I said! If you must smoke, go outside. If I catch you at it in here I'll throw you out at once – I won't have it!

LAURA. But I do love to smoke in bed before breakfast.

VALENTINA. Well sleep out there in the fresh air, by the fire bucket. . . .

LAURA. Strict rules. . . .

VALENTINA. A fire's all I need here. Stand by the door if you want to smoke.

LAURA (*lighting up*). The journey's tired me out. . . .

VALENTINA. So where d'you live? What's your address?

LAURA. It's a funny story. My relations moved into Granddad's university flat when he died. Granny and I moved to Sudak, in the Crimea . . . I grew up there in a tangerine grove. . . .

VALENTINA. Where the late flowers bloom?

LAURA. Granny died, and left me the cottage – well not so much a cottage as a two-storey villa, overlooking the sea . . . You must come!

VALENTINA. You're registered in Sudak?

LAURA. Yes . . . I came here to stay with my friend, the one I told you about. . . .

VALENTINA. I see. . . .

Silence.

LAURA. What a lovely view you have up from here. What's that – a river?

VALENTINA. Uh-huh.

LAURA. And a forest with mushrooms in it?

VALENTINA. And blackberries . . . (*Suddenly raising her voice.*) Why's that door wide open?

LAURA. Are you asking me? (*Pause.*) Funny way to behave, shouting like that. . . .

VALENTINA. Do you work, Laura? Got a job?

LAURA. Granny never worked, but Granddad did a lot of good through his work. . . .

VALENTINA. Granny this, Granny that – tell me about *yourself* . . . Don't you have a job?

LAURA. I'm an aerialist – trapeze artiste. I'm hauled into the big top, and I fly from hand to hand, dressed all in red. . . .

VALENTINA. Like a red relay baton. . . .

LAURA. It's so sad a girl has to worry about earning her keep. Granny used to hold me in her arms – Laura, why should a woman need a job? Women are born to beautify this world!

VALENTINA. So you beautify the world, do you? How? Plant trees?

LAURA. Do you never stop asking questions? You've been questioning me for nearly an hour. Let's have a rest now, OK? Here's my passport. It's genuine. . . .

VALENTINA. All right, all right. Anything nice to sell? What's the matter? Why d'you stay out there? Come on in, dear. . . .

LAURA. I don't like this sort of talk. . . .

VALENTINA. Any women's things?

LAURA. I've come for a rest, Valentina dear – I've brought a book and some wool.

VALENTINA. You knit?

LAURA. To calm my nerves.

VALENTINA. You'll get plenty of rest with us. There's nobody here. (*Raising her voice again.*) *Why* was that door left open?

Silence.

Come in, Laura. What are you looking at out there?

LAURA. Who's that boy there? (*Pointing into the yard.*) Funny looking fellow.

VALENTINA (*coming up behind her*). Who? Oh, him, He's not a boy . . .

LAURA. Is he local?

VALENTINA. Don't bother about him, we'll send him away. Do come in and at least look around – you're going to be living here.

LAURA. My friend said it was a summer place.

VALENTINA. This *is* a summer place! You couldn't live here in the *winter* – no radiators!

LAURA (*walking round the hut*). It's big. . . .

VALENTINA. The electricity's been cut off, but I'll wire up a bulb so you don't mess around with matches.

LAURA. But how do we heat water and wash our hair?

VALENTINA. You're not lighting anything here! You must go to the river in the wood. No smoking, no fires – I'll keep a strict watch on you, d'you hear? Tell that to your friend when she comes – is she another little hothouse flower, then?

LAURA. No need to talk like that. . . .

VALENTINA. You can sleep here – no strings attached. I don't care who you are or why you're here. Just don't make trouble. No parties, no orgies . . . The doors are unlocked, and I keep the keys. What's in that suitcase? Any dresses? No one wears your size here. You're like a doll! I was amazed when I saw you – the risks men run for women like you. They'd need binoculars to see you!

LAURA. Don't, I hate remarks like that. . . .

VALENTINA. Ooh, hoity-toity, aren't we touchy! Don't sulk. Three stops from here is the heart clinic. Maybe one of them'll risk it. You and your friend are going to raise the death rate! Don't worry. You'll get no guests up here. It's an awful place, no one ever comes. You'll rest alone on the mountain top, like Queen Tamara. . . .

LAURA. What was this place before?

VALENTINA. Used to be for patients. They've a new building now, four miles away.

LAURA. I wondered what all the beds were for. What patients?

VALENTINA. Mental patients – but harmless ones, don't worry. They slept here, and worked over there, making little boxes. Now choose a bed – there's enough of 'em – and make yourself at home. How long did they give you?

LAURA. What d'you mean?

VALENTINA. Did Klepov send you here?

LAURA. Better ask my friend. She knows all about it. . . .

VALENTINA. All right, ducky . . . I know who you are, with your 'friend' and your 'granny'. They've taken you lot off the streets of Moscow for the Olympics, and put you here, so's you won't spoil the picture for the foreigners . . . out of sight . . . out of mind. . . .

LAURA. We've come here for a holiday, of our own free will. . . .

VALENTINA. If you hadn't come they'd have slung you out of Moscow within twenty-four hours – or back to Sudak. No visitors, do you hear! They'll only get drunk and burn the place down. There'll be four of you beauties in here. (*Picks up the suitcase and walks round the hut.*)

LAURA. How many?

VALENTINA (*loudly*). Anna! Anna!

A groan comes from a dark corner of the hut. A heap of rags stirs on one of the bunks, and ANNA *sits up.*

ANNA. Mother, I'm dying!

VALENTINA. There's another, dreaming of love! (*Loudly.*) Look at the birdie that's flown in to see us, Anna!

ANNA. Oh Mum, I'm dying. . . .

VALENTINA. Yesterday she was an orphan . . . Anna, I've brought you a room-mate.

ANNA (*weakly*). I'm dying! I was dreaming about my mother. She was standing behind my bed, looking down at me. Before that I was dreaming the house had collapsed . . . It was just a cloud of mortar dust . . . A man came out of it, all white and covered in blood. . . .

VALENTINA. So your mum's still a virgin and your dad gave birth to you. Take some of your medicine, dear, and you'll feel better.

She produces a bottle, which ANNA *hides carefully under her pillow.*

So you'll be living here now, Laura. Or don't you like it?

LAURA *puts on a pair of large round sunglasses, and paces around the hut.*

ANNA. I've heard of two cases of that in Africa. Listen Valya. There was this black man gave birth by caesarian, and they kept it in an aquarium.

VALENTINA. What?

ANNA. This black man gave birth – some sailors told me. . . .

VALENTINA. What's an aquarium to do with it?

ANNA. Don't be thick, Valentina – they showed the thing for money! He was from Indonesia – or India. . . .

VALENTINA. Haven't you ever seen a map of the world?

ANNA. You mean a globe? But have you ever seen the evening light over the island of Sicily? Or the hot midday sun on the savannah?

VALENTINA. No, but you're my sunshine, Anna!

ANNA. You should've seen the postcards the sailor from that
freighter brought me! There was some sort of carnival scene,
or harvest festival. . . .

VALENTINA. You never showed us!

ANNA. I threw them in the saucepan with the food, and boiled
the hell out of them – so I suppose someone ate Sicily . . . I
told that sailor – you should've brought me stockings, mine
are all darned. No, says he, stockings are for my wife. For
you – the whole world. . . .

VALENTINA. Well, you've perked up, all right. (*To* LAURA:)
Don't mind her. She'll have a drink and go to sleep.

They both look at ANNA, *who is mumbling.*

LAURA. Valya, my friend and I were thinking of renting
something a bit nicer . . . Maybe your neighbours have a
place. . . .

VALENTINA. Who'd have you?

LAURA. But must we stay *here*? They told my friend to leave, but
they didn't mind where she went . . . So. . . ?

VALENTINA. It's up to you. Go! I'm not stopping you. It's
probably better . . . (*Pointing to* ANNA.) OK, so she drinks –
but she's harmless.

LAURA. I'll just wait for my friend, if you don't mind . . . She
gave me your address, and told me to wait for her. . . .

VALENTINA. Wait then . . . ! (*She goes up to* ANNA *and sits on the
bed opposite.*) Anna, haven't you something to tell me? (*Pause.*)
Don't mess me around . . . Has anyone else come?

ANNA. Oh yes, a man – no, a girl came. . . .

VALENTINA. Who?

ANNA. Some girl.

VALENTINA. Was her name Maria?

ANNA. That's it, Maria.

VALENTINA. Well?

ANNA. That's all.

VALENTINA. Is that her case?

ANNA. Could be. How should I know?

VALENTINA (*fetching the case and putting it down on a bed*). This'll be her place, here. (*Pause.*) Tell me more, Anna.

ANNA. What's there to tell? I scrubbed your floors, cleaned your house from top to bottom, came back here, had a drink – there was a drop left over from what you gave me for yesterday's washing. I kept it specially. Then I dropped off – and there was my mother, wandering about our yard with a bucket of mortar, but I couldn't see the house because it had been smashed to the ground, and I'd never seen that bloke before either. . . .

VALENTINA. Where's that Maria, then?

ANNA. How should I know? I'm not her minder. Your son came too. They both came here, then went off.

VALENTINA. Why didn't you tell me before, instead of spouting all that drivel? Did you see where they went?

ANNA. I was cleaning the verandah. I'd just started. . . .

VALENTINA. Did I tell you to? Give me that bottle! (*Snatches it from under the pillow.*)

ANNA. So now I'm to spy on Maria! Are you paying me to?

VALENTINA. Which way did they go?

ANNA. Down to the river. Give me my bottle – I'll put a match to this place!

VALENTINA. I'll put a match to *you*!

ANNA (*gets out the matches*). Doesn't bother me. You're the fire-warden here – you'll cop it.

VALENTINA. Put those matches away!

ANNA. Scared, eh? Then give me back my bottle . . . You've no right!

VALENTINA. Yes I have, you whore!

ANNA. You'll pay for that! I've got a witness. (*Turning to* LAURA.) You heard – *you'll* back me up, won't you?

LAURA *gazes out through the open door, paying no attention to them.*

VALENTINA (*to* ANNA). You can pack your rags and go! I took
you in out of the goodness of my heart, because I felt sorry
for you . . . Go on, pack up and get out!

ANNA. 'Took me in' – hah! You were paid! Klepov's happy, 'cos
you're keeping an eye on us, and he's in the clear. And your
son Kolya is under his orders . . . So why was Kolka sent
here? I'll tell them he's been mending your roof while he's
on duty!

VALENTINA. That's a load of rubbish!

ANNA. I speak as I find. I don't make things up.

VALENTINA. Well you can shut up, then.

ANNA. Why should I worry . . . it's your roof!

VALENTINA. And remember . . . in future just you stick to that
Maria, and don't let her out of your sight. Here's her case.
Go and find them, and tell her her place is here in the hut,
not in my house.

ANNA. What's it to do with me?

VALENTINA. Find them, I said. . . .

ANNA. I will not. Your son's in the police, and I don't want to
get on the wrong side of him. Give me back my bottle.

VALENTINA. Earn it first.

ANNA. Well, give me back my matches . . . There's no light in
here, and I'll trip over the bed in the dark.

VALENTINA. You're going to find them, d'you hear?

ANNA. All right, give me that bottle.

VALENTINA. Don't worry, it won't run away. (VALENTINA *goes
out.* ANNA *gets up, goes to the door and watches* VALENTINA
leave, then returns.)

ANNA (*animated*). She left work early on account of that girl. I was
washing her floors yesterday – no today, yes, this morning.
Listen: there was a knock at the door, and in walks a little
skeleton, stands to attention, eyes down, and says: 'Hello, my
name is Maria. Are you Kolya's mother?' 'No', I say. 'I'm the
maid' – no, I don't really. 'She's out', I say, 'Call Nikolai'
And there he was – been there all the time!

LAURA. Who's Nikolai?

ANNA (*even more animated*). The landlady's son, see? He's in our district, patrols the Savelev station. I've met him before – he pulled me in twice. Great big bloke. He'd brought the girl's things into the house – in that suitcase. First there was whispering and giggling in the next room, then off to the woods! So she's another Olympic girl! (*Pauses, waiting for a response.*) Dodgy ring on her finger, dodgy eyes . . . Are *you* an Olympic girl?

LAURA. What?

ANNA. People call us 'Olympic girls' – I'm one. Klepov told me not to show my face in Moscow till after the Olympics. What about you? Do you work the bars, or go with foreigners? I can't stand those 'gentlemen' – I'll go with anyone for a drink, so long as it's one of ours . . . Well, say something. . . .

LAURA. What d'you want, you old slag?

ANNA. What d'you mean, old slag! Once I've had a wash I'll look younger than you! How old *are* you?

LAURA *silently takes out a cigarette.*

No smoking in here!

LAURA. Oh?

ANNA. Yes! You can go out to smoke! You're not with your gentlemen now! I'm in charge – you'll burn down the hut and I'm head girl!

LAURA. Oh?

ANNA. Stop mooing like a cow!

LAURA. And you stop shouting!

ANNA. Why? Show me your papers.

LAURA. What have I done? Leave me alone!

ANNA. All right, we'll be friends. Who are you?

LAURA. Are *you* questioning me now?

ANNA. All right, I'll say sorry – there, sorry. (*Silence.*) Such a young kid, that Maria – never been married, either. Our fire-warden's really worked up about her, isn't she?

LAURA. Who's the fire-warden?

ANNA. Valentina. Used to work here. Now she's moved to the
new building – rides a motorbike, just like a man. Did
Klepov send you here, then?

LAURA. They hauled in my friend – I was staying with her.

ANNA. Klepov's all right. Others would've been rude . . . But
he's polite . . . Asked nicely. Vanish for a while, he says. He
comes to my home, unofficial like, says he doesn't want to
round me up like a sheep, and it'd be better if I just beat it
. . . Where would I go? He gives me Valya's address, says
she'll take me. So I took my mother's pension, and off I went
. . . The rule is – Valya checks up on us every evening. I
suppose Klepov was taking no chances, and just sent us here.

LAURA. *I* don't know. . . .

ANNA. Oh, he was worried. They're obviously putting the
squeeze on him because of the Olympics . . . Mother's been
left on her own. Valentina says when the games have started
and it's calmed down a bit, I can go and see how she is. (*Gets
out a bottle.*) To us! (*Laughs.*) Thought I had none left, eh? This
is my reserve supply!

LAURA. I don't drink that stuff.

ANNA. There's nothing else. I'm offering to share my last drop
with you. Remember that, and next time you can treat me.
From now on, everything's communal, OK? I'll drink to that
anyway. (*Drinks.*)

LAURA. Go ahead, drink . . . And I'll smoke, OK?

ANNA. Smoke if you like.

LAURA (*pointing to the door*). There he is again. Has he come to see
you?

ANNA. This is all I need! (*She drinks.* LAURA *smokes.*) Well,
darling, I suppose you thought there'd be lots of your foreign
gentlemen over for this jamboree . . . A big choice, and all of
them handsome. 'The pride of the planet', they called 'em on
Valentina's telly. (*Silence.*) What's the matter?

LAURA. Drink, and leave me alone!

ANNA. Don't cry, love . . . I'm sorry. Forgive me. (*Silence.*) So
we've a women's collective in the making. A bit a gossip, a

bit of a cry . . . Don't you cry now! We'll watch telly! Valentina said we could if we behaved ourselves. (*Silence.*) Now I remember where I've seen you!

LAURA. Where could you have seen me?

ANNA. I used to work as washer-up in a restaurant. Whenever I had a spare moment, I liked watching real life through a little window. Didn't you used to go to the 'Peking'?

LAURA. I live in Sudak. D'you know it? In the Crimea.

ANNA. Never been there. (*Gets up and goes to the door.*)

LAURA. Wait, don't go.

ANNA. It's time for Annie to have a wash. She's not just any old boozer. She's a naughty girl. Other girls stay at home and drink, but when Annie's had a few, she goes and finds a bloke. She was caught a couple of times . . . and she went on the police list . . . What's it they say? When you're on the list, you're on the game for real.

LAURA. Look!

ALEXANDER *appears in the doorway.*

ANNA. You can stop moaning now! Soon as you arrive, the men show up . . . (*To* ALEXANDER:) Look, dearie, why keep coming here? Aren't there any nurses for you over there?

ALEXANDER. Just out of curiosity. . . .

ANNA. Well, you won't have any luck here. We're on holiday . . . Laura, if a bloke and a girl come, tell 'em Valentina's looking for them . . . and about the suitcase. I'll go and see if I can find 'em . . . He's in the police. . . .

LAURA. Wait. . . .

ANNA. Don't worry – he's safe. They don't let the violent ones out. Shout if you need me . . . I won't be far. . . .

Exit ANNA. ALEXANDER *remains standing in the doorway.*

ALEXANDER. I didn't see you. . . .

Silence.

Haven't we met before? Why don't you say something?

LAURA. I'm deaf.

ALEXANDER. May I . . . come in?

LAURA. Stay there . . . better still, clear off.

ALEXANDER. All right . . . I'll stand by the door.

Silence.

LAURA. Why d'you stare like that? Just you try pestering me. . . .

ALEXANDER. Excuse me, but were you ever a patient here?

LAURA. Do I look like one?

ALEXANDER. Then why are you here?

LAURA. Just passing through . . . I'm with some people . . . waiting for a friend. . . .

ALEXANDER. If any of our people come here . . . let me know. . . .

LAURA. So I'm to sit here waiting for your people! *You're* not cured yet, are you?! Idiot!

ALEXANDER (*smiling*). I'm not an idiot, actually. I'm a physicist.

LAURA. Your name's obviously Newton.

ALEXANDER. My name's Alexander.

LAURA. The first or the second?

ALEXANDER. Goodbye. someone's coming – must be your friend.

LAURA (*shouts*). If it's your people, tell 'em no one's allowed in here!

LAURA *stubs out her cigarette to be on the safe side, and withdraws into the darkness. Enter* MARIA *and* NIKOLAI; *both have wet hair after bathing.*

NIKOLAI. You should've told me you couldn't swim.

MARIA. You should've warned me the water was deep.

NIKOLAI. The bank slopes suddenly to five metres. Anyway, you survived. . . .

MARIA. You saved me . . . You should get a medal for life-saving. . . .

NIKOLAI. I'll have to report it.

MARIA. You won't get a medal from me, you'll get jankers . . .
My saviour. . . .

MARIA *kisses* NIKOLAI; *he turns away.*

What's the matter?

NIKOLAI. Nothing.

MARIA. I see. . . .

NIKOLAI. 'Jankers' is an army word. . . .

MARIA. What do they call it in the police?

NIKOLAI. Forget that army slang. Were you in the army?

MARIA. Haven't been called up yet.

NIKOLAI. So don't use army slang.

MARIA. Why? Did I say a dirty word?

NIKOLAI. When I was doing my service, girls who went with
soldiers did it the army way – you know: Attention! Stand
easy!

MARIA. Coming to bed?

Silence.

I don't know who you slept with when you were in the army,
but in our hostel the girls always tried to get off with cadets.
They're future officers, and they never gave orders like that.

NIKOLAI. Have you finished?

MARIA. Ah, there's my suitcase . . . Will you see me to the
station? I'm off back to my village . . . perhaps my mother
will forgive me and take me in. 'Your girlfriend's brought all
her things . . .' So your Mum'll be lying on one side of the
blanket, with you and your morality on the other. . . .

NIKOLAI. Don't work yourself up. . . .

MARIA. She doesn't know about the baby yet. Know what my
own mother wrote to me? Give the kid to an orphanage, then
you can come home. Oh, I should've gone earlier, and
walked round the village with my belly out to here. But I
spared her that . . . Now she can unpick the bootees she
knitted. For ages I've been longing to go to the Black Sea. . . .

NIKOLAI. When you talk like that, I could punch you up the
throat. . . .

MARIA. That's it, I'm off. . . .

Picks up her case and suddenly sees ALEXANDER *standing in the doorway.*

Look, Kolya, who's that?

ALEXANDER. Excuse me, I thought we knew each other. . . .

NIKOLAI (*going up to him*). Don't think so . . . Where are you from, comrade?

ALEXANDER. From the madhouse.

NIKOLAI. I'm serious.

ALEXANDER. So am I, comrade.

NIKOLAI. What d'you want?

ALEXANDER. Nothing . . . Just thought I'd seen you here before, a few years ago . . . I wondered whether you were a patient or not. There's another girl here, by the way. . . .

LAURA (*from the darkness*). Stop pestering me, you bloody cretin!

ALEXANDER. I just wanted to invite you out for a walk. Sorry to have troubled you.

Exit ALEXANDER.

NIKOLAI (*to* LAURA). What are you doing here?

LAURA. I came to pick wild flowers . . . Like our 'nature walks' at school. . . .

NIKOLAI. Cut out the jokes.

LAURA. Why are you hassling me? I'm not hurting you, am I?

NIKOLAI. There'd be trouble if you did. Come on: Surname. . . .

LAURA. Surname indeed! Listen to him!

MARIA. Leave her alone.

NIKOLAI. I'm not talking to you.

MARIA. Well, lay off her.

LAURA. Give your name? . . . Our answer to that is – look on the 'Wanted' notices . . . (*To* MARIA;) Is your name Maria?

MARIA. Yes. . . .

LAURA. Valentina's looking for you.

MARIA. Who?

NIKOLAI (*to* LAURA). Go on – clear off!

LAURA. What a way to speak to a lady . . . *officer*.

NIKOLAI. That bloke just now – is he with you?

LAURA. He was with *us* . . . He's an atomic physicist. Do you realise the *daily* amount of mental strain on him? As much as you get in five years . . . Put yourself in his place . . . Yet he can still manage to joke with you. . . .

Silence.

Well, I'm going out for a walk . . . Aren't you going to ask me if I need an umbrella? Does it rain here at this time of year?

Silence. Exit LAURA.

MARIA. Cheap tart. . . .

NIKOLAI. Language!

MARIA. Why d'you always lecture people like a school master! Your job's to catch 'em – it's the judge who passes sentence. If you don't like it – don't listen! I never learnt any other words . . . He doesn't like anything . . . even my eyes don't look right. . . .

NIKOLAI. I like your eyes.

MARIA. Do you?

NIKOLAI. I just don't like the way you always look at the floor. Drop that habit. People talk to you, and you look at the floor . . . you should look them in the face.

MARIA. I don't want to look at just anybody . . . But I can't take my eyes off you.

NIKOLAI. You should get used to people.

MARIA. No, they've hurt me too much. You're the only man I want . . . If you cheat on me, I'll put my head in a noose. . . .

NIKOLAI. Then listen to what I tell you. . . .

MARIA. I will . . . I even like it when you tick me off! You made love to me almost the first day after I got here. (*Laughs.*) And you a policeman! When it gets dark – will you come?

NIKOLAI. Where?

MARIA. Here . . . I'll stay here . . . You don't have to tell *her*.

NIKOLAI. Get your suitcase and let's go down there. . . .

MARIA. No . . . she shoved me into the hut like I was a sheep or something. I'll be better off here. You're near by.

NIKOLAI. You can't stay here. Look at these bottles. The place has started to fill up.

MARIA. It was good in the forest . . . If only I could live there with you. Then no one'd know who you were carrying on with.

Enter ANNA.

ANNA. Look out, boys and girls, Valentina's on her way. . . .

NIKOLAI. I'll handle her . . . (*To* MARIA:) You sit down. . . .

MARIA. Can't I stand?

NIKOLAI. Stand, then!

MARIA *sits down; after slight hesitation,* NIKOLAI *sits down beside her.*

NIKOLAI. Mind if I sit here too?

MARIA. Please yourself.

ANNA. How cosy – all set for a nice little chat!

NIKOLAI (*to* ANNA). Go on, you – push off. . . .

ANNA. Kolya – sorry to use your first name – I'm hungry. I was going to have some dry bread for my lunch. Here Maria, have some bread, you can't live on love. I went into a vegetable garden just now. This old man says: 'What d'you want?' So I say: 'Give us something to eat.' He says: 'Why should I feed you for nothing?' So I say: 'I'd pay you with a fuck, only you're so old you'd die on the job, and it'd be my fault. I could work as a scarecrow, take it in turns with you. . . .'

Enter VALENTINA; *she looks around. Silence.*

VALENTINA (*to* NIKOLAI). Look here, son, how many times do I have to tell you not to break the rules? This is a women's hut – no men allowed.

NIKOLAI. All right, mother.

Silence.

ANNA. Valya, who's that old bloke who lives near you? First house after the turning? Says he'll pay me two cucumbers a month if I'll work for him. Can't pay more, he says – been a bad year. . . .

Silence.

Brought any food with you, Maria?

MARIA. No, and I don't want any.

ANNA. What?! Suppose the local shop's closed for stocktaking? Who d'you think'll feed you then? The fairies? (*Breaking off a chunk of bread, offering it and a cucumber to* MARIA.) Here, take this. . . .

MARIA. No thanks.

ANNA. Go on, the cucumber's fresh. . . .

Silence.

VALENTINA (*quietly, to* NIKOLAI). They're looking for you . . . I told the lieutenant you'd come home for lunch. His big boss dropped in out of the blue to check the posts and you weren't there. . . .

NIKOLAI. Don't worry about it, mother.

VALENTINA. You're beat's down there . . . on the main road. . . .

NIKOLAI. That's right, at the flyover. . . .

VALENTINA. So what're you doing here? If they ask, say you came home to fetch your binoculars.

NIKOLAI. All right.

VALENTINA. What's your job today? To stop people going to Moscow without a permit. Am I right?

NIKOLAI (*pointing to* MARIA). There's one of 'em. She can come home with us.

VALENTINA. Who is she?

NIKOLAI. Name's Maria.

VALENTINA. Your home's in Moscow now, and I'm chock-a-block with people. . . .

NIKOLAI. All right . . . let's go outside and talk about it. . . .

VALENTINA. What? I've my hands full here . . . Got to fill the fire-buckets with sand. Check the hoses. Everything's dry as tinder. Had to bring 'em a light bulb, too. And *you're* not doing your job properly, my boy. Thank God the lieutenant's a decent bloke. Said you ought to be manning your post.

NIKOLAI. All right, that's enough about that.

VALENTINA. You're s'posed to be on duty, but your tunic's off and your shirt's unbuttoned to the navel. Huh! You look terrible. Get out of my sight! And come straight home this evening. I've invited the lieutenant. . . .

NIKOLAI. Listen to me, mother. . . .

VALENTINA. You're not meant to be hanging around these sluts! You clear off!

ANNA. Hey, come off it! She's not a slut!

VALENTINA (*brusquely, to* ANNA, *handing her a bottle*). Here, have a drink and go to sleep.

ANNA (*takes the bottle*). Thanks . . . Maybe I'll have a drink, maybe I won't . . . But I'm not going to sleep. It's my business, whether I sleep or not . . . You can't *make* me – I've had a good sleep. Or am I supposed to knock myself out?

NIKOLAI. Maria – I'm off down there to find out what's going on. When I get back, you can come home with me. OK?

MARIA. OK.

VALENTINA. Look, son, the lieutenant's coming this evening. I can't have one of these Moscow tarts at table with him. Don't pull faces, you might stay like that. . . .

ANNA. She's not one of them. She came to see him off her own bat – she could've gone anywhere. . . .

VALENTINA (*to* NIKOLAI). Don't get in my way here. Go on – off you go, before you get into trouble. (*Referring to* ANNA.) Look who's teaching me to suck eggs!

NIKOLAI. Haven't you got the message, mother? She's going to stay at our place. I'll fetch her kid, and you can look after it.

MARIA. I won't let her. She'll smother him!

NIKOLAI. Shut up, you!

ANNA. That's right. No one's asking you.

NIKOLAI (*to* ANNA). You shut up too.

ANNA. I never said a word!

VALENTINA (*going further into the hut*). Phew – this place is filthy!

ANNA. What kid? Have you got a kid, Maria? Whose is it? Don't say it's his! Tell us: the law's on your side. . . .

MARIA. I don't know whose it is!

ANNA. Can't remember what the father looked like? You idiot, you should've said it was his.

MARIA. He's a son of the regiment. . . .

Silence. VALENTINA *produces a length of wire.*

Let's have some more of your food, Gran.

ANNA. What's all this? First I'm 'old slag', now I'm 'Gran!' . . . Hey, Valya, I'll weed your vegetable patch, so will you take me to the hairdresser? Otherwise I'll kill myself using the poker for curling-tongs.

MARIA. What's the booze?

ANNA. Just eat – fancy an unmarried mum *drinking*!

MARIA. Gimme some, I said!

After some hesitation, ANNA *pours out a drink for herself and* MARIA. VALENTINA *is busy doing something with the wire.*

ANNA. Anyone else want to join us?

Silence.

All right, then . . . sorry . . . The guests drink, while the hostess looks on. . . .

VALENTINA *disentangles the wire.*

MARIA. After lunch I'll sing a song. What'd you want? A gypsy song? Prison-camp songs? Or a proper song?

ANNA. A proper song.

MARIA *sits quite still for a while, then suddenly starts singing a song in a fine, clear voice:*

MARIA (*sings*): On Nevsky Prospect, near a bar there,
　　Pounds a grim-faced old copper his beat;
　　There's a spot, just a little bit farther
　　Where a lad and his girl-friend did meet.

　　'Go away, for from now on I hate you,
　　Go away, for I love you no more –
　　The Komsomol won't let me meet you:
　　You're a thief, and I'll see you no more'

　　He wept, for she wouldn't stand by him;
　　And to do his dark deeds he set forth;
　　But the coppers did catch him and tie him,
　　Packed him off to the cold, frozen North.

　　Come along, girls, to us in Siberia,
　　To the camps, where the cold winds do blow;
　　You may think that Moscow's superior,
　　But *we'll* pay three roubles a go!

　　If only you knew, you good people,
　　What it's like 'mid the stench and the grime,
　　How we slave till we're worn out and feeble –
　　How a young lad must serve out his time!

ANNA (*thrilled*). Oh, it gives me goose-pimples, it really does. . . .

MARIA. Probably because you need a wash . . . (*Holds out her glass.*) More, please!

　　NIKOLAI *snatches the bottle from* ANNA, *spilling the wine.*

ANNA. Hey – don't grab! I was pouring some for myself!

NIKOLAI. Give her any more and I'll thump you. (*To* MARIA, *quietly:*) Stop playing the fool. . . .

MARIA. You will *not* tell me how much I may drink! Go on – they're looking for you out there!

VALENTINA (*matter-of-factly*). There was a spade here, Anna. Where is it?

ANNA. It must be outside, Valya. I used it to clear up the yard this morning. You told me to. . . .

MARIA. I s'pose you used the broom to dig ditches?

ANNA. I keep it for flying on!

Silence.

VALENTINA. The bulb's in the socket now, Anna – twist to the right to turn on, to the left to turn off.

ANNA. I don't want light – I'd rather be in the dark.

VALENTINA. It's all insulated – just don't leave it on at night. I kill myself making you lot comfortable.

ANNA. You'd better run us a wire from a pocket torch as well!

MARIA. Off you go, Kolya, you're late already because of me.

NIKOLAI. Relax . . . pull yourself together . . . I'll be right back as soon as I've shown my face there. . . .

Silence.

MARIA. Couldn't you stay with me?

NIKOLAI. Back soon. . . .

MARIA. Stay . . . don't go . . . I'll never ask you for anything again. . . .

NIKOLAI. Won't be long . . . you heard: the big boss is around . . . The flame will be coming soon. . . .

MARIA. What flame? (*Pauses, then understands.*) Ah-ha!

NIKOLAI. I must go.

MARIA. Couldn't you get sick?

NIKOLAI. Not a chance.

MARIA. There are so many of you there. . . .

NIKOLAI. An animal or a person might run in front of the man carrying the torch – you never know. . . .

MARIA. Take me with you!

NIKOLAI. Civilians aren't allowed. The flame's coming at night, so I might in the morning, then it'll be easier. We'll see.

ANNA. Could I come too, Kolya? Just for a peep? You wouldn't mind, would you, Maria?

NIKOLAI. I'll see – when I get there. . . .

Silence.

Anyway, don't do anything stupid, everything's fine.

MARIA. Go then! . . . Wait . . . a goodbye kiss. . . .

NIKOLAI. Goodbye?! I'm only going down there and back.

NIKOLAI *kisses* MARIA, *who hugs him.*

ANNA. Valya, look . . . Aren't they sweet? (VALENTINA *pays no attention.*) Take her, lad . . . she'll never fail you . . . she'd do anything for you . . . anything. . . .

NIKOLAI. Let me go now. . . .

ANNA (*weeping*). Oh mother, why was I ever born? . . . Life's so unfair . . . I'll never cope, mother.

Exit NIKOLAI. ANNA *sobs.*

Only you remember what I was like once . . . golden plaits. . . .

VALENTINA. Yesterday you said you had brown hair . . . Any wine left?

ANNA. Are you going to drink with us?

VALENTINA. Go down to my motorbike at the bottom of the hill. There's a bag in the sidecar. Bring it here.

Exit ANNA. VALENTINA *looks at* MARIA.

VALENTINA. My husband was a ganger on the railway. But people called him a . . . gangster. He left me . . . All sorts of riff-raff used to settle here, people who weren't allowed into Moscow, gypsies . . . he ganged up with them. he was a Tartar . . . from the south . . . The Crimea. Clever, he was. Read a newspaper once, and he knew it all by heart . . . Even remembered the printing-works where it was printed. Couldn't bear sitting indoors all day . . . he felt boxed in. I thought he was up to no good and decided to follow him. Are you listening?

MARIA. I can hear you . . . I'm not deaf. . . .

VALENTINA. He'd walk down the track at night. I followed him along the path. He'd stop, throw back his head and stand there . . . for ages. I thought: it's the Tartar blood in him. Is he praying? Suddenly he began to howl like a wolf. It knocked me over. I fell down and bit my fist . . . I crawled

back home, my legs wouldn't carry me. Later I understood –
he was singing . . . Every night, when the wind was blowing
our way, you could hear him. . . .

VALENTINA *suddenly lifts her head and starts chanting a wordless
song.* ANNA *appears with a bag; she stops in the doorway, transfixed.*

ANNA. Valya, what's the matter?

VALENTINA. It's a song. . . .

ANNA. Call that moaning a song? (*Enters.*) You ought to be a
soloist, Valya, We could put on a show here.

VALENTINA. Why am I telling you this? Because there's a lot of
his father in my Kolya. He can go crazy . . . You're the last
thing he needs. I could hardly keep control of him till he did
his army service. After that he calmed down a lot, but even
that didn't knock all the nonsense out of him. With you he's
different . . . But you could be real trouble. You might find
another man tomorrow, and he'd crack up . . . you're under
age. . . .

MARIA. How d'you know? Seen my passport?

VALENTINA. You're too young to have a passport, my girl –
you're under sixteen.

MARIA. I am not '*your girl*'.

VALENTINA. Seems you spun him a hard luck story. he said
he'd bring your little kid here.

MARIA. I have a mother. . . .

VALENTINA. Course you have – only she disowned you. I've not
been wasting my time. Went to town and made some
enquiries . . . I know all about you – how you went thieving
and who made you do it. (*Pause.*) If you were just a mite
older, I'd turn you in – Klepov's my brother. My maiden
name was Klepov. But I feel sorry for you. I'm talking to you
as one woman to another . . . so don't be offended. As soon
as I had Kolya, I had the Tartar put in this loony bin . . . He
sang here . . . So you see, for me my son is. . . .

VALENTINA *produces some packages out of her bag.*

There's something to eat for you both.

ANNA. Thanks, Valya. That'll go down a treat.

Silence.

VALENTINA. Have some, Maria . . . You'll find a husband yet
. . . you're young. . . .

ANNA. You'll find a taker, even with a kid. That won't spoil your
chances. Your parents did a good job – nice legs, tits, good
teeth, too.

VALENTINA. Does that make people happy?

ANNA. No, it doesn't. . . .

VALENTINA. You've found out the hard way.

ANNA. My only happiness now is a drop of the hard stuff.

VALENTINA. Hand me my bag. Here's the timetable. There's a
train due soon, Maria . . . You'll easily catch it . . . can you
pay for your ticket? (*Produces money.*) There. . . .

MARIA. I won't look a gift horse in the mouth. . . .

ANNA. That's not enough.

Silence.

VALENTINA. Well come down to my place, and I'll give you
some more.

MARIA. No, I'll stay here for now. Kolya's promised to teach me
to swim.

VALENTINA. You'll find others to teach you that. Or anything
else for that matter. There's plenty more fish in the sea.
Klepov can be very useful. He'll fix you up with a job. And
good luck to you. You've got to pick yourself up off the floor.
Go away from here . . . get a job . . . no one'll know about
your past.

MARIA. Stop nagging me, you old bag, I'm sick of it . . . I'm not
that set on your Kolya either.

ANNA. You fool! He loves you! A lad like him wouldn't put his
mother before his wife – Maria'll make a man of him. . . .

MARIA. And clean his boots.

ANNA. I'd go with any of those blokes, however much of an idiot
he was . . . Its not hard to get one – you just shout: 'Hey,
Vanya, or Petya! We're looking for some talent!' . . . And they
all come flying – like the Tushino air-show.

MARIA. Will everyone stop preaching at me! Why do they all lecture me, Anna?

Picks up her case.

ANNA. Where are you off to? He said wait.

MARIA. I'm not his spaniel. . . .

ANNA. Listen!

MARIA. What?

ANNA. Listen! A car's coming. . . ! Hey, it's a fellah! A prince in a car! Maria, they've come for you in a car! The tomcats are on the prowl. (*To* VALENTINA.) You've lost, Valya. Better put a good face on it. Put yourself in her place! Why're you still eating? Are you starving?

VALENTINA *silently goes on eating. Suddenly they hear the strains of cheerful music, and in the doorway, blocking the light, appears* KLARA, *cheerful, powerfully built and drunk.*

KLARA. Lau-ra! Surprise! Guess who we've brought! Laura! Greetings, girls! What a carry-on! Cops everywhere, asking for your papers! Bushuyev was holding his in his teeth! I slipped a lieutenant a packet of fags and told him we weren't going to Moscow, but leaving it. He took one and handed the packet back . . . What the hell are things coming to – Bushuyev could hardly believe his eyes! (*Shouts.*) Lau-ra!

VALENTINA. Don't shout like that! Who is Bushuyev?

KLARA. *The* Bushuyev – he can squeeze blood out of a stone. Takes hold of it and squeezes. . . .

VALENTINA. What exactly does that mean?

KLARA. Like I said. (*Cheerfully.*) So how's the holiday camp, girls? What are the contacts like?

ANNA. Another flower from the hothouse – a cactus. What *are* you talking about?

KLARA. We learnt about contacts at school, in physics – where *is* Laura?

VALENTINA (*cheerfully.*) Any of you girls know Laura? Our little prairie flower?

KLARA. That's a good one. . . .

VALENTINA. So *you're* her friend, are you?

KLARA. Where's Laura, girls? Have you buried her?

VALENTINA. Anna, you're in charge. You tell her.

ANNA. Maria. . . .

MARIA. Leave off. . . .

ANNA. Don't be so touchy. . . .

MARIA. Get lost.

Silence.

KLARA. *Where* is Laura? Will nobody tell me?

ANNA (*slowly.*) Laura's not here . . . She's gone out.

KLARA. Out on the town, eh? Has she gone far?

ANNA. Taking a stroll, out for a breather, breathing oxygen, bags of it.

KLARA. Who with?

ANNA. Bloke from the loony bin.

KLARA. You're joking! You're going to get me into a lot of trouble. Bushuyev had a hell of a job persuading Ovsyannikov to drive us here. Find her for me at once, there's no time to waste, or he'll knock my teeth in.

ANNA. It's *your* teeth – *you* look after 'em.

KLARA. Don't wind me up. I'm in a good mood, but I'll knock you into next week if you don't watch it.

ANNA. Come off it!

Pause.

KLARA. A sculptor once did a model of me – did it first in plasticine, then cast it in bronze, put it in an exhibition and got first prize, the bastard. And d'you know what he called it? 'Girl with Sledgehammer'. Then he took it off to the country, and traded it in for a hundredweight of pork. . . .

VALENTINA. I'm Valentina.

KLARA. Valyusha! So here we are, then! The neighbours said, get on up there to your reservation! Up that bumpy track.

Ovsyannikov was furious – he's just got a brand-new car, he kept saying I was too heavy and I'd strain the engine. . . .

VALENTINA. So people know all about this place? A 'Reservation', eh? Have you been blabbing, Anna?

ANNA. I don't use such nasty words. . . .

VALENTINA (*to* KLARA). Your friend doesn't like it here. And *you'd* have done better to arrive sober. You'll get the place a bad name! That's Anna, that's Maria . ., . Somebody else may be coming too.

KLARA. Look, I've got the keys here to a dacha. Ovsyannikov gave me them . . . You don't imagine we'll be staying in this dump, do you?

MARIA. She asked us to wait.

KLARA. Found your tongue, then? Ovsyannikov'll be biting his nails. We can't hang around any longer – they're closing the road. . . .

VALENTINA. What shall I tell Klepov? Where will you be?

KLARA. He'll be overjoyed. I didn't leave Moscow by court order, but because I wanted to, and where I stay is my affair!

VALENTINA. Then off you go, and don't make such a racket.

KLARA. I can't go without *her*, can I? (*Pause.*) But quick, before they close the road . . . The Olympic flame is coming that way. . . .

VALENTINA. How do *you* know about the flame?

KLARA. 'Cos there's a cop behind every bush, that's how. (*Silence.*) Come on, girls, help me out, let's have a nice cosy evening in the dacha. There'll be music, and lots to drink. (*Silence. To* MARIA:) Hey you, what's your name, kid?

ANNA. Leave her alone!

KLARA. What's your name?

ANNA. Leave her be!

KLARA. What's your name?

ANNA. Get away from her!

KLARA. Want to come for a ride in a car?

ANNA. She's not going!

KLARA. Let *her* decide!

Silence.

MARIA. Where to?

ANNA. Maria, he promised . . . he asked you . . . Valya, tell her. . . .

MARIA. For a long ride?

Silence.

ANNA. Valya!

VALENTINA. *You* sort it out. I'm only the fire-warden.

MARIA *gets up.* ANNA *pushes her back on the bed.*

ANNA. Sit down!

MARIA. What kind of car?

KLARA. The latest model.

MARIA. I've never been in one of them.

ANNA. Hey, wait, listen. . . ! Valya, Valentina . . . (*To* KLARA:) Wait! How can I explain . . . Look, she's got a boyfriend here . . . Wait, why don't *I* go instead?

KLARA. You? (*Slowly looking her over.*) No, I'm afraid *you* wouldn't do.

ANNA. Well, if you'll do, Miss Sledge hammer, I'll have no problem. Where are they? In the car? I'll put on my best dress at once. (*Rummages amongst her things.*) Where's my mirror and lipstick. . . ?

KLARA. Don't bother, you'll still look a fright.

ANNA. Say I'm a shepherdess, up from the country . . . Tell 'em Laura's just coming . . . She can't decide what to wear . . . But you keep your hands off *her*, or I'll scratch your eyes out. . . .

KLARA. She your daughter?

ANNA. Daughter? Think I'm past it, do you? I worked in the docks once. I even had first officers – been to Rio, Marseilles, Karachi . . . Wait, girls, be with you in a tick! Give me a fag . . . (*Rehearses a few sophisticated gestures, then trips out of the hut.*)

KLARA *goes over to the door, and peers out across to the far side of the yard.* VALENTINA *finally fixes the bulb. Neither of them speak, or look at* MARIA.

MARIA (*to* VALENTINA). Have you been checking me out at the police-station?

VALENTINA. No one else knows anything about you. . . .

MARIA. You go to the superintendent at the girls' hostel. Number 40. She'll remember me, and the date – the 28th of March. She called the whole hostel together and read out an urgent message from the Komsomol patrol. A girl had been found in the men's hostel, drunk and naked, and she'd given my name. Let her come forward, she says, so everyone can see who's disgracing us. She pushes me out, and everyone laughs. Next thing, the girls catch me on the windowsill. Then they tied me to the bed to stop me hanging myself. They call for my mother, and she gets me in the head's office and belts me so hard they have to pull her off. Then some of the blokes from the men's hostel come in. It was *another* girl with them, from my dormitory, and she'd given my name . . . She married a student the other day. . . .

Enter ANNA, *who walks silently past* KLARA.

ANNA. She didn't come. There were two arseholes sitting in the car. They bought me off with a bottle of pepper vodka.

KLARA. So what did they say?

ANNA. They want you.

KLARA. That's that, then. Bushuyev'll skin me alive.

Silence.

MARIA. I want to go for a drive!

KLARA. Come on, we'll go for a drive!

MARIA. On one condition: you slow down at the flyover.

ANNA. Does no one care about this poor kid? (*To* MARIA.) He'll come for you, Maria . . . Think of your child. . . .

MARIA (*shouts*). Shut up, d'you hear? Shut up!

KLARA. She your mother? (*Pointing to* Anna.)

MARIA. First time I've clapped eyes on her.

KLARA (*to* ANNA). Sit and drink your pepper vodka, shepherdess!

MARIA (*to* KLARA). Let's go. But on that condition – OK?

KLARA. OK, we'll slow down.

MARIA. I'll take my things. You can drop me off at the station. . . .

KLARA. Tell 'em your name's Laura.

MARIA (*to* VALENTINA). Thanks. I'll always remember you. . . .

ANNA (*quietly*). Fool! You'll regret this all your life!

> MARIA *goes out.* KLARA *takes* MARIA'*s suitcase.*

VALENTINA. What'll we tell Laura?

KLARA. Tell her if I don't come for her she must shift for herself.

VALENTINA. So she can stay here, is that it? I s'pose we'll be seeing you again. . . .

KLARA. All the best, folks. Here, I've got something for you. (*Takes some glass-stoppered bottles out of her case.*) Some little presents. Do you have a bath-house here, Valya?

VALENTINA. I don't – my neighbours do.

KLARA. I fancy a nice long steam. Could you ask them?

VALENTINA. I can *ask*, but I don't expect they'd want *you*. 'Cos you're on the game – know what I mean?

KLARA. Even if I paid them?

VALENTINA. Well that's different – I'll ask.

> *Exit* KLARA. ANNA *goes to the door.* VALENTINA *sits down heavily on the bed.*

VALENTINA. Have they gone?

ANNA. Yes. You bitch.

VALENTINA. Shut up. . . .

ANNA. I hope you rot, you bitch . . . Want to hit me?

VALENTINA. No, Annushka. No, my love.

ANNA. What's up?

VALENTINA. Annushka. . . .

ANNA. What is it?

VALENTINA. I'm so tired, I can't see straight. Come here.
(ANNA *goes to* VALENTINA, *and supports her.*) Come home
with me and help me make a cake for this evening. . . .

ANNA. I'm not coming. I never want to see you again.

VALENTINA. Don't leave me alone. . . .

ANNA (*looking out of the door*). There's their car, they've reached the
flyover. . . .

VALENTINA. Everything'll work out, you'll see. . . .

ANNA. The car's stopped. . . .

VALENTINA. The lieutenant's coming to supper. You can help
me . . . please come.

Exit VALENTINA. ANNA *looks through the open door, then retires
into the darkness and stretches out on her bed. A motor cycle engine is
heard starting up and driving away. Enter* LAURA *and*
ALEXANDER.

LAURA. Life's full of surprises, as some great writer said. Who
was it? Stendhal, I think . . . Granny used to say when I was
little I always ran around with my arms out . . . They said if
you dreamt of flying it meant you were growing. I tried to fly
when I was awake too, but I never did manage to grow. I
jumped off mountains, flew over the sea . . . I still have those
dreams sometimes.

ALEXANDER. Funny you should say that – I was thinking along
rather the same lines. There was once a Greek who lay on
this bed. Called Illiadi. They nicknamed him Odysseus.
'How's things, Odysseus?' they'd say. (*Pause.*) 'I'm lying on a
cloud', he'd say.

LAURA. It's all right for loonies, they can lie on clouds when
they want to. My story's quite simple – I'm a trapeze artist.
In the circus all my life. When I was little my parents used to
saw me in half. I was nice and small, and I'd nip out of one
box into another . . . But now I'm a trapeze artist. I'd like to
do my act in Moscow. How d'you like the idea? I'm all in
red, being thrown from hand to hand like a relay baton. Not
bad, eh? So how did you end up here?

ALEXANDER. I came to look up my old haunts.

LAURA. But over there, in the new buildings . . . did you go there of your own accord?

ALEXANDER. I've been there nearly a month. My doctor sent me to rest and do a bit of work . . . I've been here, off and on, before. Got a lot of work done here – it was here I wrote my master's thesis. . . .

LAURA. You're an M.Sc.?

ALEXANDER. I did my doctorate in those new buildings. . . .

LAURA. You're taking my breath away! You're married, of course.

ALEXANDER. Not any more.

LAURA. Listen, you're my last *chance*! I wondered why I liked talking to you so much. Because you're my *chance*! D'you know what's so unusual about you, Sasha? You know how to listen. Men never listen to women. Bed's all they can think of. That's all right in the end, but it's nice you've waited so long to make a pass at me. I thought you'd be rough, but not at all – if anything you're too gentle . . . Am I beginning to lose my touch, I wonder, doctor?

ALEXANDER. There've never been so many pretty girls in this hut before. . . .

LAURA. Stop, don't . . . I'm nothing really, just a nice piece of skirt . . . God, how I chatter on! I can't even talk decently any more! Nothing but the circus, tours and being tired . . . Now don't try anything yet. Just stay sweet and gentle, for a while, anyway . . . But no kissing, all right?

ALEXANDER. I don't mind. It's up to you.

LAURA. But you're thinking you'd rather we kissed, eh? All right, if you insist. . . .

They kiss.

ANNA (*quietly*). Larissa. . . .

LAURA. Anna! Are you here?!

ANNA. Yes, I am. Your big friend came.

LAURA. I saw her, thanks.

ANNA (*gets up*). I'm going down to Valentina's. I'll be out late, so you can settle in . . . You're in charge while I'm gone.

LAURA. Wait, he's leaving. I'll be scared on my own here. . . .

ANNA. Let him stay till morning. (*To* ALEXANDER.) See? You're in luck! Be nice to her.

LAURA. She's joking. Don't go, Anna! Sasha can't stay, they'll be looking for him.

ANNA. Seems everyone needs me. Stay here, lad . . . I'll bequeath you the pepper vodka – for the repose of my soul . . . I won't hurry back, so feel free. Don't suppose anyone else'll come tonight. . . .

Exit ANNA. LAURA *nervously lights a cigarette.*

LAURA. I'm in trouble now. Will they really be looking for you?

ALEXANDER. They don't know I went out. . . .

LAURA. So you can stay for a bit? Just for half an hour?

Silence.

ALEXANDER. Well . . . all right then. . . .

LAURA. You're an angel, thank you.

ALEXANDER. Won't your friend come back?

LAURA. She's not really a friend. Chance threw us together. I don't think she needs me any more . . . Now we've got a bottle, Sasha dear, and some cigarettes – and I'm going to change. I didn't bring my whole wardrobe here for nothing! (*Goes off into the darkness.*) Can you see me?

ALEXANDER. No.

LAURA. Are your parents alive?

ALEXANDER. I've got no one – I'm not so young.

LAURA. Nor am I. Here, d'you know any poems by heart? Will you recite some later? There's a good one by Lermontov – *The Novice.* (*Emerges from the darkness wearing a beautiful dress, and stops in the doorway.*) I thought I'd be wearing this one day at a reception for some champion. Klara stayed with me in Sudak last summer. Said she'd put me up during the Olympics. Lots of opportunities, she said . . . And this is where I've landed up . . . Ah, well . . . a mad doctor'll do just as well. Come here, my last chance. (ALEXANDER *goes to* LAURA, *who kisses him.*) Only don't rush it. Do you like me?

ALEXANDER. Yes. . . .

LAURA. I knew you did, when you came back . . . Now then, silly, take it easy, all in good time . . . Everything we do has to be beautiful. Look, it's still light, but there's a star already . . . It's Venus, the goddess of love. She's in a hurry to show herself. Wants a husband. Where is she? She's gone out. . . .

ALEXANDER. It was a signal rocket.

LAURA. And there's another. . . .

LAURA *stands at the door, lifting her head up to the darkening sky. Down below is the road, dipping downhill and climbing up again to the horizon.*

ACT TWO

Moonlight pours through the open door of the hut. A lamp shines dimly.
ALEXANDER *is asleep.* ANNA *is cutting a cake into slices.* LAURA,
*wearing another beautiful dress, is holding a cigarette and a drink; standing
in the doorway, she is waving to someone in the yard.*

LAURA. Say what you like, Anna, there's more variety in
European men . . . Asians have only one sort of face. Even
Indians, especially the ones who wear turb . . . what d'you
call 'em?

ANNA. Turbans.

LAURA. . . . on their heads . . . I get drunk so quickly . . .
Anyway, that Indian head-dress. I don't like Indian men. The
women are all right. Wear a jewel on their forehead. Poor
women, it's hard for them in these days of headlong change.
What can they hope for? I'd like to go to India, you know,
and ride on an elephant. Go to the embassy, and say: 'Listen,
what's-your-name, Raj Kapur, I want to ride on an elephant,
if it's the last thing I do. What's it to you, Raj?' Of course I
could go to the zoo, get the keeper drunk and have a ride
there. No, I'd have to get the elephant drunk, or it'd trample
me to death. How d'you like that, Anna – a ride on a drunk
elephant?

ANNA. How many bottles would it need? (*Laughs.*) I had an
Indian once, or a Korean, from those parts, anyway. . . .

LAURA. You're a real international *femme fatale*, Anna. (*Sees
someone, smiles and waves.*) You again? Come on in, there's still
some left. Look Anna, we're being watched. A young man in
his prim.:, with time on his hands. We need another man . . .
This girl's called Anna. . . .

ANNA. Does he look nice?

LAURA. God knows, all I can see is his cap-badge. (*Loudly.*) Hey,
you – got red blood in your veins? A lady's calling you!
Invite her behind a bush, stupid – she'll come . . . Why're
you grinning like that, you spastic?

ANNA. Cut it out, stop making trouble. . . .

LAURA. Know where they've put us? It's where the dacha folk
walk their dogs! Look – two bulldogs, or rather dog and
mistress. Here lady – yes, you! Why don't you swap harnesses
with your dog? Come closer, then you can hear me! What's
the time? My watch stopped at midnight, but my prince
hasn't come. He's very handsome. Don't smile – hasn't it
happened to you? On the dot of midnight the door opens,
and in comes this gorgeous man. Give him your hand to kiss,
and he says: 'I cannot, madam, I am just an official witness
to your arrest. . . .'

ANNA (laughs). You'll get us slung out, you slag. . . .

LAURA. Don't go, dear . . . Know what's happening on the main
road today? One mass of police. That's a nice dog you have.
People say dogs end up looking like their owners. I used to
think it meant just their characters, but now I see it's their
ugly mugs too . . . Oh, what have I said – call the police, call
the police!

ANNA. No need for that – they're everywhere.

LAURA. Nice doggie, don't go away . . . I'm drinking to you – I
was looking for someone to toast. Cheers. . . ! (Drinks, and gets
out another cigarette.)

ANNA. You're smoking too much, you're wheezing. . . .

LAURA. We're having such fun today – that's why I'm smoking.

ANNA. OK, you've had your fun, now wake up your bloke and
eat. You must have fucked him to a standstill, he's slept
nearly three hours. You haven't killed him, have you?!

LAURA. Let him rest. Dear Sashenka, darling boy . . . Just can't
hold his drink. I more or less drank the whole bottle myself.
One gulp and he was nodding. Dropped off so peacefully
too, I hadn't the heart to wake him. . . .

ANNA. Have you tried my cake? I baked it for Valentina, and this
is our share. Eat, you parasite. . . .

LAURA. Tomorrow I'll cook for you. Tell me what you like best.
We'll buy milk and vegetables from the peasants.

ANNA. And plant them on my grave.

LAURA. Are you planning to die?

ANNA. Sing, little songbird, little Thumbelina, and wake your mate . . . What vegetables? Bet you haven't a penny to your name . . . Eat properly, girl, stop pecking! Take more!

LAURA. I'm not a hen!

ANNA. Don't peck, then! Like this – only don't choke yourself. . . .

LAURA. Why do you call me a songbird?

ANNA. Blabber on, dear, as long as it keeps you off the booze and fags.

LAURA. D'you know what parasites are?

ANNA. 'Course I do! Worked in an isolation hospital once. My job was to get rid of 'em. Soon as those cockroaches saw me they'd run like hell. Got short shrift from me.

LAURA. Anna, parasites are rich people, the bourgeosie. . . .

ANNA. Wouldn't know about that, I'm working-class myself.

LAURA. Yes, we're proletarians – or worse . . . The only chains we have to lose are our necklaces.

ANNA. What's necklaces to do with it? You can start by unfastening your tongue and talking properly. . . .

LAURA. It's heavy going with you. You need to go back to school. (*Gets up and goes to the door.*)

ANNA. Is that all you're eating?

LAURA. Why do I keep thinking about the ballet? I remember the Bolshoi Theatre . . . While you were talking about cockroaches, I was imagining the stalls . . . plush seats and diamond earrings in ugly ears. . . .

ANNA. Go to bed . . . with him. You're not making sense.

LAURA. You know, there's some stuff for killing cockroaches – 'Prima'. What a misuse of the word. (*Looking out through the door.*) Bonjour, comrades . . . are you training today? Yes, you – I'm asking you, don't gape like that. A toast to the two sexes. Pass *that* on to your gallant comrades . . . Why do you turn away? It's so rude. Why are there so many of you? Want to have a drink with us? Which sex are you, lads? What sex d'you put when you fill in forms? D'you cross it out, or paste in glowing references to your prowess? Here's another one,

Anna. *Je . . . du ist. . .* What's the matter with you? You're
ignoring us. Well, I'll just have to console myself elsewhere
. . . (*Smokes.*) Anna, did you really have an Indian? What was
he like?

ANNA. *I* can't remember!

LAURA. I just want to know, do they take off their turbans in
bed, or what? Did you notice?

ANNA (*struggling to remember*). He was a student. . . .

LAURA. Tell me, tell me . . . And was he thin? Like a
skeleton. . . ?

ANNA. Not much meat on him. . . .

LAURA. Fantastic . . . Was he bald under his turban?

ANNA. Uhuh . . . He had a string tied around his jaw to stop it
chattering.

LAURA. Fantastic . . . Why are you so sad?

ANNA. What have I got to be happy about? I can't get that Maria
out of my mind. I was like that once . . . Confident, good-
looking, loved music. . . .

LAURA. Hang on, that one's waving to me. . . .

ANNA. Off you go.

LAURA. I've got one here. . . .

ANNA. What do'you think he's after?

LAURA. Take the bottle, give him a drink and tell him to push
off. . . .

ANNA. The bottle's empty, you've drunk it all! Listen, and you'll
hear it all swilling around your gut now.

ANNA *goes out.* LAURA *goes to the bed where* ALEXANDER *is
sleeping.*

LAURA. Come on, Sashenka, up you get. You've overslept. You
said to wake you in half-an-hour and you've already slept
three-and-a-half . . . don't you recognise me? Did you have a
bad dream?

ALEXANDER. Laura!

LAURA. Yes, darling, it's me! The night's nearly over . . . Have a hair of the dog – oh, sorry it's all inside me. . . .

ALEXANDER. Was I asleep?

LAURA. Yes . . . as you fell asleep you whispered: 'Just half-an-hour' . . . But I decided not to wake you . . . You really were tired – you did well to come here, for a real rest . . . I'll rent a room nearer to you, so we can meet and talk and you can tell me about the new trends in science. . . .

Enter ANNA. *She looks around, hesitates, then goes over to* LAURA *and* ALEXANDER.

ANNA. Listen, young man, you'd better get out . . . Why d'you look at me like that? They're looking for an escaped loony. They asked me and I said he'd been here and then gone away. Tall, thin bloke, they said, just like you.

ALEXANDER. I'll go and show my face, then hide.

ANNA. Don't go. The flame's coming, they won't go looking for anyone. Sit tight. They won't come in here.

LAURA. Why are they after you? What have you done?

ALEXANDER. They must have done a head count and found me missing.

ANNA. A loony on the loose at a time like this . . . S'pose he put out the Olympic flame? Then there'd be trouble . . . Now d'you see, doll, why there are so many cops around?

LAURA (*to* ALEXANDER). I'm afraid for you. Won't you get into trouble for this?

ALEXANDER. For what?

LAURA. It's all my fault, I kept you here . . . Why don't you curse me? If you're arrested, I'll go with you . . . I'll say . . . you behaved like a gentleman . . . Couldn't leave a lady on her own. . . .

ANNA. Oh, stop whining . . . A man was sent to search our hut. He spoke to me from five yards off and turned his head away, 'cos there's a rumour we're all infected. That's good – fewer men pestering us . . . Wait long enough, and it'll all be over. (*To* ALEXANDER:) Look, you're a scientist . . . one thing's always puzzled me . . . I once heard a man could

have a baby by caesarian . . . Rubbish, of course, but what
are the reasons?

ALEXANDER. I don't understand the subject.

LAURA. God, this is wonderful, Sasha, you're priceless.

ANNA. *Subject?* What d'you mean, subject?

ALEXANDER. You should ask a biologist . . . or a doctor. . . .

ANNA. I see . . . a biologist. . . .

LAURA. What about immaculate conception, Sasha? What's the
scientific view?

ANNA. It's when a husband and wife . . . do it properly.

LAURA. But they say she had no man . . . It was a bird, or
something.

ANNA. Depends what sort of bird . . . There *were* birds, you
know, that. . . .

ALEXANDER. I think she was just an unfortunate prostitute,
who'd probably been raped, and couldn't be sure who the
father was. That's why she said: 'The father is God!' The
child was born in poverty, among cripples, probably sickly
himself, and saw nothing but pain and suffering all around.
All he asked of people was mercy and kindness, but the
world was always cruel and unjust. The strong oppressed the
weak. So he told these wretches that after their suffering
they'd be happy. Otherwise life would be unbearable:
suffering now – afterwards, nothing.

ANNA. Wait a moment – *who* do you say was a prostitute?

ALEXANDER. Perhaps Mary was, the blessed Virgin Mary.

ANNA. You shit! You bloody bastard!

LAURA. *Anna!*

ANNA. I'm going straight out to turn you in! And *that*'s for you!
(*She spits in* ALEXANDER's *face.*)

LAURA (*jumping up*). Get out, you stupid cow!

ANNA (*to* ALEXANDER). I hope you die! (*To* LAURA:) You bitch
– you listen to him talk like that after you've just had him up
your cunt!

LAURA. He only said he thought that science. . . .

ANNA (*to* ALEXANDER). Don't you dare touch her, our Queen of Heaven. (*Weeps.*) *We're* the ones who get raped! Know how many men I've had in a night? They'd prick me with pins to make me move my arse . . . She'll meet me up there . . . she's pure . . . and holy . . . she'll wash me clean . . . She *never* had a man! Not one!

ALEXANDER. She's called blessed because of what she suffered!

ANNA. She didn't suffer! An angel came down to her. . . .

ALEXANDER. All right, take it easy. . . .

Silence.

LAURA (*to* ANNA). Why d'you spit at people?

ANNA. I don't know – but I'm not infected. Anyway, so what? Spit at me, for all I care . . . I was going to give you some cake, but now I'll chuck it away. . . .

LAURA. Sasha, eat my share of the cake . . . Forgive us, we're both a bit drunk. Anna's very touchy . . . She's had a hard life. . . .

ANNA. No, I haven't . . . I had everything everyone else gets. Free schooling . . . did lots of things . . . singing, dancing . . . I had no cause to complain. I could have done anything – I could have been a cook, f'r instance, or worked on the railways. I've no one but myself to blame. Mother said: 'Don't leave home, dear!' But I did, went and worked on building sites. Far North. Far East. I wrote to my mum I was a crane-driver, but by then I was on the game. When you're young and healthy, you can make a fortune at it! I started drinking then. At first I thought I'd find Mr. Right. Lived in hostels all the time. People always helped me, though . . . My kids were taken away from me . . . they were fed, clothed and schooled . . . If I live long enough, I thought, I'll see how they're growing up . . . I wouldn't go right up to them, of course – just peep through the keyhole at them.

LAURA. Don't cry, Anna. This is turning into an interesting evening . . . We may argue and disagree, but we mustn't quarrel . . . Now I'll show you a little trick . . . See, I'm holding an empty bottle. (*Goes out and returns with her hands behind her back.*) And *now* what?

LAURA *produces a new bottle.*

ALEXANDER. That's excellent wine.

ANNA. And we don't have to hand in the empties, Laura!

LAURA. As the French say: Let me pour out. I had it in my bag
all the time. It's our local wine, Crimean . . . And to think we
were drinking that pepper vodka!

ANNA. That pepper vodka was my prize.

They drink. MARIA *appears in the doorway.*

ANNA. Look who's here. . . .

MARIA. What's going on?

ANNA. We're celebrating the harvest festival. . . .

MARIA. All the same faces here . . . Anything left to drink?

ANNA. You know that painting by Repin called *They Didn't Take
It?* You should've listened to me and brought some back with
you from those 'gentlemen'.

MARIA. Just some plain water to drink. . . .

MARIA *limps in, staggers a few steps then collapses.*

ANNA. Why're you limping?

MARIA. Been ballroom dancing. . . .

MARIA *groans, and stretches out on the floor.* ANNA *goes quickly up
to her.*

ANNA. Why did you go? Little fool . . . *(Stands looking at* MARIA.*)*
Where does it hurt? Look, she's covered in blood. (LAURA
and ALEXANDER *come up.*) Beat you up, did they?

MARIA. I jumped out of the car while it was moving. We'd
passed the flyover. 'Stop!' I shouted. 'I'm car-sick!' Klara was
in on it. 'We're driving on!' she says. So at the bend I shoved
one of them in the face with my elbow and jumped out into
the ditch.

ANNA. What did they do?

MARIA. What could they do, with cop cars everywhere?

ANNA *(gleefully).* So they dropped off their girl and didn't stop to
pick her up!

MARIA. Water . . . I want a drink. . . .

ALEXANDER. Look, she's bleeding – she's badly wounded!

ANNA. All right, she's young, it'll heal. Give her some wine, bean-pole.

LAURA. Drink some of this, it'll do you good.

ALEXANDER gives MARIA some wine. She drinks.

LAURA. How did you get back?

ANNA. Thumbed a lift.

LAURA. She may have broken her leg. Looks bad, Anna.

Silence.

It certainly *looks* broken. (*To* MARIA:) Does your leg hurt?

MARIA (*wearily*). Yes. I must go to Moscow.

ANNA. You can't – lie down.

MARIA. No . . . I've got to get the first train.

ANNA. You've had your outing today.

MARIA. My kid's with the girls in the hostel . . . I must get him back from them by morning . . . Otherwise they'll think I've abandoned him. . . .

LAURA. They won't let you into Moscow – there are checkpoints everywhere. . .

MARIA. Shut up, will you. . . .

LAURA. Don't be so rude. Do as you're told, lie down and don't get up.

Silence.

ALEXANDER. She needs help . . . She's losing blood. . . .

ANNA. Shall we go and ask Valentina for a bandage?

ALEXANDER. She needs a doctor . . . a surgeon. . . .

Silence.

ANNA (*quietly*). How d'you feel, love?

Silence.

She's passed out! Oh lord – I've started to feel funny . . .
Let's hope to God she doesn't . . . She'd bled a lot . . .
(MARIA *opens her eyes, then closes them again.*) Listen, she's
moaning. . . .

Silence. Using a torn shirt, ALEXANDER *finishes bandaging*
MARIA*'s leg, and they all stand looking at her.*

ALEXANDER. I'll go for a doctor . . . I'll tell them to send one
up from the asylum . . . There's always one on call . . . She
must go to hospital. . . .

LAURA. Don't leave, Sasha dear. They'll keep you there.

ALEXANDER. Rubbish.

ANNA. No, she's right – let me go, there'll be less fuss.

LAURA. *I* could go. . . .

ALEXANDER. You don't know the way, you'd get lost in the
dark. I know this place – it's best if I go.

LAURA. Everyone's going berserk round here – I'll be worried
about you.

Silence.

ANNA. She's looking at us. Look – she's smiling! What have you
to smile about – smashing up your life like an empty bottle?

MARIA (*quietly*). And I should have handed in the empty,
shouldn't I?

Silence.

ANNA (*to* ALEXANDER). Go on, bean-pole. *I'm* not allowed out
of here, but you'll be arrested and taken down there . . . So
when you get to the flyover, tell Nikolai that Maria's here.
Tell him everything, then it's a matter for his conscience. . . .

MARIA. Don't. . . .

ANNA. Lie down. . . .

MARIA. Please don't fetch anyone . . . please. . . .

ANNA (*to* ALEXANDER). He's a big, strong bloke.

ALEXANDER. I know, I've seen him.

MARIA. Please, please don't go!

ANNA. Don't get up!

MARIA. I just came here to rest. I'll leave tomorrow. I don't need help. I'll manage. If I conk out it's none of your business. My kid's there.

ANNA. What can you do for him? It's better if they put him in a home. Later you can find him. . . .

MARIA. I was a fool to come here . . . a bloody fool. . . .

ANNA. You see, Laura, she came here expecting something. Expecting, hoping, like any normal person. . . .

MARIA. If they put me in hospital, Anna, I'll tell you where he is – I'll give you the address.

ANNA. OK.

MARIA (*to* ALEXANDER). Wait! Please get me some water to wash myself . . . (*To* ANNA:) I'm all dirty, Anna . . . get him to bring me some water . . . I'm filthy. . . .

ANNA. What's she on about?

LAURA. You're not dirty, love!

MARIA. I want to wash. D'you grudge me some water?

ANNA. There's rainwater in the bucket outside the door.

ALEXANDER *brings in the bucket,* ANNA *helps* MARIA *to get up and* LAURA *gets her undressed.*

MARIA (*to* ALEXANDER). Go away, please. . . .

ANNA. You're right, he could be your dad. (*Washes* MARIA's *face and shoulders.*) Look at this scratch all down your back – where's your cardigan? Let's give it a shake.

LAURA. Chuck it away. (*Takes hers out of her bag.*) Here, try mine on.

MARIA. It's lovely – can you spare it?

ANNA. Say thank you.

MARIA. Laura, you used to have a pretty brooch. Let me wear it. And have you got a make-up brush? Mine's in my suitcase.

LAURA (*taking out her make-up case*). Take this. Mine's for eye-shadow. D'you want me to give you golden eyelids?

MARIA. Yes please, and a cigarette.

LAURA *gives her a cigarette and lights it for her.*

ANNA (*to* ALEXANDER). Go on, son, you might just make it if you slip in quietly. . . .

ALEXANDER. Goodbye, Laura. . . .

LAURA. Wait, I'll come with you . . . We'll say we're both from the madhouse . . . They'll believe us. I'm about ready for the place myself, anyway . . . I'm losing you, Sasha, losing you forever. . . .

Kisses him.

ALEXANDER. We'll meet again . . . Come and see me . . . It's not far.

LAURA. You might even come to the circus one day and look up and see me . . . I hope you weren't bored with me.

ALEXANDER. Or you with me. . . .

LAURA. Don't be upset that we didn't make it in bed . . . I wanted to . . . but you fell asleep . . . Who knows, maybe we'll meet again . . . Will you remember me? I'm Laura, the trapeze-artist.

ALEXANDER. I shan't forget that.

LAURA. Goodbye, my might-have-been.

LAURA *embraces* ALEXANDER. *Enter* KLARA, *her clothes torn, looking grim.*

KLARA. Break it up, Laura . . . I want to thank you. . . .

LAURA. Come in, Klara.

ANNA. So she's back! (*To* MARIA:) You lie down. They'll sort it out.

KLARA. Thanks for everything, Laura.

LAURA. What for, Klara?

KLARA. For being such a rat, Laura.

LAURA. We're not alone, Klara.

KLARA. So I see. I'm only blind in one eye. Look how Bushuyev paid me – with this shiner. What did I tell you? He talked himself hoarse, trying to persuade Ovsyannikov . . . A car-boot full of food and wine, enough to last till the Winter Olympic Games. Know why Bushuyev hit me?

LAURA. Don't, Klara – please!

KLARA. To make me pay for the petrol . . . He's furious . . . We chased all over the place. . . .

LAURA. Klara, don't – d'you hear?

KLARA. I hear. He only punched one ear. Left the other one alone. As I say, we chased everywhere looking for you . . . So you've been having fun, I see. Is this him?

LAURA. Let's go outside, Klara.

KLARA. What for? Come on, get your things . . . hurry, before they close the roads. . . .

LAURA. I'm not going . . . I'm sorry, but I *can't* – I'm frightened.

KLARA. Don't make me laugh! If you couldn't, you should've said so before. It's a bit late to start being awkward now . . . *(To* ALEXANDER:) Let her go, lover boy, don't look for trouble . . . or they'll have to take you away in little pieces. . . .

LAURA. She's gone stark raving mad. . . .

KLARA. I told you – she'll write you a letter.

ALEXANDER. Thanks . . . I'll wait for ever.

KLARA. Better still – a telegram . . . in the dark.

LAURA. Go on, Sasha, you were going anyway.

ALEXANDER. Yes, it's best of all in the dark.

LAURA. Klara, I won't go.

KLARA. Who d'you plan to stay with? Look at him, with his mouth open. *(To* ALEXANDER:) What sort of yarn did she spin you?

ANNA. Shut up! Mind your own business . . . stirring it up again. Maria's bad . . . *(To* ALEXANDER:) Go on, clear off. . . .

KLARA. Who are you talking about? I've got a bone to pick with her later!

ALEXANDER *makes a dash for the door, but* KLARA *tackles him.*

KLARA. Stop! Did you think she was a circus artiste? Did she tell you her grandmother was Spanish, her grandpa an aircraft designer? She never had a grandmother . . . Her mother was

a vagrant . . . on the road all her life . . . That's our Laura!
Every cop on the coast knows her . . . Bushuyev's her lover
. . . he promised her to Ovsyannikov on the side. . . .

ANNA. I'll kill her! It's all her fault! What can I thump her with?

KLARA (*suddenly pulling a glass-stoppered bottle out of her pocket*). Stay
where you are, everyone! (*Goes towards* ANNA.) *Who* are you
going to kill? Stop! Don't move!

ANNA *freezes.* KLARA *goes up close to her.*

If I throw this in your face, first aid won't help you . . . Right
– repeat after me . . . (*Swings round.*) Don't move, you, or I'll
burn her face . . . Repeat after me: 'Laura is a cheap
scrubber'. (*Silence.*) Repeat it, you fool. . . .

ANNA (*quietly*). Larissa. . . .

KLARA. Hurry up and say it, Anna.

Silence.

Want to drink it? Or d'you only drink liqueurs? This is much
better . . . good strong stuff. . . .

ANNA. You can't frighten me!

LAURA (*yells*). Say it, Anna, say it. . . !

ANNA. Klara, wait! I'll go! I'll go!

KLARA *puts away the bottle and produces another from her bag.*

KLARA. Take this bottle of scent, Anna . . . I always carry some
on me . . . It's cheap rubbish, but it attracts attention. . . .

LAURA. Get away from her, Anna!

ANNA. Did I frighten you? (*Cheerfully.*) I don't need my ugly mug
any more, you old bag. . . .

KLARA. What? Forget it . . . Take the scent . . . The other bottle
had the same stuff in it . . . I was joking, but you didn't get it
. . . You're too gullible! (*Silence.* LAURA *prepares to leave.*) Want
some help, Laura?

LAURA. Thanks, Klara. I can manage.

ALEXANDER. Please ring me . . . there's my phone number.

LAURA. Don't bother, Sasha, I won't phone. . . .

ALEXANDER. Please ring me. It's a shared flat, with two Alexanders. Ask for Illiadi.

LAURA. Are you that Greek?

KLARA. Get a move on!

LAURA. Doctor Illiadi! (*Laughs.*) Alexander Illiadi, Nobel prizewinner! Goodbye Mr. Might-have-been! We would have had fun! (*Laughs.*) Mrs. Laura Illiadi! OK, Klara, let's go – just let him leave first. Go on, Sasha, hurry . . . God help you!

Exit ALEXANDER.

Coming, Klara . . . Wait, Anna, here's some money. . . .

ANNA. Forget it . . . What do I want money for? I'll only drink it.

LAURA. Maria . . . I'll leave you my makeup and clothes. The skirts are probably too short, but never mind, you've nice legs. Be brave, help will come. . . .

MARIA. Thanks.

LAURA *goes to the door. Enter* VALENTINA, *carrying two large hold-alls. Looks around.*

VALENTINA. Ah, you're all together – Laura, Klara. . . .

Silence.

ANNA. Look over there, Valya. . . .

VALENTINA. I can see. It's Maria.

ANNA (*glumly*). Well, shall we take the roll-call? Line up, girls!

VALENTINA. Did you like my cake?

ANNA. We forgot all about it. How did it go down with the lieutenant and Nikolai?

VALENTINA. They ate every last crumb.

ANNA. Why lie to me? They never left their post.

VALENTINA. I took it to 'em there, and they shared it out. . . .

KLARA. Why've you brought my bags?

VALENTINA. Your boyfriends gave 'em to me . . . Theirs was the last car allowed into Moscow . . . No more traffic – all the rest are being turned back. (*Pause.*) It's so quiet here. (*Solemnly raising her hand and listening to the silence.*) Never heard it so quiet here. Even the birds are silent . . . No people. . . .

Silence.

Leaving out a few of his most unprintable words, Bushuyev told me to tell you that he'd kept the tape-recorder to cover his expenses. The rest was unrepeatable – 'if those fucking bitches show up in Moscow. . .' On and on he went. So your birds have flown.

LAURA (*from the door*). I'm ready, Klara.

KLARA (*sullenly*). No one to serve you up to now, sausage . . . All dressed up, too. . . .

VALENTINA. No one's to leave this hut without my permission. Only after the procession's passed – we can see it from the hillside. We'll all stand together – they'll all be watching you, but don't worry. Just don't try sneaking off!

ANNA. Valya, the kid's bad. . . .

VALENTINA (*loudly*). No one's to go outside! That's an order! Klepov sends his regards. He's down there, and he'll come up later. . . .

Suddenly a quiet singing is heard from MARIA's *bed.*

MARIA. 'Enchanted star of love
Star of days long past
light the sky above
And my tormented heart. . .'

VALENTINA. You've got it nice here . . . Drinking, singing . . . Your boyfriend's scarpered, though. And where's that idiot who was hanging around? Anna, are you in charge or not?

LAURA. This girl may have broken her leg. . . .

VALENTINA. I'll look in a tick . . . Anna, bring the light over here and switch it on. . . .

KLARA (*rummaging in her bag*). The bastards cleaned me out.

ANNA. You're only the fire-warden, Valya – she needs a *doctor*. . . .

VALENTINA (*going up to* MARIA). What did I tell you? Bring me that light.

ANNA *takes the light and goes to* MARIA's *bed.*

VALENTINA. Still singing, my girl?

MARIA. Who's this? Yes, I'm singing. Please don't disturb me.

VALENTINA. The trouble you give me! So you've hurt your leg?

MARIA. Anna, Larissa! I've been having such a funny dream!
(*Laughs.*) There was this woman in our village who was
terribly mean . . . she refused to have children, because they
were such an expense . . . there are bitches like that. Her
husband did odd jobs all round the village . . . She used to
hire him out – not as a stud, as you're thinking, Anna! – he
dug the pits when people wanted to build cellars, helped with
the hay-making . . . Anyway, she wore him to a shred. One
of her schemes was to distil moonshine in the washing
machine, using the spin-dryer . . . But machinery needs
energy, and the electricity is metered and costs money. So
she went into the nearest town and traded sour cream for
some crocodile-clips to clip onto the power-line direct and
bypass the meter. (*Laughs.*) Honestly . . . I'm telling you – she
did . . . Well one night some girls and I were coming back
from a dance . . . and as we got near the village we saw
something bright – at first we thought it was a shooting star.
Then as we came closer, Katya shouted: 'It's a space-man!'
And we ran towards him for all we were worth!

ANNA. What *is* all this, Maria?

MARIA. Poor chap, he'd climbed up the pole to the cables . . . to
the crocodile clips . . . and he must have touched the wrong
thing, because he was shaking and giving off silver sparks like
an angel . . . They didn't get him down till next morning . . .
Ever since then he can't stop jerking and swaying from side
to side, like a pendulum. But she even turned that to good
use: whenever anyone in the village was pickling cabbage to
make sauerkraut, she would take him there . . . tie a knife
into his fist and sit him down. And he'd slice away at the
cabbage like a machine.

ANNA. Why are you telling us all this?

MARIA. Klara was like her . . . their faces were almost exactly
alike. . . .

Silence.

VALENTINA. So why are you crying?

ANNA. Can't you see she's in pain!

Silence.

MARIA. And d'you know what we called her? 'Tombstone'!

VALENTINA (*quietly*). It's obviously broken . . . no need to look. . . .

Silence.

What a disaster – you let them in and what happens? Fag-ends everywhere, too . . . I'm responsible, it's me gets the rap! I told you not to smoke! Anna! Anna!

ANNA. What? Don't shout at me. . . .

VALENTINA. Get rid of these bottles! Sweep the dog-ends out of the hut . . . Tomorrow I'm putting you all under police surveillance . . . No more boozing then . . . You're a disgrace . . . (*To* KLARA:) You look a bit of a mess! Get up and clear away the rubbish. . . .

KLARA. What happened to a bottle of scent I had? It was called 'Natasha'.

VALENTINA. And where's that idiot who was here? Anna. . . .

ANNA. No more of an idiot than you are. . . .

VALENTINA. Drunkards, the lot of you! I'm handing you all over to Klepov – just you try drinking *then*!

ANNA (*indignantly*). Who's drunk? I'm not even pink! I'm not drunk till I'm on all fours. Ask your son . . . Kolya, tell your mother. . . .

NIKOLAI *appears in the doorway.*

Back me up – tell her I'm sober . . . Remember how we first met? That was something to remember, Laura! The square in front of Savelev station . . . I was crossing it on three limbs, not four . . . holding a string bag in one hand . . . I was on a zebra crossing, so's not to get run over – and if a car hit me the driver'd have to pay. Cars all around . . . people rushing hither and thither . . . terrible. I got half-way across . . . and there on the other side was a police drunks'-van . . . They were opening the doors for me . . . I just kept straight on, until I reached the police . . . That was how I met Nikolai . . . Remember, Kolya?

Silence.

LAURA (*coming up to* NIKOLAI). Tell me . . . where's that . . . man now?

NIKOLAI. Which man?

LAURA. From the loony-bin. . . .

NIKOLAI. They took him away. . . .

LAURA. I see. Thanks. . . .

Silence. NIKOLAI *goes to* MARIA's *bed.*

VALENTINA. Soon as all this is over we'll take her to the hospital. . . .

NIKOLAI. Go away, everyone, go away.

VALENTINA. You'd better go back to your post! You'll end up in jail 'cos of her.

NIKOLAI. Mind your own business. . . .

NIKOLAI *sits down on* MARIA's *bed and looks silently at her.*

VALENTINA. On your head be it. . . .

VALENTINA *goes to the door, where she is the first to catch the sound of a barely audible rumbling.*

There it is! It's here!

LAURA (*at the door*). Look! . . . Look!

ANNA *comes up to her.*

ANNA. Where?

LAURA. Not over there . . . far away . . . like sparks . . . d'you see?

ANNA. Those blue ones?

LAURA. Look, Klara. . . .

ANNA. Now I . . . see . . . flashing . . . Lord, there's a whole stream of 'em. . . ! Look at it winding along!

LAURA. Can you see, Klara?

KLARA (*coming up*). They look lovely. . . .

NIKOLAI (*quietly, to* MARIA). Be patient . . . Won't be long now . . . We've got Mum's motorbike . . . I can take you . . . the hospital's not far. . . .

MARIA. You'd better go – I'll wait. . . .

ANNA. Go on, Kolya – leave, don't torment yourself! You can't
. . . you mustn't . . . your place is out there . . . Go,
Kolya. . . .

MARIA. That's right, Kolya, you must go . . . Thank you for
everything. . . .

NIKOLAI. Shut up! I'm staying here with you. . . .

They watch the lights in silence.

ANNA. See the lights, Maria . . . It looks so lovely . . . But
where's the Olympic flame? I can't see it. . . .

KLARA. Still a way off.

They watch in silence.

ANNA. Why can't we go out, Valya? We can't see anything
here. . . .

VALENTINA *says nothing.*

LAURA. They're disappearing – why?

KLARA. The road bends there.

ANNA. Look at all the people on the hillside! Running up and
down . . . They can, so why can't we? . . . I'm going – I don't
care if I do get arrested. Anyway, what harm can I do?

LAURA. If you go, Anna, take me too. . . .

KLARA. I won't ask – I'll just go!

VALENTINA *(quietly).* I told you – we must all go together. . . .

ANNA. Maybe we could carry her down. We'll never see anything
like this again . . . D'you mind if we go, Maria? You'd have
to wait here anyway . . . The roads are closed. . . .

MARIA. Go on . . . I'm such a nuisance. . . .

ANNA. OK . . . I just hope there's nothing seriously wrong with
you. . . .

LAURA *kisses her.*

MARIA. You go on . . . Tell me all about it. . . .

ANNA. Can you hear that hooting?

They fall silent. From far below and far away come the swelling sounds of the procession. It's already possible to distinguish warning orders from loud-hailers, and the faint sounds of sirens.

LAURA. Klara, open that bottle of champagne!

KLARA. For this – yes! (*Uncorks the bottle.*) Gather round, girls . . . (*To* VALENTINA:) Come on, missis, this champagne's like gold-dust! Have a sip. . . .

VALENTINA. *You* drink. . . .

ANNA (*taking her glass to* MARIA). Here, have a sip of mine. . . .

MARIA. No thanks, Anna, I'm fine. . . .

ANNA. Have you sorted things out with him?

MARIA. Yes. . . .

ANNA. Thank God . . . it'll be all right . . . and you'll . . . you'll be happy, Maria . . . I can just feel it . . . You stay with him . . . he won't leave you . . . You're the only one of us who'll be happy, my precious. . . .

MARIA. Go on, Anna . . . Off you go. . . .

LAURA. What shall we drink to, signori?

ANNA. What? May our boys win. . . .

LAURA (*crying*). Yes of course . . . To our boys. . . .

ANNA. To our boys . . . Why're you crying, love? . . . To our lads, the best of all . . . our brave heroes, they can't be beaten . . . Not like your Indians. Maybe we do suffer because they're so tough . . . But we'll always love 'em . . . 'cos they always win!

The women drink.

VALENTINA (*from the doorway*). Look, they're already lining up!

LAURA (*runs to the door*). It's them!

KLARA (*comes up*). They're so close. . . !

LAURA (*shouting and waving*). Hey, you there, hallo!

KLARA (*laughing*). Why're you waving? They can't see you!

VALENTINA (*sternly*). Come on everyone, follow me! (*Goes out.*)

ANNA. We must run, or we'll only see them disappearing. . . .

KLARA. We mustn't miss 'em. . . ! (*Goes out.*)

ANNA (*shouts*). Hurrah! (*Calls.*) Maria!

LAURA (*shouts*). Hallo, there! (*Runs out.*)

All the women go out. MARIA and NIKOLAI remain in the hut. The noise of cars and people shouting grows clearer and clearer.

NIKOLAI. Not long to go now . . . Want to see the flame?

MARIA. I don't care about the flame. Laura gave me her lighter!

NIKOLAI. Maria!

MARIA. Kolya – I'm not Maria. I'm just a slut . . . Your mother was right. Go quick, Kolya, while there's still time . . . I'll only bring you bad luck. . . .

Through the open door of the hut, we can see, far below, the flashing red and blue lights of police cars racing along. They are greeted by shouts from the spectators on the hillside, and with each new vehicle the shouting grows louder.

NIKOLAI. Let's go. . . .

MARIA. No! Let go of me! No!

NIKOLAI. What's up? (*Tries to lift her.*) Why're you clinging to the bed? Let it go . . . All right, stay there . . . I'll drag the bed out!

Attempts to pull the bed across the floor.

It's screwed in!

He squats down, trying to tear the bed out of the floor. Heaving and groaning, he tries again and again to move it.

MARIA (*again losing consciousness*). Kolya, my kid's down there. . . .

NIKOLAI. Who's he with?

MARIA. Anna knows. . . .

NIKOLAI *manages to lift MARIA up and carry her out of the hut. The women are standing on the steep hillside, and the blue lights flicker across their faces. Suddenly, from quite nearby, excited shouts go up, and this noise, getting louder and louder, drowns out the sound of the vehicles below.*
ANNA *runs forward, shouting something and waving her arms. Then she stops, weeping with excitement, running alongside the column*

of vehicles with one arm raised. LAURA *stands motionless, only screwing up her eyes against the bright strips of light flashing across her face.* KLARA *seems glum and morose, but even she cannot repress a loud, animal-like cry, such is her urge to be heard by the people running below.* VALENTINA *watches* NIKOLAI *carry out* MARIA, *but she does not move.* MARIA, *with her arm around* NIKOLAI's *neck, strains to see the real living Olympic flame among all the flashing electric lights. . . .*

They watch the endless procession of vehicles, and the people rushing down the hillside to follow them. They all crane their necks to peer beyond the dark plain where lurks the huge town, its outskirts just visible in the streak of dawn which lights up the morning sky, and in which the last stars of morning are still glimmering.

A MAN WITH CONNECTIONS ■ ALEXANDER GELMAN

Translated by STEPHEN MULRINE

Dealing with a marital and professional crisis in the life of a construction-site supervisor, '*A Man with Connections* is rather like a cross between Arthur Miller and Alan Ayckbourn.' (*Guardian*) Still running at the Moscow Art Theatre, the play was first staged in Britain at the Traverse Theatre Edinburgh in 1988 and then in London at the Royal Court in early 1989.

In all essentials, this translation of Alexander Gelman's *Naedine so vsemi* was first commissioned by BBC Radio 3, produced in Edinburgh by Marilyn Imrie, with Bill Paterson and Phyllis Logan in the cast, and broadcast in November 1986. This was followed by a stage production directed by Jenny Killick at the Traverse Theatre, Edinburgh, in August 1988, which marked the British premiere of Gelman's work and was subsequently seen at the Royal Court Theatre, London, in January 1989. This stage version, which was shorter than the radio version and differed in some minor details (for instance, Golubev was called Gladkov), was published alongside the Royal Court production in a separate edition – also by Nick Hern Books. The play as published here, however, represents Gelman's full text, with the restoration of all cuts made due to the exigencies of time and medium.

Stephen Mulrine

Characters

NATASHA
ANDREI

A Man with Connections was first staged in the Traverse Theatre, Edinburgh on 4 August 1988 and subsequently at the Royal Court Theatre, London on 6 January 1989.

The cast was as follows:

NATASHA	Marty Cruickshank
ANDREI	Bill Paterson

Directed by Jenny Killick
Designed by Dermot Hayes
Lighting and sound by George Tarbuck
Costumes by Morna Baxter and Caroline Scott

ACT ONE

The action of the play begins with a prolonged impatient ringing at the doorbell of the Golubevs' apartment. The Golubevs have a three-roomed flat, but only one bedroom is visible on stage. The room is dark, now around 11 p.m. No one answers the door, and we hear more ringing – in short and long bursts, now playful, now irritated. There is no response, and we hear a key being turned in the lock.

ANDREI'S VOICE *(from the hallway, with exaggerated affection)*.
Natasha, sweetheart? *(Silence.)* Natalya, where are you? Natalya, are you there?

There is no answer. ANDREI *comes in. He is short and thickset, 47 years old. Despite his bulk, and a certain puffiness, he is well set up and stylishly dressed, wearing a fashionable raincoat, thrown open. He carries a hat. He switches on the light – there is no one in the bedroom. A little troubled, he rapidly checks out the other rooms. Finding no one in the flat,* ANDREI *returns, and now begins to inspect the bedroom more closely. The bedroom is in total disarray: in the middle of the room, clearly not in its rightful place, stands a low, wide armchair; wooden coathangers lie scattered across the floor, and a coffee table, stacked with dirty cups, pokes halfway out from under a large table. Articles of clothing, mainly women's, are strewn everywhere.*

ANDREI *(to himself, gloomily)*. Huh – a tip.

He flings his hat and coat down on the divan, crosses to the telephone. He takes a tiny notebook out of his jacket pocket, looks up a number. He picks up the receiver – there is no dialling tone. He rattles the rest, shakes the telephone, but it has obviously been unplugged. He picks up the plug from the floor, pushes it into the telephone socket. He lifts the receiver again, sits down on a chair, and dials the number.

Hello? Men's Surgical? Yes, I'm enquiring about Alyosha Golubev, in Ward 3. This is his father – oh, hello, I didn't recognise your voice. Yes, we'll be picking Alyosha up tomorrow. How long has he been in? Um, let me think . . . thirtieth of June, was the accident . . . that's um, just over a month. Actually I'm looking for my wife. *(Jocularly.)* I've lost

my spouse – she's not with Alyosha just now, is she? . . . I
don't suppose she could've come in without your noticing? I
mean, she's a pretty fast mover. Not possible? Would you do
me a favour, please – ask Alyosha if his mother's been in
today at all? Thank you, Sister. (*A pause.*) Yes, yes – I see.
(*Looks at his watch.*) No, no, don't wake him up. Let him sleep.
Right, thank you – sorry to trouble you – 'bye. (*Hangs up,
dials another number from memory.*)
(*Coldly*). Hello, Vadim – it's Golubev. Listen, I've just been
down in your section an hour ago, and you haven't got that
bloody girder up yet. OK, never mind the excuses – I won't
be in the first half of tomorrow, I'll be there about two, and I
want that girder in place by then, right? That's the first thing.
Secondly – is my wife by any chance with you? You haven't
seen her? Look, ask Olga, see if she has any idea where
Natasha might be. (*A pause.*) Oh, hello, Olya . . . no, she's not
here . . Well, she's not here now, when did she phone? Well,
I don't know, maybe she wasn't phoning from home. Look,
what are you so nippy about? Has Vadim been complaining
again? I'm giving him a hard time? I'm giving *myself* a hard
time, this job's behind schedule, he knows the position . . .
Well, if it's not that . . . oh, come off it, Olga, I know damn
well what it is! Hello? Hello? Shit!

*Slams down the receiver, sits for a moment glowering, depressed. Then
he suddenly stands up and begins to jerk his left shoulder, as if shaking
something loose, or throwing something off his back. He repeats this a
few times, and almost immediately relaxes. It is as if he has corrected a
dislocation. The gloomy and anxious expression passes from his face,
and his mood has already changed – now alert, energetic. He removes
his jacket, hangs it on the back of a chair, takes off his shirt and tie,
and carefully spreads the shirt out on top of his jacket. He keeps his
vest on, and lifts the phone again. He is in a better humour now, self-
important.*

Hello, Despatch? Golubev here. How's that cement – are we
unloading it yet or what? (*He picks up the telephone, and walks
with it to the door, talking all the while.*) Mm – what about No 3
Pump – have they given us an operator? Well, I did ask.
Look, chum, what do I need to do to get it into your skull?
You get that concrete down there right away. Oh, and make a
note in the day-book, I won't be in the first part of
tomorrow, I'm going to the hospital to pick up the boy. So
you can send the car for ten o'clock, not eight as usual . . .

ANDREI *passes from view into the bathroom. The telephone cord is very long, and it keeps unwinding until eventually it will extend no further. We hear taps turned on in the bathroom. Suddenly, with a sharp blow from inside, the doors of a roomy built-in wardrobe are flung open.* ANDREI'*s wife* NATASHA *crawls out, dishevelled and dejected-looking, wearing a dressing gown which reaches to the floor. She is 42. She seems distracted, her eyes glazed over, her breathing irregular and agitated. She makes her way unsteadily to the armchair and settles into it, tucking her legs underneath her. There is something ominous about the way she sits, shivering, pressing herself into the chairback. The water in the bathroom is turned off, and* ANDREI *comes in again, stripped to the waist and washed, drying his neck with a towel. He catches sight of* NATASHA *in the armchair.*

(*Startled.*) Where have you been? (*At the sound of his voice* NATASHA *shudders, and covers up her face.*) Eh? Natalya – where did you spring from? (NATASHA *is silent.* ANDREI *notices the wardrobe doors, makes the connection, tuts disapprovingly.*) What have you been up to? Hiding in the wardrobe? (*No response.*) Natasha? (NATASHA *looks up, seems on the point of making some kind of spiteful or rancorous response, but suddenly goes limp, drops her head again.*)

(*Gloomily.*) Have you been drinking again? Have you been drinking, I'm asking you? What are you playing at – we're supposed to be picking Alyosha up at the hospital tomorrow. How much have you had? Well, come on, how many glasses?

NATASHA *draws her head into her thin, bony shoulders – almost as if she is trying to stop up her ears, so as not to hear* ANDREI'*s voice.*

(*Bitterly.*) So, OK, you've been drinking, so what, eh? Where's the harm? It'll save me drinking on my tod, we can all get drunk together now. Alyosha can join in, make it a threesome, terrific! Only next time don't hide in the wardrobe. What were you up to in there, were you asleep? Have you been crying? (*He shrugs.*) So who's going to do the driving, eh, if we go out? Alyosha's no use now, and you're drinking. We'll just have to take the bus. Get rid of the car, I mean, what do we want with a car? Will I turn on the shower? I'm asking you, do you want a shower – bring you round a bit? (*He shakes her by the shoulder.*) Natasha?

NATASHA (*shrilly*). Don't!

ANDREI (*taken aback*). Don't what? Don't turn on the shower?
Eh? Don't what? (*Looking at her back, sighs.*) Natalya, Natalya.
Oh yes, you're OK when things are going well, but the
minute there's trouble you just go to pieces. I don't know
what to do with you. This place is like a tip, when are you
going to clean it up? You can't bring Alyosha back to this . . .
Every day for the past month I've been at you to snap out of
it – to cut the moping around and the drinking, that's not
going to help Alyosha! Crying won't give him his hands back,
you can't stick them on with tears. All right, Alyosha's lost his
hands – what are we going to do about it? We've just got to
live, and work. And plan for the future. There's no point in
piling one tragedy on top of another – we've already got one,
it's here to stay. Instead of just . . . (*Gestures helplessly.*) You
know there was a phone call this morning, from the college?
Wanting to know how he was getting on. I told them he'd be
transferring to part time. Have you decided yet which room
he's having? It was you that was doing all the shouting that
he couldn't stay in his old room. And why is his guitar still
there? I thought we'd agreed – either give it to somebody or
chuck it out. I think Alyosha should have this room – do you
agree? (NATASHA *does not answer.*) He'll have more space
here, and the verandah. Plenty of light. We can bring the telly
in. Are you listening? Natasha? You're not even with us, are
you? Anyway, while you've been otherwise engaged, I've
been looking after Alyosha's interests. You know, it suddenly
struck me – (*Taps his forehead.*) – this is a big town, there must
be other people in the same boat. So anyway, I sent our chief
mechanic along to the Welfare Office, and he turned up
three – wrote down their addresses and went to see them.
(ANDREI *sits beside her on a low stool.*) One's still quite a young
chap, thirty-two, history graduate from Kiev, stays with his
mother. The other two comrades are getting on a bit – war
invalids. But they've got families, children – grandchildren.
So it's perfectly normal, I mean, people go on *living*.
Alyosha'll take a wee while to get settled, then we'll put him
in touch with these chaps – maybe cheer him up. Also I got
our mechanic to make notes on various gadgets they had.
Like a foot-operated switch for the TV – so you can change
channels. You just press it with your foot, like so –
(*Demonstrates.*) Eh? And we'll try and get one of these push-
button phones – the mechanic was saying they're really neat.
You pick up a pencil in your teeth – beep-beep-beep-beep –

(*Demonstrates.*) – and you've dialled your number, no problem. The receiver's mounted on a sort of vertical bracket – you just put your ear against it, and . . .

NATASHA (*shrieks*). You devil! Shut up! Shut up!

ANDREI. What? (*Outraged, gets up from the stool.*) Devil? Who's a devil? Eh? Well, thanks a bunch, Natasha – that's some word you've dug up. My God, you're good at dishing it out, but you don't see *yourself*. (*Goes onto the attack.*) What was the phone doing unplugged? I've been phoning you the whole day, like an idiot. Trying to let you know I'd be late in. There was a hold up at the site, we've three projects to wrap up by the first of the month. Of course, you won't be interested in my problems, you've found yourself a devil. (*Gives the coffee table with its unwashed cups a spiteful kick.*) Who've you been drinking with, eh? Who was it? Somebody just drop in? (NATASHA *does not answer.* ANDREI *continues, angrily.*) How do you want your shower, hot or cold? I'll run it hot to start with, but you finish off with a *cold* shower, right? A really stinging cold shower, that's what you need. Bring you to your senses.

He snatches up his coat and hat and goes out. Left alone, NATASHA *reaches into her dressing gown pocket for cigarettes and a lighter. She straightens herself up in the armchair, lights a cigarette. Her expression is now cruel and cold, a spiteful resolve in her eyes.* ANDREI *comes in again, now bare-foot, wearing only his trunks.*

(*Cheerfully.*) Natasha, where's my dressing gown? It was hanging up in the bathroom. Have you seen it? (NATASHA *turns round sharply to face him, hatred in her eyes.* ANDREI *is disconcerted.*) My dressing gown, do you know where it is? Natasha, what's up with you? Is this the brandy at work? What are you staring at? (NATASHA *smiles contemptuously, her eyes ice-cold.* ANDREI *approaches and peers into her face.*) Listen, Natasha, *have* you been drinking? I think you're stone cold sober. (*Comes closer still.*) Right, then, breathe out. (NATASHA *shrinks into the corner of the armchair.*) Come on, let's smell your breath. Breathe out. (*He leans over her,* NATASHA *turns her face aside.*)

(*Coarsely.*) Come on, Natasha, bloody well breathe – (*Tries to come at her from the other side*). Goddammit! (NATASHA *suddenly spits full force into his face, several times.* ANDREI *is thunderstruck.*) What the hell was that for? Eh? What was that for? (*He wipes his face with his hand.*) You're not drunk, Natasha, you haven't touched a drop . . . what's the matter with you? Natasha, this is *me*. What's up with you? What were you doing in there? (*Indicates the wardrobe.*) Have you been seeing things, Natasha? My God, that's all we need. Where's the phone? Where did I leave the phone?

ANDREI *remembers he took the telephone into the other room, hurries out.* NATASHA *gets up, has another couple of puffs and stubs her cigarette out on the ash tray. Then she crosses to the wall socket and pulls out the telephone plug, and stands with her back to the wall, concealing the socket.* ANDREI *rushes in, holding the telephone.*

Right, plug that phone in! I've just got through to Saratov – my mother's neighbour's gone next door to get her. I want to speak to my mother – plug that back in! (NATASHA *does not react.*) Plug that phone in right now! (NATASHA *refuses to budge, and* ANDREI *goes up very close to her, his manner now placatory.*) Natasha, my mother's there. She'll be worried. She'll be expecting me to phone back. She's an old woman, Natasha, she's not well. I'm phoning her now so's she'll make the eleven o'clock train and be here in the morning. We can't cope without her, Alyosha's helpless. I've got these projects to finish, I can't take time off. We'll do a quick trip in the morning, pick up Alyosha, I'll stay for an hour or so, then scoot. I mean, just don't count on me for the next couple of weeks – this is a crucial time for me, it really is. You can't imagine. And I'm sorry, Natasha, but you . . . That's why we need Mum. Look, I'm asking you to think about Alyosha. That's all that concerns us now, right? Just get that into your head – Alyosha, Alyosha, and that's it. that's it. OK? Natasha? Sweetheart?

NATASHA. Get dressed.

ANDREI. What was that?

NATASHA. Get dressed.

ANDREI. What for? What d'you mean dressed? Trousers?

NATASHA. Everything.

ANDREI. What's the point of getting dressed? Can't I phone as I am?

NATASHA. I'm not plugging this in.

ANDREI. All right, all right. (*Sets the telephone down on the floor. Goes out. Quickly comes back, wearing his vest, trousers, slippers.*)

NATASHA. That's not dressed. Fully dressed. To the last button.

ANDREI. Listen, Natasha, my mother's waiting. Let me phone. Please? Just let me phone, then you can do what you like – choke me, stab me, drown me in the bath. Natasha! (*No response.*) Right, what do you mean, fully dressed? D'you want me to stick a hat on my head?

NATASHA. You heard me, everything.

ANDREI. Says who?

NATASHA. I do.

ANDREI. For God's sake! (*Picks his shirt up from the chairback, puts it on, stuffs his tie into his trouser pocket, picks up his jacket and puts it on.*) Now can I phone? Does that make you happy?

NATASHA. No. Coat. Shoes. Hat.

ANDREI. Natasha, give it a rest! Plug that phone in, will you!

NATASHA. You heard what I said.

ANDREI. God Almighty! (*Goes out.*) I've no time for playing silly buggers, Natasha, I hope you know that!

NATASHA *meanwhile rushes to the wardrobe, opens the door, revealing a large suitcase. She drags it out and hauls it across to block the doorway, then returns to her position at the phone socket.* ANDREI *comes back, wearing his coat and hat, and his shoes, with the laces untied. He stumbles into the suitcase and capsizes it.*

What's that doing there? Some sort of bloody barricade? Right, plug that thing in now, this minute, and I'll phone for an ambulance! They'll give you an injection, to calm you down!

NATASHA. I'm calm enough, thank you.

ANDREI. Oh yeh, well, calm people don't sit inside wardrobes, Natasha. And they don't make their husbands wear hats to use the phone! You just bear in mind Alyosha'll have to stay in hospital until my mother gets here. And you're coming with me to the doctor's tomorrow, first thing.

NATASHA. Pick up your case . . . and get out.

ANDREI. What?

NATASHA. Your clothes are packed. Your dressing gown. And don't concern yourself about my health. I've never felt better in my life. Go on, take it and get out.

ANDREI. Who have you had here? What have they been telling you? I mean, everything was fine when I left this morning, the usual peck on the cheek, a wee wave – what's going on? What have you discovered? I can see it in that face of yours. Come on, what crime have I committed? You just remember how many times we've had this before. You've found me out, kicked up hell, divorce, the whole bit, then it's turned out there was nothing in it. Well, come on, who's been here? I could see from the cups, the minute I came in, somebody's been here. So what have you found out?

NATASHA. I've found out all I need to.

ANDREI. I'm asking you to tell me!

NATASHA. You better not ask. Because if I start to speak I'll kill you! That's why I hid, so I wouldn't kill you, do you understand?

ANDREI. Kill me? Oh yes, I see – I get the message now. It couldn't be anything else, could it. Somebody's told you that when Alyosha had his accident, that evening, I was at Sonya's house. Is that it? I'm asking you, Natasha, is that what you've found out? (NATASHA *is silent*.) What kind of idiot are you, eh? God Almighty, you're a fool! All right, so I *was* at her place. It was a housewarming – her husband was there, her son was there – plus three other people out of the department! And by the time I got to the hospital you were in a terrible state – *that's* why I didn't tell you. I didn't want you thinking God knows what. As you're actually doing now. As you're *always* doing. That's why I said I was at a management meeting with Shchetinin. If you don't believe me you can ring up Sonya right now. Ask her husband. Or go and see them. If you think you're onto something. That just suits you, doesn't it – the jealous wife. God, you'll come back from the grave to keep an eye on me! There's no stopping you, is there – you've got a son lying in hospital, we're supposed to pick him up tomorrow, and you can't even find the time to tidy the place – you're too busy spying on me!

NATASHA (*interrupts him*). You shut up about my son . . .

ANDREI. Why should I? Why should I shut up?

NATASHA (*rising to a shriek*). Just shut up about my son! You butcher!

ANDREI (*aghast*). What? What was that? Well, come on, repeat that!

NATASHA. Butcher!

ANDREI. Well, thank you very much, Natasha. I was a devil a minute ago, now I'm a butcher. So how come I'm a butcher, eh? Explain, please. Have you any idea what you're saying?

NATASHA (*interrupting, with increasing vehemence*). You knew! You *knew*!

ANDREI. Knew what? What did I know?

NATASHA. Everything! You knew there was a power line there! You knew the crane could hit it! They told you! The supervisor even phoned up and warned you – he told you it was dangerous!

ANDREI (*interrupting*). Wait a minute, hold on –

NATASHA. Why did you send them?

ANDREI. Look, hold on –

NATASHA. Why did you send those men?

ANDREI. What *is* this? Are you accusing me? Alyosha's accident, is that what this is about? I thought this was –

NATASHA. You thought, you thought – you gave up thinking a long time ago! You go through life like a mechanical man – Shchetinin wound you up twenty years ago and you can't stop. You're a machine, not a human being! Why did you send those men? You knew what you were doing – why did you send them?

ANDREI. Look, Natasha, you can't just – I mean, I'm not – I don't –

NATASHA. I – I – I – is that all you can say? Why did you send them? You've destroyed Alyosha, that's what you've done! And you knew, the whole time!

ANDREI. For God's sake, Natasha, calm down! *Sit* down! I'll tell you what happened . . .

NATASHA. Don't bother, I don't want to hear it – just clear out!

ANDREI. Natasha –

NATASHA. Get out, I've told you – get . . . out! *(Pushing him towards the door.)*

ANDREI. Natasha, listen, listen – at least hear me out! It was just the way things turned out – the end of the quarter, you know what *that* means. And I was twenty thousand down on the Plan, you know, to close the quarter. And that was the last day, the thirtieth of June. So I went to the Director, I mean, his wife's my assistant, that's surely worth something! That's why I've got to keep in with Sonya, but you wouldn't appreciate that. Anyway, I went to Comrade Nikitin and asked him for an advance of twenty thousand, right? OK? (NATASHA *is silent.*) I asked him for twenty thousand and he said, get that road built by tomorrow morning and I'll sign. That's the road the accident happened on. I mean, he was expecting a visit, and he didn't want the Minister up to his neck in mud, basically. It's not his fault either, he wasn't to know. It's just that I'd asked him for an advance and he saw his chance to put pressure on *me*, right? D'you understand? Well, anyway, I promised him. I wasn't to know – nobody could have. Look, there was about a half-day's work in it, and I issued instructions to the section head to organise a crane, bring up the slabs, and get it done. Then I went back to the office. I didn't even know – I'd no idea which brigade it would be. I gave the order to the section boss, he relayed it to the supervisor, the supervisor told the foreman, and the foreman put a brigade on it. Alyosha's, as it turned out. I didn't even know the exact spot. For God's sake, I've a whole construction site, five hundred acres! It was pure chance, just downright bad luck. I mean, what can I do?

NATASHA. Get out.

ANDREI. Look, are you deaf or something? I've told you what happened, it was coincidence. There's such a thing as coincidence, you know, accidents *can* happen. You try to do what's best. I had to find that twenty thousand, so the lads wouldn't lose their bonus. I mean, you can't blame them, but if they don't get paid their full whack they'll quit, and I won't be able to replace them. And then the next quarter I'll be deficient not just twenty thousand, but fifty thousand. You thought you were acting for the best, getting Alyosha to do his work experience with us. I was against it, but you were adamant. I had to phone the college and fix it. If you hadn't insisted, Alyosha would have gone off to some other town, and none of this would have happened. But I'm not blaming you. I mean, what can you do? That's just how it's turned out. You can't foresee these things.

NATASHA. Why didn't you cancel your order when the supervisor phoned? He *told* you you weren't supposed to work there, because of the safety regulations. Why didn't you cancel? Eh? Didn't you have time to think? In too much of a hurry to get to Sonya's? Was the car waiting?

ANDREI. There's no need to drag that in, Natasha. There's never been anything between me and Sonya.

NATASHA. Oh, bugger off – there's worse things in life than sleeping around. I used to think that was dreadful, shocking. Well now I know different. What's really frightening is people like you, brass-necked, you don't give a damn about anything. Why didn't you cancel that order? I mean, you were told it was dangerous.

ANDREI. I didn't give any order. I just said, if it's at all possible, do it. And if it's too risky, forget it.

NATASHA. You said nothing of the kind. People heard you, there were other people in the office. While you were on the phone, while you were on to the foreman you said: I can't order you, but I'm asking you – please, please, *please* – it has to be done. You told him everybody's job depended on that road.

ANDREI. Well, that's right, it did.

NATASHA. What's right? What's *right*?!

ANDREI. I've *told* you – I was twenty thousand short, and Nikitin wouldn't give me an advance without that road. I had to ask him, so he asked me. It's standard practice, Natasha. If you remember, you couldn't get the books you wanted in the library last year, you and Olga – you were wanting some stuff by Trofimov, and some other –

NATASHA (*corrects him*). Trifonov.

ANDREI. Anyway, you were getting the brush-off from the department. And you came running to me – the book buyer had a burst pipe, could I do something about it? So I gave him a couple of plumbers, and *you* got your favourite author. And you were ecstatic! The plain fact is, there's a shortage of paper, and that's why there's no books. And I'm short of cement, that's why I'm down twenty thousand. I needed that, the same as you pair needed your books. That's why I sent those men – sent them to your book buyer, *and* out to that road! I thought they'd have a bit of sense, going under the wires, take it easy. As it turned out, it was an inexperienced crane-driver, a trainee. I mean, it just all came together!

NATASHA. And what would they have done, if you'd told the truth, eh? If you hadn't completed the Plan? Would they have shot you?

ANDREI. Look, for the tenth time . . .

NATASHA (*shouting*). I'm asking you – would they have shot you? I want an answer!

ANDREI. And I'm giving you an answer. If the crane-driver had been a bit more experienced it wouldn't have happened. It was pure coincidence.

NATASHA. I want to know, Andrei – was your life at stake? If you'd come clean, just told them to stuff their Plan, what could they do? Fling you in jail? Give you the sack, maybe? (ANDREI *frowns*.) If you'd told them the truth, for once, eh? Even if they did give you the push, so what? But they wouldn't do that, oh no – they couldn't get rid of you *that* easily, you're too well connected, you're like a bloody spider!

ANDREI. Natasha, I've got to work to the Plan, I have a responsibility – managing CDC's like a sacred trust, you surely understand that, you're supposed to have brains, all your bloody library books!

NATASHA. What could they have done, I'm asking you? Given you a bawling-out? Would the big chief give you a dirty look, is that what you're afraid of? Is that why you sent those men into a power line? You'd bugger all to lose, but you made those workers risk their lives!

ANDREI (*agitated, shouting*). I didn't make them!

NATASHA. Just save your strength. I'm not finished.

ANDREI (*out of the blue*). Natasha, you haven't got something I could take for a headache, have you?

NATASHA. No!

ANDREI. I've got a really splitting headache, you know?

NATASHA. Go to hell. If you were to die this very second, I'd phone for a hearse and that'd be it. I'd pack you off to the morgue, along with your suitcase. They could lay it on top of your coffin – all your worldly goods!

ANDREI. Natasha, I'll need to lie down for a couple of minutes, my head's bursting. (*Moves towards the divan.*)

NATASHA. Stay where you are! (ANDREI *stops.*) You didn't have a headache then, did you? The day after – the *morning* after your own son lost his hands, when you had to run back to your work! Straight from the hospital, you just couldn't forget your twenty thousand, could you! It was buzzing in your head the whole time!

ANDREI. Natasha, you're confusing the issue –

NATASHA. Oh yes, you could still manage a few words of comfort, for Alyosha's benefit – smiling through your tears, like a human being. The consoling pat. United we stand. Only it turns out you were just play-acting, your mind was on something else.

ANDREI. Natasha, there's no connection, they're two different things. Just stick to the point, would you?

NATASHA. Of course it had to be in on time, hadn't it. You'd already sent word first thing, to Nikitin personally – in a desperate rush. So you'd be able to include that money in the quarterly figures – creative accountancy! You knew damn well Nikitin would sign – I mean he could hardly refuse, after what had happened. He'd surely take pity on his partner in crime. That's what you were counting on, his sympathy. You made a use of your own misery, Andrei, you traded off your own pain, just so you could close your bloody quarter!

ANDREI. Natasha, there's no connection, you can't do this. Alyosha's one thing, and the Plan's another. I don't get paid for being a husband and father, you know!

NATASHA. When you told Sonya to go and speak to Nikitin, she nearly fainted, did you know that? She was *horrified*!

ANDREI (*looks up*). What? What's Sonya got to do with it?

NATASHA. Sonya left here two hours ago. I got the whole story. Your Director's wife has been here half the afternoon. I was expecting to be told one thing, and I heard another. Far worse. (*Contemptuously.*) Oh, don't think you're in the clear there. The suspicion was driving me crazy, so I asked Sonya over to find out exactly where I stood. You know, when you rushed in from the hospital that morning, to rescue your damned Plan, she couldn't believe it, you left her practically in a state of collapse! You think you're a great guy, everybody thinks you're wonderful. You think they're all on your wavelength. Well, you're wrong! Sonya had to rush home, she didn't go to Nikitin. Somebody else got him to sign for your big fiddle. And when Nikitin found out, he told Sonya she wasn't to set foot in that menagerie again! So you've lost your assistant, she's leaving. You'll find her resignation on your desk tomorrow. D'you know we sat here crying, both of us? For the first time in my life I wanted to kill – physically wanted to kill someone. Can you understand that? Watching you getting out of your flash car, swinging your keys – full of yourself – striding along as if you hadn't a care in the world. I'm deadly serious, Andrei. I would have killed you right there and then. That frightened me. That's why I had to run into the wardrobe – out of fear. (*Shouts.*) I've never felt like that before, never! (*A pause, then suddenly.*) Is it true that you went down on your knees in Nikitin's office? When you were begging him for the twenty thousand?

ANDREI (*puzzled*). What?

NATASHA. You went down on your knees. His secretary saw you, she's telling everybody. How you opened the door and dropped straight onto your knees. (*Mimicking:*) 'Look how I've come to you, Comrade Nikitin, help me!' That's the truth, isn't it? You went down on your knees.

ANDREI (*glumly*). It was a joke.

NATASHA. A joke.

She crosses to the table, pulls out a drawer and flings a bottle of aspirin at him. It lands on the floor at ANDREI's *feet, and he picks it up.*

NATASHA (*suddenly*). And what's this money? (*She takes out a wad of ten-rouble notes.*) You put this in here the day before yesterday – where did you get it? (ANDREI *turns to look at Natasha slowly.*) There's two hundred and fifty roubles here, Andrei. (*Shows him.*) Is it an advance on salary, or what?

ANDREI. The day before yesterday?

NATASHA. That's right. Day before yesterday.

ANDREI. It's bonus money.

NATASHA. Bonus for what?

ANDREI. Well . . .

NATASHA. I'm asking you, what bonus?

ANDREI. Well, it was for the quarter . . .

NATASHA. Which quarter? Last quarter? When you were twenty thousand short? When you went down on your knees? When Alyosha became a cripple?

ANDREI. Why are you asking? It was for . . .

NATASHA. Which quarter did you get the bonus for? That one? Was it? (ANDREI *is silent.*) Yes or no?

ANDREI. Yes! It was that one! (*A pause.* NATASHA *goes up to him, very close. When she speaks, her voice is filled with anguish.*)

NATASHA. That means that bonus money is for Alyosha's hands? That's right, isn't it, Andrei – I'm not mistaken? That money is for your son's hands? (ANDREI *does not look up.*) And you took it. You accepted that money and brought it into this house.

ANDREI. Well, what else could I do? They gave me it.

NATASHA. Oh, of course, I mean what else *could* you do? If they gave you it. You're not going to look a gift horse in the mouth. And if they're demanding the *Plan*, you're not going to tell them you're short! (*Suddenly.*) Right, just walk over to the mirror. Go on, go up to the mirror.

ANDREI (*stupidly*). What for?

NATASHA. What d'you mean, what for? What did you do all *this* for? For appearances' sake? To crawl a wee bit higher up the ladder? Go on – (*Pushes him bodily.*) – Go on, have a good

look, see how well you've got on. Shchetinin's wee dog! His
Master's Voice! Look at yourself. My God, somebody should
paint you right now, and stick a caption on it: 'Portrait of a
Manager that Closed his Quarter'. Put it on exhibition
somewhere, so everybody can get a good look at you! (*A
pause.*) Here! (*She thrusts the money at him.*) Take it! (ANDREI
takes the money.) Tear it up! (ANDREI *lays the money on the
table.*) What do you think I said? Tear it up! Are you going to
tear it up or not? Listen you – I'll walk right out onto that
verandah, and I'll start screaming, I'll tell everybody. I'll get
on the phone this minute to every single one of your cronies'
wives. I'll let them know what kind of dirty money their
husbands earn, what their bonus is for. Tear it up, I'm telling
you! Do it!

ANDREI. All right, all right, I'll tear it up. (*Picks the money up from
under the table, tears the notes in half.*) Huh. Is there anything
else you want ripped up? Anything still left in one piece? Just
pass it across. I'll tear the lot up while I'm at it.

NATASHA. Cut it out. You've said enough. Now stand up, and
go and flush those down the toilet. Go on.

NATASHA *watches as* ANDREI *gets up and trudges to the door.
He goes out, and we hear the toilet being flushed.* ANDREI *comes
back, sits on the edge of the divan.* NATASHA *stares intently at him
for a few seconds, then suddenly goes out. She returns almost
immediately, holding the torn notes in her hand.* ANDREI *looks
pained, hangs his head, stricken.* NATASHA *goes up to him,
scrutinises him very closely, a mocking, bitter smile.*

Still valid, are they? Still legal tender? My God, you're
pathetic. I suppose you were going to stick them together,
maybe buy Alyosha a wee gift – like a push-button phone!
Beep-beep-beep-beep-beep – there you are! (*She tears the
halved notes into shreds, flings them into* ANDREI's *face. The scraps
of paper flutter round the room.*) Right, come on, take yourself
off. Get out of this house. Go on.
ANDREI *rises reluctantly, moves towards the hall.*) The suitcase!

ANDREI (*pathetically, mutters*). I don't need it.

NATASHA. The suitcase, I said! (ANDREI *returns, picks up the
suitcase and again heads for the door.*) Wait! (ANDREI *pauses.*)
Leave the flat keys on the table! (ANDREI *returns once more,
takes the keys from his raincoat pocket, lays them on the table, lingers a
moment.*) What are you waiting for?

ANDREI *picks up his suitcase and leaves the flat. We hear him slamming the outer door. There is a long silence,* NATASHA *stands motionless in the centre of the room, her eyes closed. She is breathing heavily, clearly disturbed. She takes a few steps to the divan and throws herself on to it, face down. For a moment she lies there quite still, motionless. Then she rises, crosses to the wardrobe and takes a bathtowel out of a top drawer. She makes her way slowly out of the bedroom. For a time the stage is empty, only the sound of running water in the bathroom. Suddenly we hear a prolonged insistent ringing, and simultaneous heavy thumping at the door.*

ANDREI'S VOICE *(from the landing).*
Open up! Come on, open up! Open this door! *(We hear him beating with his fists on the door.)* Open up!

The hammering at the door grows louder – evidently ANDREI *is flinging his whole weight, and his suitcase, against it. Finally we hear a crack. He has broken open the door. Out of breath, enraged,* ANDREI *bursts into the bedroom. He flings down the suitcase and rushes out. We hear him battering at the bathroom door next, and the sound of the latch flying off as he breaks it open.*

ANDREI'S VOICE. Right, you bloody well come out of there! You can get washed later, just come out. What right have you to judge me?

ANDREI *hauls her unceremoniously into the bedroom. She is naked, her bathrobe clinging to her damp body.* ANDREI *shoves her into the armchair.*

(Shouting.) Who do you think you are – God? Mary the Mother of God? Eh? Just who do you think you are?

NATASHA *(looks at him with intense loathing).* Let me get washed. *(She makes to rise.)*

ANDREI. Sit down! *(Pushes her back.)* I don't give a damn if you never wash! What was it you called me? Brass-necked? Eh? *(*NATASHA *is weeping.* ANDREI *turns her head to face him.)* It was a different story twenty years ago, when you were in a communal flat with no bathroom – and of course, you couldn't *live* without a bathroom, not with your delicate upbringing. It was a different story then all right. Do you remember what you called me? Eh? Never mind howling, just think back to what you used to call me. *(He seizes her by the chin, she knocks away his hand.)* A dumpling! A big soft lump! Well, that's where I started out, Natasha, with your blessing.

The glory road from dumpling all the way up to brass-neck! Of course you were never like that, you were into everything, committed up to the hilt. Right from the word go. God Almighty. I'd hardly looked twice at her before she'd got me into bed! (NATASHA *rises abruptly,* ANDREI *pushes her back down.*) Sit down! And then later, of course, I see this is one smart student, definitely a whole lot smarter than me, and all mine, total commitment! My God, I was besotted! I gave you everything, body and soul, right down to my last kopeck. I carried you around in my arms like a baby. Only I could never do anything right for you. You're never satisfied, as far as I'm concerned – you've made that your life's work! You've always made me feel I had to keep at it, earn more, have more, only that means playing with the big boys, and I didn't want that. I didn't want any of this, Natasha, but you've always been at my back, driving me on. Oh, not in any obvious sense, oh no, just a wee dig now and again, typical woman. But you can be obvious when you like. I mean, what else was that carry-on with Kuzmin but another way of getting at me, giving me a shove, eh? Sit down! . . . Of course there's no lovers these days. Ever since I 'arrived', as you put it, you've been the faithful wife. That's now I'm earning three times the salary, now we've a three-roomed apartment, a phone, a car – now it's *your* turn to be jealous, not me! You wanted all this as well, if you remember. Just cast your mind back to eighteen years ago, when Shchetinin called me into his office – the same office I now occupy. 'Listen, old chap,' he says, 'there's a party meeting tomorrow, and there's somebody trying to bury me, so I'm asking you to speak up, give me your support. Unless you want to sit on your arse with the foremen forever.' That's what Shchetinin said, and I came home that evening and told you the whole story. I used to tell you everything then, if you remember, but not any longer.
Anyway, if you'd said no – if you'd said you were leaving *then* – I'd never have taken that step. But all you said was – *(mimics her)* – 'Oh Andrei, sweetheart, I don't know, it's up to you. I can't make up your mind for you.' You weren't against it, you wanted it! Because you knew damn well it was a chance to become Shchetinin's man, and that meant lift-off! Sit down! . . . I stayed awake the whole night, preparing that speech – trying to get something together even *half* decent. And all I could see was your eyes boring into my head. That never-satisfied look. So I stood up, and made that speech! (*A*

silence.) And ten years ago, or what was it, twelve? . . . when it
all got too much, and I wanted to pack it in – not even
resign, but just disappear – did you support me? I mean, did
you say, 'Right, let's go'? No, no – you clammed up. You just
shrugged it off. 'Don't do anything rash, Andrei, give it some
more thought.' That's what *you* said. Because you were scared
I *would* quit. You actually phoned Shchetinin – 'have a wee
talk with Andrei', you said, 'something's bothering him'. You
were terrified, that's the truth – shit-scared you were going to
lose it all, all the things you've got accustomed to. And
there's so much, isn't there? Plus a cushy number at the
library, drifting in and out whenever you like, free as a bird.
Only thanks to *your* job, I've got to keep on that cretin –
supposed to be a section head – because he happens to be
married to your boss, that bloody Olga! And when I *did* try
to get shot of him, you kicked up hell! Now I'm hearing it
from her as well, on the phone! D'you realise if I'd had a
competent worker in his place, possibly I wouldn't have
needed to go down on my knees for that twenty thousand?
And Alyosha would still have his hands! Well, do you still
want to get washed? Or will you pass, do you think?
(*A silence*.) I have to shut my eyes to certain things at work,
for business reasons. But you shut *your* eyes, just the same, to
things that are happening to *me*. No, I'm sorry to say it,
sweetheart, but you do it for profit, worldly goods – there's
no difference. I'm your Five Year Plan. It's a business venture
we have, not a family. And you have the nerve to sit in
judgement over me? Tearing up money? I mean, who do
you think that money was for? Eh? Why am I doing my
brains in? I've got two suits, and that'll have to do me until I
die! I've got a stomach ulcer, I can't even enjoy a decent
meal these days. And who is it all for? Eh? Right, come on,
stand up. (NATASHA *refuses to budge*.) Come on, get up – I
can't see your face. (*Tries to lift her forcibly*. NATASHA *throws
him off*.) Come on, I want to see your face. (ANDREI
approaches again.) You know, you're pretty smart. You're like a
person with no past. Born again every morning, straight out
the egg! Well, everything starts somewhere in this life,
Natasha. Somebody starts every war, every sort of rottenness.
I shoved Alyosha under that power line a month ago – I
didn't mean to, God knows, it was an accident – but you
shoved me eighteen years ago, Natasha, and that was *no*
accident! And now you have the gall to accuse me? To stand
in judgement over me? Or sit, rather – come on, get up out

of there! Tearing up money? My God, we're partners in
crime, if it comes to the bit. Side by side. Come on, stand
up! (*He seizes her by the shoulders, pulls her up.*)

NATASHA (*breaks free.*) What do you want from me!

ANDREI. I want us to *live*, that's what. You've no right to fling
me out, after what's happened.

NATASHA. All right, I won't throw you out. You have a right to
stay, the law's on your side.

ANDREI. Yes, the law *is* on my side. I'm glad *something's* on my
side, or I'd be dead long ago!

NATASHA. Oh, for God's sake! Do what you like! Just let me
finish washing, then I'll get dressed and *go*. Let me past.

ANDREI. No, I won't.

NATASHA. Andrei, I don't care, but I'm not living with you.

ANDREI. Yes, you are.

NATASHA. I'm not. You think that's the truth out now? You
wouldn't know the meaning of the word. You tell lies here,
you tell lies at work – you're an incorrigible liar, Andrei, but
you're not going to get away with it much longer. Your
'interpretation' of the facts, it's completely twisted – it's
pathetic!

ANDREI. I'm not twisting anything!

NATASHA. I didn't push you, you dragged yourself up. My God,
I'd enough trouble, trying to stay in one piece, with your
jealousy. You thought . . . you seemed to think that because I
went to bed with you so easily, I was a pushover, it didn't
mean anything to me. You couldn't believe I might have
done it for love, could you? We've lived twenty years
together, Andrei, and you still can't forgive me for that. But
you don't want to remember how I walked out on you, do
you. You've forgotten that.

ANDREI. I've forgotten nothing!

NATASHA. I was in love with Kuzmin, do you understand? I
thought I could have a new life. A different *kind* of life! Not
like this. You were having hysterics, ready to hang yourself.
You begged and pleaded, went down on your knees – you
even threatened to take Alyosha away! When I went to the

nursery to pick Alyosha up, you were lying in wait for me. My God, you practically stood guard outside Kuzmin's flat. And as soon as he went out, you smashed your way in, destroyed everything you could lay your hands on, in somebody else's flat! You phoned Kuzmin at work, you told his boss, you told his mother – you dragged everybody into it. You were like a bloody wild animal, hanging on like grim death. Alyosha doted on you, and you *used* him – running after you, 'Daddy, daddy, daddy!' That's why I went back to you. Yes. And I hadn't been back three days before you started to cast up, trying to humiliate me – even hit me. You did some terrible things, Andrei, and I said nothing. You made out it was all my fault, and I believed it. But it wasn't my fault – I just wanted to live like a human being for once! And then something happened – something very interesting. Actually the worst experience in my whole life.

ANDREI. What are you talking about?

NATASHA. I'm talking about when Shchetinin was to be made Group Manager, and you were in line for *his* job, running CDC. And your promotion could depend on Kuzmin – he was stepping up as well, you all were. But I knew nothing about this, until Shchetinin suddenly phones me up and says 'Oh, Natalya, I'm sorry to bother you, but you know what's happening here – do you think Kuzmin's likely to make trouble?' And I said, 'What's it got to do with me? Why are you asking me?' I said, 'Does Andrei know you're phoning me about this?'

ANDREI. I didn't ask him to phone – I didn't!

NATASHA. And he said – 'He knows the general outline!'

ANDREI. That's a lie!

NATASHA. Just calm down. Anyway, you came home eventually, and I said Shchetinin had phoned. I said, 'Maybe I've done the wrong thing, but I phoned Kuzmin and he wasn't there.' I was waiting for you to go berserk. I thought you'd half-kill me. But no – all you said was, 'Oh, give it a rest, Natasha – I'm fed up hearing about Kuzmin.' Fed up! For a whole year I hadn't been allowed even to mention his *name* in this house, under pain of death. Just the week previously, when Alyosha needed medicine, and Kuzmin's mother could have got hold of it – Alyosha's lying burning up, and you wouldn't let me phone! Then suddenly it's, 'Oh, give it a rest, I'm fed up hearing about Kuzmin' – as if it was some old crow next door!

ANDREI. I don't remember this.

NATASHA. Really? And how about that same night, when you answered the phone, heard Kuzmin's voice, and hung up – do you remember that? And when he rang back, you said, 'You answer that, Natasha, I'm going to the loo.' You knew it was Kuzmin, and you went and sat in the bathroom! You didn't even hang yourself! And when I got dressed – at ten o'clock at night – and went out to meet him –

ANDREI. You told me you were going to Olga's. I remember that quite distinctly – you said you were going to Olga's. D'you mean to say you were with him?

NATASHA. Whether I was or wasn't, that's my business. You and Shchetinin needed help, and I gave it! You should have asked me then where I'd been. It was after one when I got home, you were pretending you were asleep –

ANDREI. I *was* asleep!

NATASHA. Oh, give over. Once you'd decided I was asleep, you got up and went out into the corridor. Walking up and down, smoking, a nervous bloody wreck. But you recovered, soon enough, eh? Crept back into bed. And you cleared off out to work a bit smartly, so you wouldn't need to ask what time I'd come home at. Or did it just slip your mind?

ANDREI. I didn't force you.

NATASHA. Oh no, you didn't force me – you just didn't *stop* me! And you didn't force Alyosha, you just wanted that road – please, please, *please*!

ANDREI. That's two different things – you never stick to the point.

NATASHA. That *is* the point! There's no difference, it's the same thing. It's all the same to you, that's all you think about, your damned self-conceit! Getting your name everywhere, so you'll be an even bigger fish! Why didn't you just speak to Kuzmin yourself? How about it, old boy? Don't you screw up my career, and I'll let you screw my wife! What stopped you? Eh? You haven't a shred of decency – what stopped you? (*Suddenly.*) Did you know it was Kuzmin on the phone?

Answer me? Did you know it was Kuzmin? (ANDREI *is silent*.) Oh my God. All these years. All these years I've been telling myself you didn't hear him, you didn't know where I was going. I mean, it was so obvious, but I was afraid to believe it, I was afraid even to mention it, in case . . . (*A silence*.) I can't take this . . . I can't take any more. I wish I was dead.

ACT TWO

Fifteen to twenty minutes have passed, about the time of an act interval. The lights go up to reveal the Golubev's bedroom as before. ANDREI, out of breath and dishevelled, blocks NATASHA's way to the wardrobe. She stands white-faced and determined, her hair still wet. She is now wearing a skirt and sweater, and carrying a suitcase . . .

NATASHA. Get out of the way!

ANDREI. No.

NATASHA. Come on, let me past – I need my . . .

ANDREI. No.

NATASHA. Look, what is it you want?

ANDREI. I want us to be together, Natasha, that's what I want. For you to stay. I'm sorry for what I said just now – sheer stupidity. You know me, I just come off the top of my head. Then I see sense. I mean, you're not like that, it's not true, and what you said about me isn't the whole truth either. There's a bit more to us, surely. And we can't do without each other.

NATASHA (*shouting, each word distinct*). What . . do . . . you . . . want!

ANDREI. I want you to put the kettle on, right? We'll have a cup of tea, and go to bed, get up a bit earlier in the morning, tidy up, and go for Alyosha . . .

NATASHA. What?!

ANDREI. We're going to the hospital . . .

NATASHA. Just you dare – you dare! I'm warning you, if you turn up at that hospital, I'll tell Alyosha, right in front of everybody – I'll tell him the whole story, how you've made him an invalid for life!

ANDREI. I'm past caring, Natasha. Tell him. I'll tell him myself,

the whole story, I'll do anything to keep us all together. I
mean, do you think I can just walk away from it? Where
would I go? You're like a god to me now, Natasha. The way I
see it, it'll be a *different* life from now on. It's up to you,
Natasha, whatever you fancy, whatever you decide, whatever
you want. From here on in, Natasha rules!

Without replying, NATASHA *crosses quickly to the wardrobe.*
ANDREI *bars her way.*

NATASHA. Let me past, till I get my things.

ANDREI. Natasha, no. I'm serious. You've never heard me like
this before. You could scream and shout and stamp your feet
– I just did as I liked. But what I'm saying now is you're in
charge. If you want your mother to stay with us, that's fine.
I've always been against it, but now I'm saying she can come
and live with us. I'm tearing up the house rules, Natasha. If
you want to have Olga here, you go ahead – invite the whole
crowd. You wanted a dog, you can have one. I'll even find a
wee dog *for* you, bring it home. I'll take it out for walks
and . . .

NATASHA. For God's sake!

ANDREI. I know, I know, I'm talking rubbish, trivial details – but
I want everything to be how *you* want it. You asked a while
ago if you could have the car in your name – that's OK.
Anything you say. And not just some time, but right now,
this minute. You go ahead and draw up a . . . oh, I don't
know, a list of conditions, under which you agree to stay with
me. And I'll ratify them. Item by item – you just tick them
off as I . . .

NATASHA. Shut up! Shut up! You're disgusting! (*Mimics him.*)
'Item by item', 'ratify' – what kind of language is that!

ANDREI. I'm sorry. That's garbage. But I'm giving you my word,
Natasha, you can have whatever you want.

NATASHA. I want you out of here.

ANDREI. Natasha, no.

NATASHA *turns and moves decisively towards the door.* ANDREI
catches her up, stops her.

Natasha, you're not leaving! Listen, listen – let's give it ten
days – give me a trial period of ten days, and if you're still

determined after that, then I'll go, I'll just disappear out of
your life. But you'll be satisfied, I *know* you will. Even before
the ten days is up. We've been together for twenty years,
Natasha, all I want is ten more days. All right? Come on, say
yes. Say yes and that'll be it. And I'll put on the kettle. And
you'll see. Come on, say it. Nod your head. A wee smile?
Natasha?

NATASHA *turns, crosses to the table, and takes out a cigarette.*
ANDREI *follows her.*

Natasha, sweetheart? Ten days? OK? (*She lights up her cigarette.*)
Is that it? Yes? You're lighting up a cigarette, that's a sign of
agreement! Can I take that as a sign of agreement? Right, I'll
take that as a sign, and I'll put on the kettle, OK? A cup of
tea, right? Fine, I'll put on the kettle . . . (*Hurries out to the
kitchen.*)

NATASHA *immediately stubs out her cigarette, opens the wardrobe,
flings a few things into her travel bag, snatches her coat off a hanger
and rushes to the door. In the doorway, she collides with* ANDREI.

What's going on? I thought we'd agreed ten days! I've got the
kettle on!

NATASHA. I'm leaving.

ANDREI. No! No! No! No! . . .

NATASHA. Oh, stop it, for God's sake! Cut the hysterics.
(ANDREI *is silenced.*) Take off your coat! (*He removes his coat
and hat, flings them on the divan.*) Sit down! (*Indicates the armchair.*
ANDREI *meekly complies, and* NATASHA *moves to confront him.*)
What's bothering you – that I'm leaving, and you'll be stuck
with the flat? You needn't worry, Alyosha and I'll have
somewhere to live.

ANDREI. What's this about?

NATASHA. I couldn't stay here. I'm going to stay at Olga's
mother's. She's at her sister's in Leningrad for the whole
summer. Olga's giving me the key. I can't bring Alyosha back
to this, I hate this flat, and you along with it. I don't want
you in the same –

ANDREI. What's this for? I've told you, I know how to sort this
out now.

NATASHA. No, you don't. You can't fix it this time, like you fix

everything else. I don't want to see you and Alyosha in the
same room, do you understand? I can't just pick up the
pieces, and go on as if nothing had happened. I can't do it,
Andrei. You wouldn't be able to stand it, either – I'd be a
constant reminder, the slightest thing . . .

ANDREI. Natasha, I know what we have to *do*! It'll be all right!

NATASHA. There's nothing you *can* do.

ANDREI. There is.

NATASHA. There isn't!

ANDREI. Well, all right, just kill me. (*Shouts.*) Kill me! Either that
or trust me. I know what to do –

NATASHA. For God's sake, what can you do, what can anybody
do!

ANDREI. Natasha, I can do anything now!

NATASHA. Like what!

ANDREI. I'll quit work.

NATASHA (*pulls a face*). You what?

ANDREI. I'll pack in my job.

NATASHA. Am I hearing right?

ANDREI. I'll quit the job, pack it in. I mean, that's at the root of
it, all the rottenness and lies. I'm jacking it in. Straight.

NATASHA. You'll never give it up!

ANDREI. Natasha, I'm quitting. I'm just not cut out to be a
manager, I haven't got the temperament. I don't know what
it is, but I just can't be a boss, *and* a human being. I'm
incapable. Maybe some people can, but I can't. I realise that
now, it's finally got through to me, Natasha, I can see it all
now.

NATASHA. What do you mean, *now*?

ANDREI. I mean right now, this very minute. (*Rises from the
armchair.*) You just don't know what's been happening with
me. This while back. I've been a sick man for a good number
of years now. It's the truth, Natasha, what are you looking at
me like that for? I'm not a well man. I can't put a name to it,

all right, but it's frightening. The fact is, I'm just not normal. I mean, I'm scared of everything. Like, for instance, if I get word there's been a District Committee meeting or something, and they haven't invited me, I start getting jumpy, it preys on my mind for days. What's the significance of it, what have I done wrong, whose nose have I put out of joint? I'm frightened to unplug the phone at nights, in case they're suddenly looking for me and I can't be reached. And holidays are just blue murder. Dear God, if it wasn't for you, I probably wouldn't take *any* leave. I keep waiting for something – that they'll sack me, that they're out to get me. Because they could give me the bullet anytime, you know. Not a day goes by but there's something I could be sacked for. The fact is, in twenty years I haven't once – in any single year, quarter, month – not once have I completed the Plan straight. There's always some sort of fiddle going on, even if it's only petty. But if I play it by the book, and report a shortfall, I'll be out the door. If they take a notion. Somebody's just got to want a new face, and I'll be finished. That's all it needs, Natasha. That's why I have to keep at it the whole time, diving about all over the shop – so nobody'll get any ideas. I've got to watch I don't get stomped on. *That's* why I'm hanging onto Shchetinin – for stability. One thing I do know, you can't make it on your own. They'll just brush you off, like a bit of dirt. And another thing – there's always less seats than arses to cover them. D'you want to know what I dream about at nights? *Who* I dream about? Shchetinin. I dream about Shchetinin. Shchetinin at work, Shchetinin on the phone, Shchetinin at home, Shchetinin in my dreams! There's not just *one* Shchetinin, there's thousands of them. When he's not in his office, he's inside my skull! He's got an armchair, a desk, a bed even – all in my head! D'you know the only time I'm happy? When Shchetinin's happy. When Shchetinin's pleased with me. When I've pulled off some cowboy stunt or other, for the Group, and carried the whole can myself – kept his name out of it. Then he's absolutely delighted. And I'm ecstatic, like a bloody idiot. You know how I gave up smoking? God, the number of times I tried to give it up. My ulcer was killing me and I still couldn't do it. I hadn't enough willpower. Then Shchetinin announced *he* was giving up and suddenly I found the willpower. I didn't tell you that. I was too ashamed. But I chucked smoking because Shchetinin did. He didn't like it at meetings,

everybody puffing away, so I had to set an example. Then
everybody chucked it, the whole Group. We're practically a
smokeless zone. You want to know how I see myself? Eh? I
mean, you tell me often enough, I've no decency, no
conscience. No feelings. But it's not true, Natasha – I have all
these things – decency, conscience, feelings, the whole kit.
But that's exactly what it is, a kit of parts. I can play it smart
when I have to, or I can be dumb. I can be deaf and blind as
well, if that's what they need. Whatever's required I'll dredge
it up from somewhere. Mister Versatile, that's me. You're
dead right, it's all show. You know, when I went to Sonya's
housewarming that night, I was in a cracking good mood –
I'd done the business, wangled the twenty thousand, wrapped
up the quarter. Who cares if the job's only half-finished, it's
party time, let's celebrate! Anybody that stands in my way,
any voices raised in protest, well, they're just beneath
consideration – simple-minded souls. Actually it's worse than
that. Deep down, I really believe everybody's on the fiddle,
and if they're not, well, they're just thick. You know what
really pisses me off about Vadim? I mean, he does what he's
told, he'll go along with it, but he's not happy, his heart's not
in it. And I want him to be like *me*. He's got to join the club,
and he will do, soon enough. And look at me, eh? 'Portrait
of a Manager that Closed His Quarter'. And what about us?
What about *our* relationship?

NATASHA. Forget it!

ANDREI. Forget it? You can't do that, Natasha. It's got to come
out. All right, I did know, or at least I'd a good idea you
were going to Kuzmin that night. I was in a cold sweat, I was
shaking all over, but I said nothing. I was frightened to ask,
same as you were. I didn't *want* to know. I just hoped I'd got
it wrong, somehow. I closed my eyes to it!

NATASHA. Andrei, forget it!

ANDREI. How can I! I'm not a man, Natasha – I may look like
one, but I'm not, I'm not human! You were right – I'll do
anything to keep people sweet – things no human being
would do, even with a gun at their head. But that's it, I'm
finished. I'm through.

NATASHA. You'll never be any different.

ANDREI. You don't think so?

NATASHA. No, I don't.

ANDREI. All right then, don't. I'm not asking you to believe me, not right away. I can hardly blame you. It's bad enough trying to believe myself. I'm only asking you not to throw me out, or leave me. To give me a chance.

NATASHA. I don't trust you, Andrei. I asked you to quit a year ago. Maybe you really *could* change, if you wanted to. But you won't do it.

ANDREI. I will!

NATASHA. No, you won't.

ANDREI. Yes, I will! I can do it, Natasha, you just don't know me. Nobody knows the real me. Besides, I've no option, have I. I can't carry on the way I've been doing, you've made that abundantly clear. I stand to lose you *and* Alyosha. And for what? What can I leave behind that's more important, more precious than my own son? I've already left him a . . . cripple. What else has to hit us before I come to my senses?

NATASHA. It was a different story when it happened, wasn't it! A different bloody story altogether!

ANDREI. That's right, it was. I was totally wrapped up in myself, you'd every right to do what you did. God, no wonder you lashed out, I deserved to have my head kicked in. But that's it over now, finished. I'll find the strength. I've found it before, when I needed it. You've no idea what I went through, Natasha, what it cost me to take you back . . . after Kuzmin. I've got my pride, you know, where women are concerned. Everybody knew you'd run off with another man. Shchetinin and his wife – I've never told you this, but they were all on at me – she's not worth it, Andrei, let her go to hell, don't lower yourself. The minute Zina found out, she started pushing all sorts of women at me, but I didn't even the score, Natasha. I swallowed my pride. I mean, did you ever think I could control my jealousy? You didn't think I could. You didn't believe me. But I managed it!

NATASHA. The situation changed, that's all. You became a big fish in a small pond, and that's why you stopped being jealous. You felt sure of yourself.

ANDREI. What's this next? Do you want to turn everything against me now? Go ahead, it's dead easy, it's simple. I

mean, you can see I'm even doing myself down. But I
definitely *did* straighten myself out, Natasha. And I'll do the
same again, no more ego-trip, just squash it flat, like a bug.
Right? I mean, it takes me a long time to make my mind up
to a thing, but once I do, you watch my dust. It's always like
that with me – the pressure builds up and builds up, till the
moment arrives and that's it – kaboom! Like an atom bomb.
Do you know how an atom bomb works? (NATASHA *does not
respond.*) You don't know how they make an atomic bomb?
Seriously? Well, to produce an atomic explosion you have to
have a very precisely calculated amount of uranium, right?
Critical mass, it's called. Anyway, they take this mass and
divide it in two, and as long as the two halves are kept apart,
it can't explode. But as soon as they remove the shield, and
the two halves come together, that's it – goodbye, Hiroshima,
farewell, Nagasaki! (ANDREI *suddenly falls onto his knees before*
NATASHA.) Natasha – give us a kiss, eh?

NATASHA *remains motionless. He takes her hand and places it on
his own head. Then removes his hand, leaving* NATASHA's *in place.*
NATASHA *is soundlessly weeping.*

ANDREI (*tenderly*). Come on, love, you'll see – everything'll be
fine. Don't cry. It's not worth it – I mean, what's it all for if
this is what it's going to cost? Let's go to bed now . . . we'll
get up a bit earlier in the morning. I'll give you a hand to
tidy the place. From now on, I really am going to be a help,
in every way. All right? Will I make up the bed? (NATASHA
is silent.) You wait and see, Natasha, there'll be big changes
once I pack in this job. God's sakes, I don't want to dream
about Shchetinin. I want to dream about the sea, or the sky –
I want to dream about you, Natasha. I mean, was I put on
this earth to be a manager? No way! And I'm not going to
drop dead if I have to give it up. Damn right I'm not – we'll
be together all the time now, evenings, weekends. I won't be
so tied up, we'll go for drives in the country, get a bit of
fresh air. You'll see, Natasha, we'll make something better of
our lives. I feel I can do it, I have the strength now. I don't
know where from, but it's there, it's definitely there. I'll do
anything so we can live like human beings again. You know,
it really pains me to see you drinking, Natasha – you
shouldn't do it, love, please don't. Please, give it up, eh?
Promise? OK? (NATASHA *is silent still.*) Will I make up the
bed?

NATASHA *removes her hand from* ANDREI's *head, where it has lain all this time, as if stuck there, and wipes away her tears.*

NATASHA (*quietly*). Where will you go?

ANDREI. What do you mean?

NATASHA. Where will you get a job?

ANDREI. I'm not bothered. I'll find some nice peaceful, ordinary job. Something human. I'm a simple bloke at heart, Natasha. I can swan around like now, in the big limo, or I can live on the basics. I'll go into teaching.

NATASHA. To do what?

ANDREI. To lecture. In the Building College.

NATASHA. What, for a hundred and twenty roubles?

ANDREI. Natasha, sweetheart, people get by – we'll manage on that, it's not that desperate.

NATASHA. We'll have to look after Alyosha his whole life, have you thought about that? We don't even know if he'll be able to work. Or if he'll get married – it's not everybody that'll want to marry him now. You know what I dreamt last night?

ANDREI. No, what?

NATASHA (*intensely*). I dreamt Alyosha was married, and his wife was throwing him out of the house. You were there, and we were trying to talk her round. She was . . . she was a dreadful person, a big fat woman, hard as nails, and she was shouting, 'I've been running after this cripple of yours for three years, the flat's mine, I've paid for it!' You said something to her, and she started bawling into the other room, 'Volodya, come and fling these people out!' And then this Volodya appeared – with *huge* hands, enormous, and a big moon face. 'This is my new husband', she says, 'I've been living with him for three months now.' And then she turns to Alyosha. 'Go on, Alyosha, tell them', she says.

ANDREI. That's awful!

NATASHA. And this Volodya comes up to you, and starts shoving you out, punching you in the face –

ANDREI. Natasha, that's hellish!

NATASHA. And Alyosha was just standing in a corner the whole time, crying.

ANDREI. Natasha, love, it was only a dream.

NATASHA. It wasn't a dream! That's what's ahead of us! (*Tearfully, wiping her eyes.*) We've got to leave him something, we've got to save. You've made him a cripple, and now you're going off to lecture. About what? How to live on a hundred and twenty roubles?

ANDREI. All right, love – look, I don't have to quit, it's not as if they want rid of me. Quite the reverse –

NATASHA. And I'm not living with you if you *don't* leave! I've had it, Andrei! You're giving in your notice, then we'll see . . .

ANDREI. OK, fine. I'll pack it in.

NATASHA. When?

ANDREI. Well, I don't know.

NATASHA. Can you do it tomorrow?

ANDREI. Tomorrow?

NATASHA. I want you to resign tomorrow.

ANDREI. Well, OK, if that's what you want. But I mean they won't just let me go at a day's notice. They'll have to find somebody to take my place.

NATASHA. No, they won't. I'll go with you to Shchetinin. I'll have a talk with him. And if I have to, I'll go to the District Committee – I'm a wife and mother, I've got rights as well! OK, now you can phone.

ANDREI. Phone who?

NATASHA. Shchetinin. So he'll see us in the morning. Just remember, we're not going for Alyosha until you've got your release date. Now phone. (ANDREI *checks his watch.*) It's early yet. Phone.

   ANDREI *crosses to the table, where the telephone has been left.*

ANDREI. What have I to say?

NATASHA. Get him to see us tomorrow. Tell him what it's about. Well, go on – lift the phone!

ANDREI. Right, right. (*Lifts the receiver, then suddenly.*) Oh, bloody hell! Shit! (*Slams the receiver down.*)

NATASHA (*alarmed*). What's up?

ANDREI. I forgot!

NATASHA. What?

ANDREI. I forgot! I can't phone Shchetinin now – something else happened today, I was going to tell you about it, and I forgot. I mean, when you jumped out of the wardrobe, it flew right out my head.

NATASHA. So what was it?

ANDREI (*stalling*). Well, actually . . . it's a bit . . . well, to cut a long story short, I've been promoted. I've been appointed Group Manager.

NATASHA. You've been appointed what? (*Agitated.*) I don't understand this. Would you please explain exactly what's going on?

ANDREI. Shchetinin's being transferred to Head Office – Deputy Controller's job. He's due to retire, Shchetinin's taking over. And they've appointed me Manager. The Minister signed the order today.

NATASHA. What order?

ANDREI. About my appointment.

NATASHA. Do you mean to say you've been made Group Manager in place of Shchetinin?

ANDREI. That's right, Natasha – I've been made Group Manager in place of Shchetinin.

NATASHA. You?

ANDREI. Me.

NATASHA. Do you take me for a fool? They've suddenly made you Manager?

ANDREI. It's not sudden. You heard about it before, last winter, I'm sure, when the Controller was here from Head Office. We were at Shchetinin's place for dinner, if you remember. And there was talk about it then – you were there, you heard it – about the possibility of a general shake-up, when the Deputy Controller retired.

NATASHA. Don't lie to me! You told me it had all fallen through.

ANDREI. That's right, I did say that! That was because at one time they were going to take another manager into Head Office, not Shchetinin. Then they started to say it *was* Shchetinin. Then next it *wasn't* Shchetinin – they were a whole year sorting that one out. And now it's settled – he goes, and I move up.

NATASHA. And does that mean you'll be in charge? That huge organisation? Three thousand men?

ANDREI. I won't be in charge of anything, don't worry. I'm leaving. I'll do whatever you say, Natasha – only not immediately, not tomorrow. I can't do that, there's –

NATASHA (*interrupts*). Why can't you do that?

ANDREI. Natasha, let me finish. You see, there's a whole chain – I'm taking over from Shchetinin, one of the section heads takes over from me, somebody else takes his place, somebody else takes his, and so on, and so on. If I hand in my resignation now, that'll all fall apart. I'll be letting people down. That's why I'm asking you to wait a wee bit with the resignation. I'll accept the Group job, everybody'll move into place, and then I'll quit straight away. No problem. No unpleasantness.

NATASHA. No!

ANDREI. What d'you mean no?

NATASHA. I don't believe a single word of it! Why didn't you tell me this when you came in? You forgot? A likely story.

ANDREI. All right, I didn't forget. I was frightened to tell you. I mean, it really isn't my fault – the rotten bad luck and this promotion just happen to have coincided. I can't help that, can I? I was going to tell you tomorrow, when you'd calmed down a bit.

NATASHA. Just a coincidence, eh? Well, Alyosha's paid for that coincidence! Going through channels, was it? Was that why you couldn't report a shortfall in the Plan? Was that why you sent those men under that wire? Because your wee link in the chain might just snap? Well, as it turned out, your luck was in – it wasn't just anybody that got hurt, it was your own son! Yes, you'd have wound up in court if it had been anybody else! It all worked out nicely for you, didn't it? They felt sorry for you – poor Golubev, he's had to suffer. Only he *hasn't* suffered, he's positively bloody thriving on it! Now I know why you were grinning when you came home. Promotion! Victory!

ANDREI *crosses to pick up the phone, grim-faced.*

NATASHA. Who's that you're phoning now?

ANDREI. Shchetinin. I'm telling him to stuff his job, and I'll give him my resignation tomorrow. (*He starts dialling the number.*)

NATASHA. Put the phone down.

ANDREI *stops dialling, turns round to face her.*

NATASHA. Put it down.

ANDREI *replaces the receiver.*

NATASHA. Switch off the kettle!

ANDREI. What?

NATASHA. The kettle, switch it off. You've left it on, did you forget?

ANDREI *goes out.* NATASHA *sits at the table and lights up a cigarette.* ANDREI *re-enters, carrying two glasses of tea, in holders, in his outstretched hands. He puts one glass down for* NATASHA, *and sits at the opposite side of the table. They remain silent, not looking at each other, sipping tea.*

NATASHA (*setting aside her glass*). Well, what are we going to do?

ANDREI. Just keep going. Stay alive. What else can we do?

NATASHA (*after a pause*). I suppose I should congratulate you, on your promotion! (ANDREI *does not respond.*) Well, what are we going to do? (ANDREI *is silent.*) I'm asking you, what are we going to do?

ANDREI *looks intently into* NATASHA's *face, gets up and goes towards her.*

ANDREI. Natasha, love, listen – hear me out. OK? I'm sorry about all this, I really am. I've made a mess of it, just lost the head completely. I mean, it all happened so suddenly, first one thing, then another. Please, Natasha, we've got to sit down calmly now and talk this out. I mean, essentially why is it you want me to quit? You want it, and I want it – why?

Because it's nerve-wracking, chaotic – my head's nipping with it the whole time. Eh? But it doesn't have to be like that, it could all be different. I mean, look at what's happening now. Shchetinin'll be leaving. That means I won't have him breathing down my neck any longer – all that pressure, do this, do that, come on, chop-chop, jump to it! From now on, I'll be in charge of the situation, do you understand? Group Manager's not like running CDC – it carries a lot of clout, you know, you're practically a free agent. I mean, there's one level of activity, where you're dependent on circumstances, like managing CDC, and then there's another level, where you *create* those circumstances. Group Manager's on *that* level, it's like stepping out onto the strategic heights. And if you think about it, here I am forty-seven years of age, and for the first time I've got an opportunity to really *do* something! And do it *my* way. I won't get an opportunity like this again, it just won't happen. D'you understand? All right, so it's come up at the wrong time, it's not exactly the happiest moment of my life. It's actually the bloody worst imaginable. But if I *am* going to carry on living, what am I supposed to do – bury myself? I want to give it a try, Natasha. I've got ideas, and know-how – I can turn this job around, I've got the experience. I've got the drive! I'll pick out some really bright people, genuine grafters. I mean, I know where to find them – first-rate qualified people, out in the cold. And I'll bring them in, put together a team. We'll have a real think-tank, Natasha.

NATASHA. And what will you do with the people you've got now?

ANDREI. Get shot of them! We're needing to turf half of them out anyway, and I'm just the man to do it!

NATASHA. Oh yes? And how are you going to do that? They're all Shchetinin's people. The first sniff of trouble, they'll be on the phone to Shchetinin and he'll tell you to lay off. And you won't go against Shchetinin. He set you up in the job, after all. He doesn't know you're lying awake nights, getting big ideas. The only Golubev he knows is his faithful wee dog, that does whatever he tells it. He doesn't know the night-time Golubev, only the day-time dog.

ANDREI. Well, that's life, Natasha. He picked out the kind of Golubev he needed, but when I take over the Group I'll be the kind of Golubev *I* need – that *we* need. I've kept my head

down long enough, I've paid in full, Natasha, we're quits. So
OK, I know there'll be trouble, it's unavoidable. But what the
hell, I'm ready for it. I'm not looking for an easy life. They'll
maybe even end up giving me the sack. But I want to give it
a shot. I want to *try*, Natasha! And if it doesn't work, well,
that's too bad. I'll have learned a lesson and I'll just fade out
of sight. I'm not scared of anything now. I'm not going to be
sitting at night, gripping the chair-arms. I'll be able to relax
now, because I'll know you're behind me, Natasha, and that
you want me as a human being, even at a third of my present
salary! I'm not going to take on more than I can realistically
handle, like Shchetinin. That's the cause of this whole mess:
he promised them too much and it all started to hit the fan.
Well, I won't do that – I'll tell them straight: these are the
resources you've given me, this is what I can build, and that's
it. That's your lot. And if they don't like it, then sod them,
I'm off. But if I just quit like this – neither one thing nor
another – well, it's a bit dumb.

NATASHA. Listen, they *know* you – organisation man – they've
got your number long ago. How are you going to walk in as
somebody else – plastic surgery?

ANDREI. I've thought about that as well, Natasha, I really have.
Maybe it's a terrible thing to say, but that's exactly where
Alyosha'll be a help. Everybody knows why my son lost his
hands. That gives me the right just to walk in and tell them –
that's it, the game's up. And it'll be accepted. A month ago,
it would have been different, but I have the *right* now. You
know, when I was a wee boy, listening to the grown-ups
going on about how complicated life was, I thought it was a
big joke. What's complicated about it, I thought, they're just
trying to frighten me. And now look at the godawful mess
we're in. A shambles. And don't think I don't know what's
ahead of me. This big clear-out's going to need God only
knows what sort of strength and persistence. And the kind of
good health I frankly don't have. I'll tell you the honest
truth, Natasha, I'm not at all sure I'll be able to cope, that
I'll not just cave in. You don't know the full story. The ulcer's
one thing, that's OK, it comes and goes. But this last while
back, I've been tiring very quickly, as if I'm carrying this
heavy weight on my shoulders. In the middle of the day I've
been asking my secretary not to let anybody in, and getting
the head down on the desk, for a half-hour or so. Otherwise
I just can't work . . .

NATASHA. That's because you haven't had a break two years on the trot. How many times have I told you – bugger the job, you need a rest, Andrei. *That's* what's weighing you down.

ANDREI *smiles affectionately, draws* NATASHA *to him, a chaste kiss.*

ANDREI. Never mind, love, I'll survive. You've no idea how grateful I am for the way you've supported me. (*Kisses her warmly.*) Natasha, I swear I'll do whatever you want, I promise – I love you, Natasha – I'll do everything I possibly can, you'll see –

NATASHA. Andrei, if there's going to be any more lies . . . the way it's been – I just couldn't . . .

ANDREI. I know.

NATASHA. This past month's turned me inside out, Andrei. I'm not the same person.

ANDREI. I know . . .

NATASHA. I just couldn't take any more lying – physically I couldn't. The slightest . . .

ANDREI. I know . . .

NATASHA. You've got to promise me, if it doesn't work out, you'll quit right away?

ANDREI. Of course.

NATASHA. And you can change, Andrei, if you really want to.

ANDREI. I can. And I will.

NATASHA. I sometimes wake up in the middle of the night and look at you. You look nice when you're asleep, when your face is relaxed – it's sort of friendly and open, like a wee boy. *My* wee boy. I look at you, and I start to cry. That's him, I think, that's the man I married, and now he's going to wake up and that'll be it, and . . . Andrei, I don't know . . . I'll really do something to myself this time, if you . . .

ANDREI. Natasha, love, don't – I know, I know.

NATASHA. I wasn't going to tell you . . . but when you came home tonight, and you were standing laying it off on the phone – I was in there (*Indicates the wardrobe.*) and this terrible feeling came over me. It was all just too much, you sounded so obnoxious. And then what Sonya had told me . . . And the darkness . . . I was searching around for a belt or something. I'd found a place I could hook it onto . . .

ANDREI (*starts up*). You what?

NATASHA. It's the truth. If you'd stayed there five more minutes, it would have been all over. You just left the room, and I fell out onto the floor. Like out of a grave.

ANDREI. Natasha, for God's sake, don't! Don't say any more – we'll get through this, we will! We'll still dance at Alyosha's wedding – *and* we'll babysit for him when the grandchildren arrive! We'll get this business up and running, Natasha, we'll *build* something in this town, eh? What d'you say? Natasha, honey, come on, Natasha, sweetheart. (*Kisses and cuddles her.*) I love you, Natasha, you know I do . . .

NATASHA (*tearfully*). Oh, Andrei, Andrei – will you do something for me?

ANDREI. Of course I will, pet – what is it?

NATASHA. I mean, if you did agree, then I really *would* believe you were serious . . . Andrei, I want to get out of the library. I want to leave the library, so you can take me on at your place. I want to work alongside you, Andrei, to be *involved* . . . so I'll understand.

ANDREI. Yes, sure, love – no problem. I'll give it some thought.

Kisses her.

NATASHA. Do you mean that? Really?

ANDREI. Why not?

NATASHA. We're not young any longer, Andrei, and this has been a terrible blow. We've got to live right, what's left to us, do you see? I deliberately didn't get involved before, I didn't want to . . . I mean, that was *my* fault, and I'm sorry. I knew things were going badly, but I just turned my back on it, didn't want to know. Couldn't care less, you're absolutely right. And that's no way to live, if I'm to be a wife to you, Andrei. I couldn't stand that Shchetinin, but if there's going to be other people now, then I would have them here, put on a bit of a show. You could all get together here, discuss things . . . and I'd know everything that was going on. Please, Andrei, I really mean it, I want you to find me a job with the company. If you do that, then I definitely *do* think we could make a go of it. Will you do that? Andrei?

ANDREI. Mm, yes. Natasha, love, I'm just not sure what you could do in our set-up.

NATASHA. It doesn't matter. You have a records office, I could do that – any sort of paper work.

ANDREI. Mm. To tell you the honest truth, Natasha, it's a wee bit inconvenient.

NATASHA. Why is it inconvenient?

ANDREI. Well, I mean . . . I mean, how will it look if the new Group Manager arrives and the first thing he does is set up his lady wife? It's a bit off, you know?

NATASHA. So what are you saying, Andrei? That you haven't understood? That you don't agree to it?

ANDREI. No, no, love, I understand. And I *do* agree. I'm all for it. Only not right away, OK? Give it time. I mean, if I bring you into the office on day one, it might be misinterpreted. It could actually interfere with what I'm trying to do, you know? We'll definitely do it, but we'll need to wait a wee while. OK? (*Kisses her.*) And you'll be able to help me at home meanwhile . . . I'll tell you everything. Every last detail, all right?

NATASHA. Andrei, I think it's important that we do this from the very beginning. That we're together from here on in. It's crucial, Andrei.

ANDREI. Natasha, honey, you just don't know what these people are like. I promise you, it *will* happen. Only not right away. I can't just assemble everybody and explain why I'm taking you on.

NATASHA. That's all right – if they want an explanation, I'll give them one. If necessary I can tell them why we've decided to –

ANDREI. God's sakes, Natasha, you're not serious! We *can't* do it, they won't buy it.

NATASHA. Is that the only reason?

ANDREI. Of course it is. What other reason could there be?

NATASHA. And when do you have to take over?

ANDREI. Well, there's no hurry. The Deputy Controller still has a leave due. They'll give him his place for a wee while after he comes back. Then the usual send-off. I'll be at CDC for another six to eight weeks.

NATASHA. Well. that's fine!

ANDREI (*guardedly*). What d'you mean, that's fine?

NATASHA. Because *Shchetinin* can give me the job. Now, while *he's* still in charge. D'you get it? Shchetinin'll take me on, and when you arrive I'll already be there, nothing to do with you! (NATASHA *is overjoyed.*) A brainwave, eh? Pretty good, huh? (NATASHA *presents her cheek for* ANDREI *to kiss.* ANDREI *obliges.*) So that's it, then. I'll give in my notice to Olga tomorrow, and go and see Shchetinin. In fact, I'll ring him up right now and arrange it! Oh, Andrei, it'll be so nice working together, you can't imagine. And I know how to behave, you needn't worry . . . I won't even come to work in your car. (NATASHA *crosses delightedly to the phone, lifts the receiver.*)

ANDREI. Natasha, hold on. Wait.

NATASHA. What for? It's a fantastic idea, a stroke of genius. Who knows, Andrei, you're maybe just about to acquire the most valuable member of your think-tank! You can put me in charge of public relations! (*Begins dialling the number.*) I'll congratulate old Shchetinin on his promotion first, and fix a time.

ANDREI. Natasha, put the phone down! (*She carries on dialling the number regardless.* ANDREI *crosses to the table, clicks off the rest.*) It's too late. They'll be asleep.

NATASHA. So what? He's not slow to phone you up at two and three in the morning – why shouldn't I phone him at half-twelve? I'm sure he'll be delighted. Andrei, take your hand off the phone. Come on, love, move your hand.

ANDREI *does so, and* NATASHA *dials again. This time, however, he crosses to unplug the cord at the wall, and the line goes dead.*

What are you doing? Plug that back in, Andrei!

ANDREI (*coldly*). You're phoning nobody, Natasha. I'm not having you working beside me.

NATASHA. What?

ANDREI. It's just not on.

NATASHA. Why not?

ANDREI. It just isn't! I mean what's the point? I don't need help at work. You can help me here. But not there.

NATASHA. Huh! (*Disgusted.*) My God. Is that your last word?

ANDREI. Yes.

NATASHA (*pathetically, confused*). Andrei . . . I wanted it for us . . . for your sake. I wanted us to be together . . . so we could be responsible for each other . . I . . .

ANDREI. I'm sorry, Natasha, but you're talking rubbish.

NATASHA. And what about the promise you made, to do what *I* want?

ANDREI. Yes, well, *except* that. And you needn't think there's any funny business going on – that I'm scared in case you find me out.

NATASHA. I don't think that, Andrei, it's *worse* than that! Keep off, eh? Give you a completely free hand? Oh yes, of course, that's all you need, so you and Shchetinin can electrocute people!

ANDREI. I damn well certainly don't need *you* checking up on me! No way, sweetheart! There's enough folk doing that! Oh, no, maybe I got slightly confused. These past couple of hours it's been like a madhouse. But that's it over, I've come to my senses now. What's yours is yours, sweetheart, and what's mine's my own!

NATASHA. Oh, of course, that's typical – what's yours is yours, so far and no further. A madhouse? That's right, anything the least bit human *is* mad, as far as you're concerned. You'll end up putting me away in an asylum!

ANDREI. Oh, leave off, Natasha.

NATASHA. Oh, I'll leave, don't you worry.

ANDREI. I know damn well what you're after. You think you've got me by the throat? Well, you just remember, Natasha, who's got the brass neck – you won't squeeze me!

NATASHA *turns pale, anguished, gasping for breath.*

NATASHA. God Almighty! I don't believe this . . . it's not possible . . . What am I doing here? Why am I still here, and not thousands of miles away? It's a judgement on me, I'll pay for this! One of these days I'll be judged for it, that I stayed married to you for twenty years! Nobody forced me, nobody made me do it. (*She picks up her coat and makes her way to the door.*)

ANDREI. Just stay there! (NATASHA *stops.*)
   Turn round. Oh, don't worry, I'm not stopping you, you can go. But first let's get a few things straight. I have *never* lived with you on the kind of basis you're now proposing, and I don't intend to, so you can just get your head out of the clouds. And what do you mean . . . you can't live like this? As if you're superior – well, you're *not* superior. If it hadn't been Alyosha that suffered, but some other kid, you wouldn't have turned a hair! You'd have been tearing round the management trying to rescue me – you'd have run to your precious bloody Kuzmin, to keep me out of jail! And rightly so! That's how it should be. Instead of taking bloody refuge with Olga! You're supposed to be my wife, then *be* a wife. A bit of support, and help when I need it, not a bloody take-over bid! It's Olga that's put you up to this. She's actually said it to my face, I remember distinctly: 'You know, Andrei, Natalya should never have married you – her kind of man would despise people like you!' Bloody cow! Telling me who my wife should have married! Well, you *do* that, you go to her. She'll keep you right. Only you just remember, you're going of your own accord. And I'm staying put, right here. In my own place. I'm not just a husband. I'm an engineer, a manager, in charge of hundreds of men – huge resources. If you can't stand the heat, you stay out of the kitchen. And you can't make an omelette without cracking a few eggs. I'm a builder, for God's sakes, not a bloody librarian! It's people like me that have to carry the whole show on our backs!

NATASHA. Carry it where?

ANDREI. Wherever! And if you leave me now, Natasha, you're on your own. I'm warning you, you step over that door and there's no way back! Once before I let you back in, I'm not doing it a second time. You walk into that lift, press the down button, and that's it. As far as I'm concerned you're down and out forever. Now go!

ANDREI *turns sharply on his heel, and sits in the armchair, his back to the door. After a moment's hesitation,* NATASHA *goes.* ANDREI *jumps up.*

ANDREI. Natasha, come back! (*He runs out into the hall.*) Come back here! Natasha, for God's sakes! (*Comes in again and stands in the middle of the room.*) Bloody hell! Shit! (*He flings open the verandah door, goes out and begins shouting from the verandah down to the street below.*) Natasha, come back here! There's no need for this! Natasha! Driver, don't you dare take her! Bastard! Bloody swine! (*Comes in again.*) Shit! (*Stands in the middle of the room, and begins to jerk his left shoulder in the now-familiar stretching movement, as if trying to correct a dislocation. He jerks his shoulder several times, with increasing force, but it doesn't seem to help. Eventually he stops, and crosses to the telephone, breathing heavily. He dials a number.*) Hello, Despatch? Golubev here. What took you so long to answer? How's that concrete, is it in the pump yet? How many cubic metres? Yes, well you just remember, I'll be checking it in the morning. Oh, and by the way, I asked for the car at ten o'clock, I won't be needing it now. Have it outside here at eight, same as usual. (*Slams down the receiver. The phone instantly starts ringing, he picks it up again.*)

(*Gloomily.*) Hello?

ALYOSHA'S VOICE. Dad?

ANDREI. Alyosha?

ALYOSHA'S VOICE. Did I wake you up, Dad?

ANDREI. No, no. What's up, son? Is there something you want? You know it's after one o'clock? I phoned earlier . . . they said you were asleep . . . what's wrong, are you OK?

ALYOSHA'S VOICE. No, I woke up again – just feeling sort of rotten. I'm sorry, Dad.

ANDREI. No, no, that's OK, son. I'm glad you phoned. Listen, is there something up? I could drive over right now, no problem.

ALYOSHA'S VOICE. No, no, I'm fine, Dad. It's gone now, anyway. I just felt kind of frightened, you know? And then I heard your voice, and everything was all right again. Is Mum asleep?

ANDREI. Your Mum? Yes, she's asleep.

ALYOSHA'S VOICE. What time will you be coming for me tomorrow?

ANDREI. Tomorrow? Before lunchtime. We'll be there before lunch.

ALYOSHA'S VOICE. Am I keeping you out of bed, Dad?

ANDREI. No, don't be daft – I could chat away to you the whole night.

ALOYSHA'S VOICE. No, that's OK. I'll get back to sleep. Dad . . . everything's going to be all right, isn't it? Dad?

ANDREI. Yes, sure. Just you put it out of your mind.

ALYOSHA'S VOICE. Good night, Dad.

ANDREI. Good night, son . . .

> ANDREI *lowers his hand, holding the receiver, and we hear* ALYOSHA'S VOICE *continuing at the other end, trying to summon assistance to replace his receiver.*

ALYOSHA'S VOICE. Nurse? Nurse, will you help me, please? Nurse, I can't put the phone back, will you help me, please? . . .

> ANDREI *remains motionless, still holding the receiver. His eyes are glazed, a distracted look, off in another world somewhere, while the 'line open' tone is heard, growing louder and more insistent, like an alarm signal.*

FORGET HEROSTRATUS! ■ GRIGORY GORIN

Translated by MICHAEL GLENNY

Written and staged in the pre-Glasnost era, *Forget Herostratus!*
shows Gorin disguising a political message in a classical allegory –
in this case the burning of the Temple of Diana and the trial of its
perpetrator – provoking comparisons with Hitler, the Reichstag
fire and the then prevailing Soviet judiciary system. It was first
performed in Britain on Radio 3 in November 1986.

Characters

MAN OF THE THEATRE
TISSAFERNES, Ruler of Ephesus, Satrap of the King of Persia
CLEMENTINA, his wife
CLEON, Archon or Chief Magistrate of Ephesus
HEROSTRATUS
CHRYSIPPUS, trader and money-lender
ERITA, priestess of the temple of Artemis
JAILER
FIRST CITIZEN
SECOND CITIZEN
THIRD CITIZEN

Place – the city of Ephesus, Asia Minor
Time – 356 B.C.

Forget Herostratus! was first performed in English on BBC Radio 3 on 25 November 1986. In this version the name of CLEMENTINA was changed to KALLISTA and the name of ERITA was changed to AGLAIA. The cast was as follows:

HEROSTRATUS	Mike Gwilym
TISSAFERNES	Joseph Marcell
KALLISTA	John Moffatt
VISITOR	Edward de Souza
CHRYSIPPUS	John Church
AGLAIA	Rachel Gurney
JAILER	George Parsons

Directed by John Theocaris

PART ONE

Confused noise, shouts, groans, the crash of falling masonry, followed by an ominous silence, lasting a few seconds – long enough for people to realise what has happened and then to give way to tears and despair . . .

MAN OF THE THEATRE. In the fourth century before Christ, in the Greek city of Ephesus, the temple of Artemis was set on fire and destroyed. It had taken many master-craftsmen a hundred and twenty years to build it. According to legend, the goddess herself had helped the architects. The temple was so magnificent that it was numbered among the seven wonders of the ancient world. Crowds of people flocked to its portals to worship the goddess and to marvel at the grandeur of human achievement. The temple stood for a hundred years. It might have stood for a millenium, but it stood for no more than a century. On that fateful night in the year 356 BC, an inhabitant of Ephesus, a market trader by the name of Herostratus, burnt down the temple of Artemis. The rulers of the ancient Greek states issued a decree forbidding the name of the arsonist ever to be mentioned again. Kings and priests demanded: 'Forget Herostratus!' Tyrants and dictators gave the order: 'Forget Herostratus!' 'Forget him . . !' 'Forget . . !' But do decrees have any power over human memory? . . . Today, when the whole planet shudders to the sound of gunfire and explosions, when crime in some places has become the normal state of affairs, when cruelty is an everyday occurrence, I am reminded more and more often of what happened then, three hundred and fifty-six years before the birth of Christ . . .

Scene One

The MAN OF THE THEATRE *lights a dull unpolished bronze candelabrum. The light reveals a prison cell.*

MAN OF THE THEATRE. We are in the prison of the city of
Ephesus, a stone cell in a grim underground vault. The
ancient Greeks excelled in building magnificent palaces and
temples but their prisons were awful. Prisons in all ages are
ugly, utilitarian structures . . . (*Looks for somewhere to sit down,
but finding none he withdraws to the side of the stage.*)

Noise and cursing off-stage. The door is opened and a powerfully-built
JAILER *drags* HEROSTRATUS *into the cell.* HEROSTRATUS *is
in a dishevelled state: his tunic is torn, his face and arms are covered
in bruises. Having deposited* HEROSTRATUS *in the cell, the*
JAILER *suddenly turns on him and knocks him to the ground with a
smacking box on the ears.*

HEROSTRATUS. Don't you dare hit me!

JAILER. Shut up, scum! I'll hit you as much as I like. Why d'you
suppose the soldiers dragged you away from that crowd? You
could have been torn to pieces in five minutes out there on
the square. But no, the law must be observed, someone has
to get his hands dirty and haul you into prison . . . (*Spits at*
HEROSTRATUS.)

HEROSTRATUS (*getting up from the floor*). I still say you have no
right to hit me. I'm not a slave, I'm a free man.

JAILER. Huh! Call yourself a *man*? You're nothing but a mad
dog. You burned down the temple! How could any sane man
do such a thing . . ? Well, anyway, you're here now.
Tomorrow they'll tie your feet to the cart's tail and your head
will go bouncing over the cobblestones, a sight that I for one
will enjoy watching, believe me.

HEROSTRATUS. Go on, bark away, you mangy old dog. I heard
worse from the people out there. (*Groans*). Oh, my shoulder!
They almost broke my arm . . . Aaah, how it hurts . . ! Give
me some water.

JAILER (*sarcastically*). Anything else you want?

HEROSTRATUS. Give me some water, my throat's so dry I can't
swallow. Then you'd better wash my wounds or they'll start
to fester and go rotten.

JAILER. You really are off your head, my lad, aren't you! You're
going to be executed tomorrow and you're worrying about
your wounds festering . . .

HEROSTRATUS. Bring me some water, I tell you! It's your duty!

JAILER (*lunges at* HEROSTRATUS *and gives him another punch on the ear*). There's your water – and your wine and everything else! (*Starts to go.*)

HEROSTRATUS. Stop! I'll make you an offer.

JAILER. I don't want any of your offers.

HEROSTRATUS. Wait! Look what I've got here. (*Produces a silver coin.*) An Athenian drachma! If you do as I ask, it's yours.

JAILER (*laughs*). I'll get it anyway. (*Advances on* HEROSTRATUS.)

HEROSTRATUS (*retreating*). You won't get it like that!

JAILER (*still advancing*). Think you can fight me, you wreck? You're done for. Well?! (*Stretches out his hand.*) Come on, hand it over!

HEROSTRATUS. I said you wouldn't get it like that, and you won't! (*Puts the coin into his mouth and with a great effort, almost choking, swallows it.*) There! I've swallowed it. Now you'll have to wait till I'm dead.

JAILER (*taken aback*). Well I'm damned! (*Stares at* HEROSTRATUS *for a second, wondering whether there is any way of shaking the coin out of him, then spits with annoyance and turns to go.*)

HEROSTRATUS. Wait!

JAILER. What is it now?

HEROSTRATUS. I've got another one. (*Produces a second coin.*) Look!

The JAILER *immediately makes a lunge at* HEROSTRATUS.

Stand back, or I swear it'll land up in my stomach along with the other coin. Will you do as I ask or not? Well? Please don't make me swallow all this silver on an empty stomach.

JAILER (*relenting*). Well, what do you want?

HEROSTRATUS. That's more like it . . . Do you know where Chrysippus the money-lender lives?

JAILER. Yes, I do.

HEROSTRATUS. Go there and tell Chrysippus that I'd like him to come and see me at once.

JAILER. The very idea! Making a respected citizen come to see a criminal in prison . . .

HEROSTRATUS. He'll come! Tell him I've got a business deal for him – a profitable deal. Do you hear? A *very* profitable deal. What I'm going to propose will be worth a fortune to him – got that? And when he comes I'll give you this drachma . . . and another one, too. (*Produces a third coin.*) These are real silver drachmas, none of your Ephesian rubbish. Well? Why are you waiting? Or have they raised the jailer's wages lately?

JAILER. You blackguard! I've never seen a villain like you. All right, I'll go. But I warn you – if you cheat me, I swear by the gods I'll rip your guts open and get back what you owe me. (*Exit.*)

HEROSTRATUS *paces thoughtfully up and down, rubbing his injured shoulder. The* MAN OF THE THEATRE *watches him.*

HEROSTRATUS. What are you doing here?

MAN OF THE THEATRE. I'm curious to find out what happened – and why it happened – two thousand years ago in Ephesus.

HEROSTRATUS. You fool! Why bother about what happened so long ago? Haven't you got enough problems of your own?

MAN OF THE THEATRE. Some problems are eternal and puzzle men in all ages. If we want to understand and solve them, it's not a bad idea to remember what happened yesterday, what happened recently and what happened long ago.

HEROSTRATUS. All the same, it's tactless to interfere in events so long ago in time.

MAN OF THE THEATRE. Unfortunately, I can't interfere in them. I can only try to find out what actually happened.

HEROSTRATUS. So are we just the objects of your research?

MAN OF THE THEATRE. Of course. Just as we shall be to our descendants.

HEROSTRATUS. What interests you at this moment?

MAN OF THE THEATRE. I want to know whether you're afraid.

HEROSTRATUS (*defiantly*). Not a bit!

MAN OF THE THEATRE. That's the sort of answer you give for the benefit of the historians. But what do you *really* feel?

HEROSTRATUS. Yes, I'm terrified, I admit. Only I'm not quite as frightened as I was. What I feel is the fourth fear.

MAN OF THE THEATRE. Why the fourth?

HEROSTRATUS. I've already been through three stages of fear. The first was when I thought of doing what I have now done. That was the fear caused by the boldness of my idea. It wasn't a very terrible fear, and I fought it down by thinking of how famous I would be. The second fear gripped me in the temple itself, while I was pouring pitch on the walls and throwing tinder all over the place. That fear was stronger than the first. It made my hand shake and my mouth go so dry that my tongue stuck to the roof of my mouth. But that wasn't the worst fear; I suppressed it with wine – a dozen or so mouthfuls. Not enough to get drunk, but it chased the fear away. The worst was the third fear: the temple was burning, the roof-beams were starting to crack and one of the pillars came down – it collapsed like a felled oak, and its marble capital was smashed to fragments. And then people came running from all directions. No festival had ever brought so many people to the temple! Women, children, slaves, Greeks, Persians . . . People on horseback, people in chariots, rich and poor – they all came to see the bonfire I had lit. They shouted and wept and tore their hair, while I ran up to a mound beside the temple and shouted: 'People! I set this temple on fire!! My name is Herostratus!!' They heard what I was shouting, because all at once they were silent, and the only sound was the crackling of the flames as they devoured the beams. Then the people started to close in on me. They came silently. I can see their faces now, their eyes reflecting the tongues of flame. It was then I felt the most terrible fear – it was the fear of my fellow-men, and there was nothing that could make it go away . . . What I feel now is the fourth fear, the fear of death . . . But it's weaker than all the others, because I don't believe in death.

MAN OF THE THEATRE. You don't believe in death? Surely you don't expect to avoid paying the penalty for what you've done, do you?

HEROSTRATUS. So far, as you see, I've managed to stay alive.

From outside come shouts and the sounds of a fight.

MAN OF THE THEATRE. I fear you're not going to have much more time for these reflections, Herostratus. There's a crowd at the gates, and . . . yes, now they've broken into the prison . . ! They're coming this way . . .

HEROSTRATUS (*terrified*). They have no right to do it . . ! They can't take the law into their own hands! (*Shouts:*) Hey, guards! Soldiers! Help! (*Dashes frantically around the cell.*) You – do something! Stop them . . ! But they mustn't do this! Law and order must be preserved!

MAN OF THE THEATRE. Strange to hear that coming from *you* . . !

The door bursts open and three CITIZENS *run into the cell.*

HEROSTRATUS. Who are you? What do you want? . . . Get out of here!

FIRST CITIZEN. Come on out, you!

HEROSTRATUS. You'll pay for this, you hooligans, you brainless cattle! Don't you dare touch me!

THIRD CITIZEN. He's still barking, the mad dog! Tie him up!

SECOND CITIZEN (*advancing threateningly on* HEROSTRATUS). You're coming out of here with us, Herostratus, you'd better try and face death like a man.

HEROSTRATUS. What right have you to break in here? Idiots! (*Almost weeping:*) Don't touch me . . . I beg you . . .

SECOND CITIZEN (*grabs* HEROSTRATUS *by the shoulder*). Come on!

Enter CLEON, *the Archon or Chief Magistrate of Ephesus. A tall, grey-haired man aged about fifty, he is wearing a white cloak of rich material adorned with a red border.*

CLEON (*to* CITIZENS, *in a commanding tone*). Let go of him!

Seeing CLEON, *the* CITIZENS *obediently release* HEROSTRATUS.

CLEON. Who are you?

FIRST CITIZEN. We are citizens of Ephesus.

CLEON. Your names?

SECOND CITIZEN. What's that to you, Cleon? We're nobody special. I'm a stonemason, he's a potter, and he (*Pointing to* THIRD CITIZEN.) is a barber.

CLEON. All the same, why won't you tell me your names?

SECOND CITIZEN. We're not acting on our own, Archon. We've been sent here by the people.

CLEON. What do the people want?

FIRST CITIZEN. They want to bring Herostratus to justice.

CLEON. His trial will take place tomorrow or the day after – when I say so.

FIRST CITIZEN. The people are mad with fury. They don't see why his death should be put off . . .

THIRD CITIZEN. Our hands are itching to get hold of this bastard, and we . . .

CLEON (interrupting angrily). The people have elected me as Archon of this city – or does the name of Cleon no longer mean anything to the Ephesians? If so, they must either re-elect me or banish me from the city. But as long as I am your chief magistrate, law and order will prevail in Ephesus. So tell that to the mob that sent you here.

FIRST CITIZEN. We'll tell them, but who knows if they'll obey you?

CLEON. I will not allow an illegal lynching to take place! Due process of law must be observed. The law says: He who kills a felon before his trial is himself guilty of murder. That law was passed by the People's Assembly, and no one has yet repealed it. Herostratus will be punished, I swear to you. don't you believe my word?

SECOND CITIZEN. We believe you, Archon . . . You've never deceived us yet.

FIRST CITIZEN. So mind you keep your word this time, too.

THIRD CITIZEN (to HEROSTRATUS). We'll get even with you yet, Herostratus!

Exeunt CITIZENS. *For a little while* CLEON *and* HEROSTRATUS *look at each other:* CLEON – *calmly, and with a certain curiosity;* HEROSTRATUS, *recovered from his fright, now stares back at* CLEON *with a bold, challenging look.*

HEROSTRATUS. Greetings, Cleon!

CLEON *is silent.*

Greetings, Cleon! Do you think it unworthy to greet a free citizen of Ephesus?

CLEON *remains silent.*

All right, be silent if you like, although it's a stupid way to behave. After all, you came to see me, and not the other way round.

CLEON. We shall indeed speak. I merely wanted a good look at you.

HEROSTRATUS. Didn't you expect to see a normal human being? I suppose you thought I would have fangs instead of teeth or horns growing out of my head.

CLEON. No, I imagined you would be more or less as you are. But I thought you would have pimples all over your face.

HEROSTRATUS. Why?

CLEON. Oh, I just imagined it.

HEROSTRATUS. No, Cleon – my skin is clear, I have white teeth and a healthy body.

CLEON. Well, so much the worse for you. Tomorrow that healthy body of yours will be flung into the city's garbage pit. Is that what you wanted, Herostar?

HEROSTRATUS (*angrily*). My name is Herostratus! And it's no use pretending you don't know my name.

CLEON. Your name will be forgotten.

HEROSTRATUS. No! Now my name will be remembered for all ages. And you, Cleon, will only be remembered because you sat in judgment on me.

CLEON. I hope my descendants will at least sympathise with me for being forced into this unpleasant duty . . . However, enough of this chatter about eternity, Herostratus. You have only one night left to live. You had better tell me about yourself. The court will want to know who you are and where you come from.

HEROSTRATUS. With pleasure! I am Herostratus, son of Strato, born in Ephesus, a free citizen. I am thirty-two years old, by profession a trader. I used to sell fish, vegetables and wool in the market. I had two slaves and two oxen. The slaves ran away, the oxen died . . . I went bankrupt, so I abandoned trade and became a professional burner of temples.

CLEON. Did you have any accomplices in your crime?

HEROSTRATUS. I did it all alone!

CLEON. Don't try and lie to me, Herostratus, otherwise you will be made to tell the truth under torture.

HEROSTRATUS. I swear I was alone. What would be the point in sharing the glory?

CLEON. How did you get into the temple?

HEROSTRATUS. The usual way – by the main entrance. I went in during the evening, hid in one of the side-chambers, and then at night, after the priests and priestesses had gone, I set to work.

CLEON. How did you manage to smuggle a jar full of pitch into the temple?

HEROSTRATUS. I didn't smuggle it, I carried it in for all to see. The priests are only interested in the expensive gifts that rich people bring to the altar of the goddess. Nobody paid any attention to my cracked jar.

CLEON. Were you drunk?

HEROSTRATUS. No. I'd only had a few gulps of wine to give myself courage.

CLEON. The man who owns the market-stall next to yours says that one day in the market you fell down in a faint.

HEROSTRATUS. True, Cleon – and more than once. But that doesn't mean that I'm an epileptic . . . (Laughs) It's really a very funny story! You see, when my business went completely on the rocks, the money-lenders took so much from me that I didn't know where the next meal was coming from. I wasn't fussy about what I did, so long as I got well paid for it. As you know, the laws that regulate market trading forbid a stallholder to pour water on the fish he's selling, because it makes them twitch and look fresher than they really are. The overseers make any trader pay a heavy fine if he breaks that rule. So then I thought up this 'fainting' dodge . . . you walk along past the fishmongers' stalls and suddenly – oh dear! – you fall in a faint all over the baskets of fish. The stallholders douse me with water to revive me and they 'accidentally' splash water on the fish too . . . It's foolproof: the fish get a sousing and I get paid!

CLEON. Cunning!

HEROSTRATUS. Even so, the overseers caught on in the end. They realised we were making fools of them and they gave me a good flogging.

CLEON. I expect you got flogged quite a few times, didn't you?

HEROSTRATUS. Now and again. People never forgive anyone who's cleverer than they are.

CLEON. People don't forgive those who treat them as fools. Are you married?

HEROSTRATUS. I was, but I got divorced. My wife was Theophila, the daughter of Chrysippus the money-lender. He paid ten thousand drachmas for her dowry. I grabbed the money and I somehow forgot that along with the dowry I had to take a stupid and ugly woman into my house . . . On top of that, she gave birth to a baby boy four months after the wedding. I realised I'd been fooled, and I went to law about it, but that swindler Chrysippus won the case by convincing the court that I'd seduced his 'innocent' little girl long before we got married. Well, we were divorced, and according to the law I had to give back the whole dowry to Chrysippus, plus eighteen per cent interest for breach of contract. So that crook even earned a tidy sum by exploiting his own daughter.

CLEON. I realised as soon as I saw you that you were one of the world's unlucky ones.

HEROSTRATUS. Yes, I am. I never win arguments, I never win at dice or cock-fighting.

CLEON. And so because of all this you decided to take revenge on the whole of Ephesus, is that it?

HEROSTRATUS. I wasn't taking revenge on anyone, Cleon. It was just that I suddenly got fed up with wasting my life away as a nobody . . . I knew I deserved a better fate. And now *everybody* knows my name.

CLEON. Wretched man! Now everybody in this city is cursing your name.

HEROSTRATUS. Let them . . ! They're cursing me today; tomorrow they'll begin to think I'm someone interesting; in a year's time they'll love me – and in five years from now they'll worship me. It's quite something for a mere mortal to challenge the gods, you know. Apart from me, who else has ever dared to do it? Prometheus, perhaps?

CLEON (angrily). How dare you compare yourself to him, you wretch! Prometheus stole fire from the gods to give it to men, but you took fire and used it to rob your fellow-men of a priceless possession. The temple of Artemis was the pride of Ephesus. For decades we have admired it, treasured it and cared for it, because we knew that in every marble column, in every carved figure there lay a hundred and twenty years of human genius and human toil. Do you hear, Herostratus? A hundred and twenty years! Generations passed, master-craftsmen built and sculpted and passed on their art to their sons that they in turn might teach their grandsons . . . And what did they do it for? Just so that one day some miserable scoundrel could come along and reduce it all to ashes? No, Herostratus, you don't know your fellow-men at all. They will forget your name, just as they forget their nightmares.

HEROSTRATUS. Well, we shall see.

CLEON. You will not see! By tomorrow evening you will no longer exist.

HEROSTRATUS (defiantly). We shall see about that, too . . .

CLEON. I don't understand exactly what you're relying on to save you.

HEROSTRATUS. My fellow-men, Cleon!

CLEON. Which of your fellow-men?

HEROSTRATUS. Well – you, for instance. After all, you have just saved me from death.

CLEON stares suspiciously at HEROSTRATUS, shrugs his shoulders in perplexity and stalks out.

MAN OF THE THEATRE. Have you really not lost hope, Herostratus?

HEROSTRATUS. Of course I haven't. There is a wise proverb that exactly applies to my case. It says: when you lose money, you gain experience; when you lose a wife you gain freedom;

when you lose your health, you may have gained pleasure
from indulgence . . . but you must not lose hope; when you
lose hope, you lose everything . . .

MAN OF THE THEATRE. But you're bound to be executed! The
logic of events, the law . . .

HEROSTRATUS. Forget about logic, man. Logic is a bad
counsellor. Why wasn't I killed last night, outside the temple
– or just now, here in the prison?

MAN OF THE THEATRE. Because, after all, people are
humane . . .

HEROSTRATUS. If they're so humane, why do they want to
execute me tomorrow?

MAN OF THE THEATRE. You have caused people grief, scorned
their cherished beliefs and insulted their dignity, so you must
suffer the penalty prescribed by the law.

HEROSTRATUS. Rubbish! Where was the justice when the
Greeks sacked Troy and murdered all the Trojans just
because one woman had been abducted? Where's the logic in
such savage cruelty? A little time passes – and the great
Homer sings their praises in the *Iliad*. No, it's not logic that I
need, it's strength, inner strength. I only have to be confident
of my strength and I can start to control events and people.
Afterwards, the philosophers will find some convincing
justification for everything that happened.

MAN OF THE THEATRE. Possibly. But then other philosophers
will come along and get at the truth of the matter.

HEROSTRATUS (*irritably*). Oh, I can't be bothered to argue with
you! I have too little time. Where is that rogue Chrysippus?
Go and fetch him, he's taking too long to come . . .

MAN OF THE THEATRE. I'm not here to run errands for you,
I'm afraid! (*Retires to one side and continues to observe the action.*)

Enter CHRYSIPPUS, *a fat old man wearing a rich purple cloak.*

HEROSTRATUS (*delighted*). At last! Greetings, Chrysippus!

CHRYSSIPUS. Busy though I was, I could not resist the pleasure
of coming here to spit in your face.

HEROSTRATUS. Spit away, Chrysippus. Right now I can bear
even that.

CHRYSIPPUS. No, but seriously! You know very well how busy I am. A cargo of goods has just arrived from Crete and I must go and inspect it, after which I have to go to the money-changers in the market, then I have to go to court, where I'm suing two of my creditors, and later I have a business meeting with a Persian merchant . . . But my wife clutched me and screamed: 'Chrysippus, put off all your business affairs and go and spit in Herostratus' face!' How could I refuse the pleas of the woman I love? (*Spits in* HEROSTRATUS' *face.*) That's from her!

HEROSTRATUS (*wiping his face*). Good! Now spit again on your daughter's behalf, and let's get down to business.

CHRYSIPPUS. My daughter told me to scratch your eyes out and tear out your tongue.

HEROSTRATUS. No, that won't do. I must be able to see you and talk to you.

CHRYSIPPUS. What do we have to talk about, you miserable wretch?

HEROSTRATUS. About money, Chrysippus. Isn't that something worth talking about? I owe you a hundred drachmas.

CHRYSIPPUS. Indeed you do, you scum. But how am I going to get them now? Villain that you are, I've no doubt you burned down the temple simply to avoid paying your debt to me.

HEROSTRATUS. I want to pay that debt.

CHRYSIPPUS (*astonished*). You do? Well, I suppose you still have some honourable feelings left; a scrap of your conscience seems to have survived. (*Holds out his hand.*) Hand it over!

HEROSTRATUS. I only have two drachmas, and I've promised those to the jailer.

CHRYSIPPUS. In that case I shall have to carry out my daughter's instructions. We have no more to say to each other.

HEROSTRATUS. Don't be in such a hurry. I'll repay your debt, and with more interest than you could imagine in your wildest dreams. I want to sell you this . . . (*Produces a scroll of papyrus.*)

CHRYSIPPUS. What's in that papyrus?

HEROSTRATUS. The story of my life. The memoirs of the man who burned down the greatest temple in the world. There is everything here: my autobiography, some verses, my philosophy.

CHRYSIPPUS. And what use is that rubbish to me?

HEROSTRATUS. You fool, I'm offering you pure gold! Give this to the scribes to copy, and you can sell each scroll for three hundred drachmas.

CHRYSIPPUS. You can keep that sort of gold. Where's the money to be made in writing nowadays? We live in unsettled times. People eat a lot nowadays and have no time or money for reading. The papyrus-sellers can hardly make ends meet. Nobody buys Aeschylus any more, Aristophanes sells for chicken-feed. And that's not all – they can't even sell Homer, the great Homer! Who's going to buy the work of a scribbler like you?

HEROSTRATUS. You're a fool, Chrysippus. I'm sorry, but you're a terrible fool. You're so stupid, in fact, that I don't know how you've managed to stay in business for so long. Don't you see? You're comparing wine with milk! I'm not offering you a lot of boring old myths that everybody knows by heart already. I'm offering you 'The Confessions of the Man who Burned Down the Temple of Artemis'! When you put a papyrus like this on the market, they'll tear it out of your hands to get a copy! Just think, Chrysippus. People will be fascinated to read the thoughts of a monster like me. The man in the street will relish every line – I can just see him reading the manuscript aloud to his wife, while she squeals with terror and excitement over it!

CHRYSSIPUS (*thoughtfully*). Perhaps . . . but the rulers of the city will ban your manuscript.

HEROSTRATUS. So much the better! It'll double the price!

CHRYSIPPUS. You're not as stupid as you look . . . All right, give it to me.

HEROSTRATUS. What d'you mean – *give* it to you?

CHRYSIPPUS. You wanted to settle accounts with me, didn't you? Well, I'll take this papyrus in payment of your debt.

HEROSTRATUS (*indignantly*). What? Do you imagine you're going to get this deathless work for a hundred drachmas? Really,

Chrysippus! This is a unique original. Look, there's my
signature. A thousand drachmas – no less!

CHRYSIPPUS. Ye gods! This man really has gone off his head. A
thousand drachmas!!

HEROSTRATUS. Calm down – it's less than a thousand. I owe
you a hundred drachmas, so you only have to pay nine
hundred. Shall we shake on it?

CHRYSIPPUS. Never! Nine hundred for a risky deal like this?
I could never look myself in the face again.

HEROSTRATUS. All right – what's your price?

CHRYSIPPUS. My price? . . . Well . . . Listen, what use is money
to you anyway? You're going to be executed tomorrow.

HEROSTRATUS. That's neither here nor there. I'm selling, you
want to buy – so pay up!

CHRYSIPPUS. But a corpse doesn't need cash. They don't take
silver in Hades, you know.

HEROSTRATUS. That's none of your business. Name your price.

CHRYSIPPUS. Well, I'm a kind-hearted man . . . Just for
curiosity's sake . . . So that I can read it myself at my leisure
. . . A hundred and fifty drachmas!

HEROSTRATUS. Get out, Chrysippus. (*Puts away the papyrus.*) Go
on, off you go . . . Go and buy dates and sell figs. Go on
charging one per cent interest on your loans, and don't forget
to tear your hair out when you realise you've thrown away
the chance of making millions. As soon as you've gone, I'm
going to send for Menander the money-lender; he'll shell out
fifteen hundred drachmas without a moment's hesitation . . .

CHRYSIPPUS. But that's not fair! We were once related, you and
I, after all!

HEROSTRATUS. When you stripped me of everything I
possessed, you weren't too worried about family feelings
then. Go away, Chrysippus.

CHRYSIPPUS. Two hundred!

HEROSTRATUS. Not interested.

CHRYSIPPUS. Two hundred and fifty!

HEROSTRATUS. You old skinflint! I'm offering you a work of
genius. (*Produces the papyrus.*) Listen to this. (*Reads:*)
'Ephesus lay in the arms of all-healing Morpheus;
Tinder and pitch in my hand, in the goddess' temple I stood'
. . . It's enough to make your flesh creep!

CHRYSIPPUS. Three hundred!

HEROSTRATUS. ' "O Herostratus", I cried to myself with a
challenge:
"Do not relent now, be bold, man, and do what for so long
you planned to do"!'

CHRYSIPPUS. That last line's a false hexameter . . . Four
hundred!

HEROSTRATUS. 'Sun-like, the torch in my hand flared up into
brightness,
Lighting before me the huntress's countenance: Artemis!'
(*To* CHRYSIPPUS:) Seven hundred!

CHRYSIPPUS. Four hundred and fifty, Herostratus – I can't pay
more.

HEROSTRATUS. ' "Hear now, O goddess!" I cried to the statue
– "Hear me and tremble, for I, Herostratus . . ." '
(*Stops reciting.*) All right, make it five hundred. Agreed?

CHRYSIPPUS (*tauntingly*). A pentameter with only four feet! Huh!
Illiterate scribbler. (*With a sigh:*) Very well, agreed . . .

HEROSTRATUS. Done! Give me the money.

CHRYSIPPUS. I haven't got it with me. Give me the papyrus, I'll
go home and . . .

HEROSTRATUS (*interrupting*). It's no good trying your tricks on
me. People in your profession never go out without their
purse.

CHRYSIPPUS (*spreading his hands*). I swear I haven't got it on me!

HEROSTRATUS. You shouldn't wave your arms like that – I can
hear your purse clinking.

CHRYSIPPUS (*gives in*). Oh, very well . . . I hope the money
chokes you, you robber! (*Counts out the coins, takes the papyrus.*)
This poem will be the ruin of me.

HEROSTRATUS. Don't lie, Chrysippus. You've never yet paid

out a single drachma if you didn't believe it would earn you a hundred more . . .

CHRYSIPPUS (*putting away the papyrus*). Thanks for the compliment. Your head seems to be screwed on the right way, Herostratus. Pity you didn't give me a few ideas like this one *before*, when you were one of the family.

HEROSTRATUS. You wouldn't have listened to me then, Chrysippus. In those days I was nothing but your poor son-in-law, but now – I'm the man who burned down the temple.

CHRYSIPPUS. No, you're certainly not stupid . . . definitely not . . . (*Exit.*)

HEROSTRATUS (*shouts after him*). Hurry up and have it copied, Chrysippus! Every minute counts now . . . (*Clinks the money.*) Right! That's the first step . . . (*Shouts:*) Hey, jailer!

Enter JAILER

There are your two drachmas. And three more for a job well done.

JAILER (*takes the money*). You may be a rogue, but you're generous.

HEROSTRATUS. You'll get two more drachmas if you stop insulting me.

JAILER. All right – agreed.

HEROSTRATUS. And you can earn yourself another fifty if you do what I'm going to ask you next.

JAILER. Fifty?

HEROSTRATUS. Yes, fifty.

JAILER. Tell me what I have to do.

HEROSTRATUS. See this purse? It's full of silver. Count out fifty drachmas for yourself and take the rest to Dionysios' tavern.

JAILER. That's where all the drunkards of Ephesus go.

HEROSTRATUS. Exactly. Give them the remaining money to spend on drink.

JAILER. What? Give all that money to those idle layabouts? What for, Herostratus?

HEROSTRATUS. None of your business. Throw them all the money and tell them that Herostratus the fire-raiser invites them to drink to his health. And don't think you can fool me and just pocket the money. I swear to you those bandits will find out that I meant to give it to them, and then they'll cut your throat. Got it?

JAILER *(takes the purse)*. What are you up to, Herostratus?

HEROSTRATUS. What am I up to? I'm proving to Cleon that I *do* understand my fellow-men . . .

Scene Two

A chamber in the palace of TISSAFERNES, *Ruler of Ephesus.*
TISSAFERNES *himself, dressed in a cloak of royal purple, is reclining on a wooden couch. At his side is a low table bearing fruit and wine. Nearby sits the* MAN OF THE THEATRE; TISSAFERNES *is greedily devouring a bunch of grapes.*

MAN OF THE THEATRE. Tissafernes, Ruler of Ephesus, Satrap of Persia – you seem worried.

TISSAFERNES. What makes you think so?

MAN OF THE THEATRE. I read it in the history books. Describing your character, the historians all mentioned that whenever you were nervous or worried you displayed a ravenous appetite.

TISSAFERNES. I've never noticed it myself. *(Shoves a handful of grapes into his mouth, then suddenly checks himself and spits them out again.)* Ugh! I can't even eat in peace. These chroniclers and poets slink around the palace spying on me for something to write about. This morning, for instance, my back started to itch, so I went over to a pillar and leaned against it, just to scratch my shoulder. I looked round – and there was some damned scribbler getting out his papyrus and preparing to write. How about that? It's no life, this – it's torture.

MAN OF THE THEATRE. I sympathise.

TISSAFERNES. I should have thrown them all out long ago, but it's a whim of my wife, Clementina. She's obsessed with the idea that we are fulfilling some great historic mission. Every

morning she wakes me up at crack of dawn by saying: 'Get
up, Tissafernes – history won't wait!' So because history won't
wait, I never get a proper night's sleep.

MAN OF THE THEATRE. But you are the Ruler of Ephesus.

TISSAFERNES. What is a Ruler compared to my wife? Especially
if you're old and she's young, you're a Persian and she's a
Greek. There are no bossier wives than Greek women. I don't
understand how Greek men manage to put up with them.
Socrates was the wisest man who ever lived, yet his wife did
nothing but make fun of him and insult him in public.
(*Greedily devours a handful of grapes.*)

MAN OF THE THEATRE. You are *very* worried.

TISSAFERNES. You'd be worried if people were perpetually
springing some nasty surprise on you. Don't forget that I'm
not a king, only a satrap. I have to obey the King of Persia, I
have to stay at peace with Sparta, maintain friendly contact
with Athens, keep an eye on the Thebans and be wary of
Macedonia – all at the same time. And then at a tense
moment like this, the temple of Artemis gets burnt down!
What is it – a plot, a conspiracy?

MAN OF THE THEATRE. That I don't know yet . . .

TISSAFERNES (*gloomily*). Life has worn me out, my dear fellow.
When I was young I was bold and fearless, I led my troops
into battle and the Greeks trembled at my very name . . .
Now I'm old, my physicians have forbidden me to get
excited or to eat too much . . . (*Crams a bunch of grapes into his
mouth.*)

MAN OF THE THEATRE. Cleon has come to see you.

TISSAFERNES (*joyfully*). At last! Let him in!

The MAN OF THE THEATRE *starts to go.*

No, stay here!

MAN OF THE THEATRE. Why?

TISSAFERNES. Do sit down, I beg you. You're not stupid . . .
and you can help me with your advice or you can remind me
of the sayings of the . . . the sages, the great philosophers . . .
I'm going to have to take an important decision.

The MAN OF THE THEATRE *sits down in a corner of the stage.*
Enter CLEON.

CLEON (*bowing respectfully*). Hail, O Tissafernes. The Archon of
Ephesus greets you.

TISSAFERNES. Greetings, Cleon. I've been waiting impatiently
for you to come. Have you been to the prison?

CLEON. Yes.

TISSAFERNES. Well, is it a conspiracy?

CLEON. No, Tissafernes. The temple was set on fire by one man
acting on his own.

TISSAFERNES. Praise be to the gods! One man – that's not so
bad. Who is this madman?

CLEON. A citizen of Ephesus – Herostratus, a former market
trader.

TISSAFERNES. A Greek?

CLEON. Yes.

TISSAFERNES. I thought so.

CLEON (*slightly offended*). What do you mean by that, Tissafernes?
He might equally well have been a Persian, a Scythian, an
Egyptian, or anyone you like.

TISSAFERNES. But he is a Greek.

CLEON. I'm a Greek too! And most of the inhabitants of
Ephesus are Greeks, but a whole people is not responsible
for the misdeeds of one scoundrel.

TISSAFERNES. Of course not, my dear and respected Cleon.
There's no need to get angry. I didn't mean to insult all
Greeks. I was merely certain that this arsonist was a Greek.
Ever since Ephesus became a Persian possession, I've been
expecting some Greek patriot to pull a trick of this kind.

CLEON. Greek patriotism was the last thing on Herostratus'
mind. If he had been a patriot, he would have set fire to the
barracks of the Persian garrison or tried to murder you.

TISSAFERNES (*still picking hungrily at a bunch of grapes*). You may be
right . . . But in that case, why did he do it?

CLEON. To immortalise his own name.

TISSAFERNES. What do you mean by that?

CLEON. A longing for fame and glory, vanity taken to the ultimate extreme.

TISSAFERNES. How funny . . .

CLEON. Not quite so funny as it might seem at first sight. There is a terrible, frightening urge behind what he did. It was an act of defiance of the world at large, Tissafernes.

TISSAFERNES. I still think it's funny. I've never heard anything like it in my life. Does he realise he'll be executed?

CLEON. The man is certainly in his right mind.

TISSAFERNES. Isn't he afraid of death?

CLEON. That's what I couldn't understand. When he was talking to me, his attitude was one of bold independence, almost arrogance. Herostratus described his crime with the rapture of a creative artist.

TISSAFERNES. Very interesting. You have aroused my curiosity, Cleon. (*Suddenly turns towards one of the pillars and shouts:*) Clementina, stop trying to hide behind that pillar! Come out and listen to what our friend Cleon has to say.

Enter CLEMENTINA *from behind a pillar, slightly embarrassed at being caught out.*

CLEON (*politely*). Greetings to the consort of Tissafernes.

CLEMENTINA. Greetings, Cleon. (*To* TISSAFERNES:) What made you think I was hiding? I was just passing through the room, and the lace of my sandal came undone.

TISSAFERNES. You have the most sensitive and intelligent sandals in the world, Clementina. They always untie themselves whenever something interesting is being discussed in the room.

CLEMENTINA. Are you accusing me of eavesdropping?

TISSAFERNES. I'm not accusing you, my beloved. I'm thanking you. When I know that whatever I say will reach your ears, I try to add some extra wisdom to my words . . . Well, what have you got to say about this fire?

CLEMENTINA. It is a terrible thing, but it seems to me that this arsonist is an intelligent man, and that it was not vanity that made him do it.

CLEON. But he confessed to me that his motive was vanity.

CLEMENTINA. You're the Chief Magistrate, Cleon, and an accused will never be wholly sincere in what he says to a judge.

TISSAFERNES. You think he had some other motive?

CLEMENTINA. Yes! I'm sure he did it because he was unhappy in love.

CLEON. I don't think so. Herostratus spoke of his former wife with nothing but contempt.

CLEMENTINA. What does his *wife* have to do with it? Men, my dear Cleon, do not burn down temples because of their wives. No, it's something else . . . It is a case of unrequited love driving a man to despair. Men like him will never admit it in court; it is a secret he will take with him to the grave. Somewhere on earth at this moment there is a woman weeping because she rejected the wretched Herostratus. She is tearing her hair and cursing the moment when she said 'no' to him. But in her heart of hearts she is glad and proud of herself . . . I envy her.

TISSAFERNES. You *envy* her?

CLEMENTINA. Of course. No one ever burnt down a temple for my sake.

TISSAFERNES. My wife should not envy anyone! Listen, Clementina – why haven't you ever told me you liked fires? I would have arranged one for you long ago.

CLEMENTINA. No, my dear Tissafernes. You might have burned down a house or two to please me, but you would never have gone to certain death just to impress me.

TISSAFERNES. Of course I wouldn't! If you love a woman, you don't want to make her a widow!

CLEON. I submit that your respected consort is wrong in her supposition, Tissafernes. She is too pure and elevated in her thoughts to comprehend the full vileness of this crime. She would like to think of Herostratus as a good but deluded man, whereas he is nothing but a self-obsessed maniac. If men are in the grip of a powerful love they *build* temples, they don't destroy them.

TISSAFERNES. Quite right! And therefore this evildoer will be executed tomorrow. (*Turns and whispers to the* MAN OF THE THEATRE.) This is where I need some suitable quotation . . .

MAN OF THE THEATRE. Will Sophocles do?

TISSAFERNES. Which line in particular?

MAN OF THE THEATRE. From *Oedipus Rex* . . . 'There is justice in this world that the gods have created: and evildoing brings retribution upon itself.'

TISSAFERNES. Excellent! (*Aloud:*) There is justice in this world that the gods have created: and evildoing brings retribution upon itself.

CLEON (*bowing*). Wisdom itself speaks from your lips, O Ruler.

CLEMENTINA. We must call the chroniclers and tell them to inscribe that sentence in the palace records.

TISSAFERNES. Unfortunately I didn't make it up, Clementina. It's from Sophocles.

CLEMENTINA. Don't be so modest, my dear. Sophocles just happened to guess what you were going to say.

TISSAFERNES. Well, perhaps he did . . .

MAN OF THE THEATRE. Tissafernes, the priestess of the temple of Artemis, Erita, has come to see you.

TISSAFERNES. Ah, the wretched victim of the fire . . . Let her come in.

CLEON. Shall we leave you, O Ruler?

TISSAFERNES. No. I always find it agonising to talk to that woman alone. Now she'll start tearing her hair and throwing a fit of hysterics. To be honest, I'm afraid of her.

CLEMENTINA. The Ruler of Ephesus has no need to fear anyone!

TISSAFERNES. Yes, I know, but that woman is closer to the gods than we are . . .

Enter ERITA, *dressed in black mourning garments.* TISSAFERNES *shows his great respect for her by rising from his couch and walking forwards to greet her.*

Hail, Erita! The Ruler of Ephesus greets you and grieves with you.

CLEON. Hail, Erita! Please accept my profoundest sympathy.

CLEMENTINA. Your grief is our grief, Erita.

ERITA. The temple of Artemis is no more! The huntress-goddess of field and forest has no dwelling! Woe is me, faithful servant of Artemis, that I did not save her house from destruction! Why did I not die? Why did the fire spare me?! Why did not the walls of the temple fall on me and crush my grey head? I must scratch out my own eyes so that I may never again see that terrible heap of ashes and rubble . . . (*In a paroxysm of religious ecstasy, she starts to claw her face.*)

TISSAFERNES (*restraining* ERITA). Oh no, no! . . . Calm yourself, revered priestess! Why hurt yourself still more? You are our intercessor – through your lips alone will the goddess listen to our prayers begging for her forgiveness.

ERITA. I dare not pray to the goddess. I am guilty of letting a robber into her house.

TISSAFERNES. How were you to know he was a robber, Erita? You trustingly assumed it was a good man coming to worship at her altar.

ERITA (*hysterically*). May the thunderbolts of Zeus strike the accursed human race that begat the evildoer!

CLEON. Why invoke the wrath of the gods upon all mankind, Erita? We are not the guilty ones!

TISSAFERNES. No, Cleon, all of us are indeed guilty and we must redeem our fault. I shall impose a tax on all the inhabitants of Ephesus in aid of the stricken goddess and her priesthood. And the vile criminal himself will be executed tomorrow on the city square.

CLEON. So be it!

TISSAFERNES. Our only task is to devise the most terrible form of execution. Which do you think is more suitable, Cleon – Flogging to death or the noose?

CLEON. The court will decide that tomorrow, O Ruler. But I would prefer not to make the execution into a public spectacle. A large crowd of people will only flatter Herostratus' vanity. He longs for a spectacular death, but he shall not have it: his trial and punishment must be no more conspicuous than those of a petty swindler . . .

TISSAFERNES. You're right. I have already issued a decree: 'All people of Ephesus are to forget Herostratus for ever!' This decree will be engraved on a marble tablet and hung in the city square.

CLEON. Which will thereby immortalise the name of the criminal. *No*, Tissafernes, no such decrees are needed; people themselves will erase his name from their memories . . .

TISSAFERNES (*embarrassed*). Ah, yes – I suppose you're right . . . I hadn't thought of that. (*Whispers to the* MAN OF THE THEATRE.) This Cleon is always correcting me and making me look stupid. Quick, give me something impressive to say . . .

MAN OF THE THEATRE. There's a line from Euripides: 'Power is given to the mighty of this world that justice may prevail among men.'

TISSAFERNES. It's rather pompous, but still . . . (*Aloud:*) 'Power is given to the mighty of this world that justice may prevail among men.' So said Euripides, and so shall I do. (*In a solemn tone:*) Cleon, Archon of Ephesus, I command you to begin the trial of Herostratus tomorrow.

ERITA. O Ruler of Ephesus, I have come to request a postponement of the trial.

TISSAFERNES. What?!

ERITA. In the name of all the priests and servants of the temple . . . (*Weeps.*) Of the former temple . . . (*Firmly:*) In the name of all the servants of the goddess Artemis of the Ephesians, I request that the trial of Herostratus be postponed.

TISSAFERNES. May I ask why?

ERITA. When Actaeon the hunter chanced to see the goddess naked, the Divine One in her anger turned Actaeon into a deer and he was torn to pieces by his own hounds.

TISSAFERNES. I have heard that legend. What of it?

ERITA. The goddess herself will punish Herostratus. And it will be such a punishment that we, weak mortals that we are, could never devise.

CLEON. That's impossible. The people are demanding that Herostratus be executed immediately.

ERITA. The people are stupid – the goddess is wise.

CLEON. But Herostratus has brought grief and shame upon the people!

ERITA. Herostratus has, above all, offended the goddess. She is powerful enough to wreak her own vengeance on the blasphemer.

TISSAFERNES. We do not doubt the might of the goddess, Erita, but you must realise that there is such a thing as the *law* . . .

ERITA. Kings govern the laws, but the gods govern kings. Do not forget that, Tissafernes.

CLEON. Forgive such an audacious thought, Erita, but does it not seem strange to you that the all-powerful goddess did not prevent Herostratus from burning down her temple? Where was her anger when that scoundrel was smearing the walls with pitch? Why did she not strike him down with an arrow from her sacred bow? Or was she otherwise occupied, and failed to notice the criminal?

ERITA. That is blasphemy, Cleon! It is not for mortals to descry the thoughts of the gods. Perhaps they are trying us, to see how we respond to such an unheard-of catastrophe.

CLEON. All the more reason for us to strive to come out of this test with honour. When they created human beings, the gods endowed them with reason and a conscience: both reason and conscience demand that this felon be tried.

ERITA. I am not asking for the trial to be cancelled, only that it be postponed. Two hours ago one of our priests left Ephesus to go to the Delphic Oracle. Let the oracle consult the gods concerning the fate of Herostratus and tell us what is their will.

CLEON. But it's a ten-day journey to Delphi! Ten days there and ten days back – or longer if the winds aren't favourable. That means we cannot convene the court for a whole month. (*To* TISSAFERNES:) O Ruler, in the name of the people's assembly of Ephesus and of all the city's inhabitants, I demand the immediate trial and punishment of this criminal!

ERITA (*to* TISSAFERNES). O Ruler – in the name of the priesthood of Artemis, I demand a postponement!

CLEON. Do not rouse the people's anger, Tissafernes!

ERITA. Do not offend the gods, O Ruler!

CLEON. Herostratus is a terrible man, Tissafernes. He is cunning, determined and unscrupulous.

ERITA. The Ephesians have nothing to fear as long as they are under the protection of Olympus.

TISSAFERNES. Quiet! Don't press me. (*Gobbles a bunch of grapes.*) Clementina, you haven't said anything. Advise me!

CLEMENTINA. You've made your decision, Tissafernes. You must keep to your word.

ERITA (*sharply*). It is not for the ruler to ask advice of a woman.

CLEMENTINA (*equally sharply*). It is not for a woman to interfere when a husband is seeking his wife's advice!

TISSAFERNES. Stop it! I must think. (*Pensively chews a grape.*)

CLEMENTINA (*quietly, to the* MAN OF THE THEATRE). Have you seen Herostratus?

MAN OF THE THEATRE. Yes.

CLEMENTINA. Is he handsome?

MAN OF THE THEATRE. Let's say he's good-looking.

CLEMENTINA. Is he young?

MAN OF THE THEATRE. Yes. Why should that interest you?

CLEMENTINA. Oh, just the usual female curiosity . . .

CLEON (*to* TISSAFERNES). What have you decided, O Ruler?

TISSAFERNES. I have decided the matter by the vote. For a postponement – Erita; for an immediate trial and execution – Cleon and Clementina.

ERITA. And you?

TISSAFERNES. I abstain. Therefore – trial and execution it is.

CLEMENTINA. Wait, Tissafernes. I have changed my mind. Perhaps it really would be a good idea to delay the trial.

CLEON. What does this mean, Clementina? Does each passing minute suggest to you some new decision?

ERITA. Have the gods made you see reason, Clementina?

CLEMENTINA. I think we should order a further investigation into this case. Cleon's version has not convinced me.

CLEON. The people elected me their Chief Magistrate, and I have never once dishonoured that office . . .

TISSAFERNES. Now, now, Cleon – my wife didn't mean to offend you . . .

CLEMENTINA. I greatly admire the Archon's public spirit and integrity, but even he can be mistaken. I think Herostratus should be questioned further.

TISSAFERNES. The situation has changed: for immediate trial and execution – one vote, against it – two. Therefore it will be postponed.

CLEON. Tissafernes, I beg you not to make a hasty decision. The laws of Ephesus will be threatened and undermined if due process is arbitrarily delayed.

MAN OF THE THEATRE. Stop, Tissafernes! Listen to me, because the moment has come for me to offer you my advice, not literary quotations. Herostratus must be tried at once. Delay would be dangerous. Evil that goes unpunished quickly gathers weight and momentum like a snowball, and could turn into an avalanche. Your city may pay dearly for the indecisiveness of its Ruler . . .

Noise and shouting are heard from outside the palace walls.

Do you hear? That sound is Ephesus in turmoil. The people await your word, Tissafernes!

TISSAFERNES (*angrily*). That's enough! I'm tired, and I've eaten all the grapes . . . You've all done nothing but confuse me. We will take a final vote.

CLEON. Execution!

ERITA. Postponement!

MAN OF THE THEATRE. Execution!

CLEMENTINA. Postponement!

ALL (*to* TISSAFERNES). How do you vote, Tissafernes?

The noise of the crowd outside grows louder.

TISSAFERNES (*wincing, as though from toothache*). What a noise they're making.

CLEON. The people demand to know your decision, O Ruler.

TISSAFERNES. I've made my decision: shut the window! (*Takes his wife's arm and leaves the room at a slow and stately pace.*)

Scene Three

The prison cell of Scene One, occupied by HEROSTRATUS. *From off-stage come approaching sounds of muttering, unsteady footsteps and drunken singing. After some fumbling with the bolt, the* JAILER *flings open the door and staggers into the cell.*

HEROSTRATUS. At last . . ! Well, you tortoise, for that much money you might have run a bit faster. And I see you've been pouring libations to Dionysios, too!

JAILER. Yes, Herostratus, I've been drinking – I've been drinking and I won't hide it . . . When I'm reduced to running errands for a man like you, it's shameful to be sober. I have to drink to keep my conscience quiet . . .

HEROSTRATUS. And has your conscience stopped troubling you now?

JAILER. It's bothering me a bit, but not so much as before . . . If it wasn't for the starvation wages they pay me, I'd never take a single drachma off such a . . . such a . . .

HEROSTRATUS. Remember – I paid you not to insult me.

JAILER. All right . . . I won't say it, Herostratus, though I'm longing to call you a bastard.

HEROSTRATUS. Did you do all I asked you to do?

JAILER. I did.

HEROSTRATUS. Well, tell me what happened.

JAILER. When I got to Dionysios' tavern, all the riff-raff of Ephesus was there to the last man. They were made up of two sorts: one sort was wanting simply to get drunk, the others wanted the hair of the dog to get rid of last night's hangovers. But neither lot had a drachma to their name . . . and then I came in! When they saw my purse, they thought Dionysios himself had sent me, but I didn't pretend the money was mine . . . I said it was yours. That got them all worked up, and they started cursing you . . . Shall I tell you all the names they called you?

HEROSTRATUS. No! Go on with your story.

JAILER. Pity! You'd have learned some really juicy new words . . . Well, then they began wondering what to do with the money. Some were for throwing it down the piss-hole, others said it was a pity to waste good money, wherever it came from, and it ought to be spent on drink – and luckily there were more of them who thought that. So we drank and talked about you.

HEROSTRATUS. What did you all say?

JAILER. Of course we all agreed you were a swine and a villain, but we thought there must be a bit of decency in you, because although you would soon be dead you still gave a thought to the poor and thirsty . . .

HEROSTRATUS. Did no one call me a fine fellow?

JAILER. We hadn't drunk enough for that, Herostratus.

HEROSTRATUS. No matter. If fate is kind to me, you may have another chance of a few free drinks. Then, I hope, you will call me a fine fellow, won't you?

JAILER. It's quite possible. Will you have any money, though?

HEROSTRATUS. I certainly will.

JAILER. I believe you. You must be a resourceful lad, judging by the way you squeezed a bagful of silver out of old Chrysippus. But the best thing is – I can now make some money out of you, too. There are some people at the prison gates who are ready to pay me to come and have a look at you . . .

HEROSTRATUS. Is that so? Well, I don't mind. It means that

people are getting interested in me. Good . . ! Who are these people?

JAILER. A few tradesmen, a stonemason, an artist called Varnatius who paints vases, and a woman.

HEROSTRATUS. Aha – I'm obviously becoming quite an attraction . . . Let's start with the woman – what's she like?

JAILER. Hard to say. She's covered her face.

HEROSTRATUS. Let her in first of all!

JAILER (*obediently*). Very good, I will. (*Remembering himself.*) Are you giving me orders, you bastard?

HEROSTRATUS. So what? I pay you well enough, don't I?

JAILER (*leaving the cell*). Gods, why didn't you tell the judge to raise my wages? . . . It's terrible, having to sell myself for your money.

Exit JAILER, *who reappears after a short while escorting* CLEMENTINA; *she is wearing a black cloak, her face hidden in a shawl.*

JAILER. There, woman, is the criminal you wanted to see.

CLEMENTINA. Thank you, jailer. (*Gives him money.*) May I speak to him alone?

JAILER (*counting the money*). . . . four, five, six . . . Yes. Go ahead. Only don't be long, other people want to see him too. (*Exit.*)

HEROSTRATUS. What has brought you here, woman?

CLEMENTINA. Curiosity.

HEROSTRATUS. Well, that's not a bad reason. If there weren't any inquisitive people, life would be much duller. What is it about me that interests you?

CLEMENTINA. Everything.

HEROSTRATUS. And what do you think of me?

CLEMENTINA. You're handsome – and you're tall.

HEROSTRATUS. Why should I be short? People are strange – for some reason they think a man who burns down a temple is bound to be small and ugly. Cleon imagined I would have a pimply face, while you thought I must be a dwarf – isn't that so?

CLEMENTINA. Everyone is saying that you destroyed the temple out of vanity. I don't believe it. I think there was another reason.

HEROSTRATUS. What can be sweeter than fame and glory? Fame is more powerful than all the gods – it can give you immortality.

CLEMENTINA. I agree. But there is one emotion no less powerful than fame.

HEROSTRATUS. What is that?

CLEMENTINA. Love.

HEROSTRATUS. Love? You're mistaken . . . Love can humiliate a man, but fame – never.

CLEMENTINA. Even if that fame is won by doing evil?

HEROSTRATUS. Even then. Who built the temple of Artemis? . . . Well? . . . Don't bother to rack your brains; you've certainly forgotten the name of the architect. But you will always remember the name of Herostratus. Now do you see how fame can make a man immortal overnight?

CLEMENTINA. Still, I had hoped that this wasn't the motive for what you did. I thought there was a woman in Ephesus for whose love you lit that bonfire.

HEROSTRATUS (*laughs*). How naive! All the women in Ephesus aren't worth setting fire to a chicken-coop!

CLEMENTINA. Come here.

HEROSTRATUS. Why should I?

CLEMENTINA. Come here!

HEROSTRATUS *goes up to* CLEMENTINA, *who gives him a resounding slap in the face.*

HEROSTRATUS. Well, now! I can pay that back with interest. (*Threatens* CLEMENTINA.) I've had enough troubles in my life. I could have done without a slap in the face . . .

CLEMENTINA. That was for all the women in Ephesus, you pathetic nonentity! (*Takes off her shawl.*)

HEROSTRATUS. Clementina! (*Laughs nervously.*) Well done, Herostratus! The wife of the ruler of Ephesus comes to you for an assignation!

CLEMENTINA (*angrily*). Our meeting is over, Herostratus. Your conversation bores me.

HEROSTRATUS. Why? In what way have I disappointed you, Clementina?

CLEMENTINA. One can be a slave, yet think like a king – but you, Herostratus, are a small shopkeeper and you think like a small shopkeeper.

HEROSTRATUS. I don't understand.

CLEMENTINA. And you never will! Your parents endowed you with a narrow, petty little mind. I don't believe you set fire to the temple on purpose at all. I've no doubt you started the fire by accident when you were drunk. That's the truth, isn't it? Admit it!

HEROSTRATUS. I don't understand what you want of me . . .

CLEMENTINA (*pacing nervously up and down the cell*). He's just a little nobody. I imagined him as a hero with a stout heart, passionate feelings and great ideas, but he is just a . . . a worm . . . You lived like a worm, Herostratus, and you'll die like a worm! Cleon was right: my mind is above being able to understand such pettiness . . .

HEROSTRATUS. Wait, wait, Clementina. I can't see what you're driving at . . . Let me think for a moment . . . (*Pause.*) Oh, I see it all! But of course! What a fool I am! (*Laughs.*) It's obvious. (*Goes up to* CLEMENTINA, *puts his hand on his heart.*) I love you, Clementina!

CLEMENTINA. You're lying, you wretch!

HEROSTRATUS. Of course, I'm lying, but that was what you wanted to hear, wasn't it? That I set fire to the temple out of hopeless love for you?

CLEMENTINA (*embarrassed*). Well, not necessarily for me . . . I thought there must be some woman who . . .

HEROSTRATUS. Don't bother playing games any more, Clementina. You can forget all the other women – everybody knows you're the most desirable woman in Ephesus. Artists

paint your portrait, poets write odes to you. A thousand
young men weep into their pillows every night dreaming of
you . . . Suddenly a terrible thing happens – the temple of
Artemis is burnt down! Why? Because some man is unhappy
in love. Love? Who is he in love with? Admit it, Clementina
– you were afraid you had a rival. Can there be a woman in
Ephesus whom a man could love more than you? You came
to me to find that out, didn't you?

CLEMENTINA. Let's suppose I did. But now I see I was wrong.

HEROSTRATUS. And has that set your mind at rest? I don't
think so! Your vanity is as great as mine. You long to go
down in history as the woman for whose sake men were
ready to face certain death . . . (*In a whisper:*) Do you know
why I set fire to the temple, Clementina? Because I think you
are more beautiful than the goddess Artemis herself!

CLEMENTINA (*frightened*). Be quiet, Herostratus – you will call
down the wrath of the gods upon me!

HEROSTRATUS. Don't be afraid, Clementina. It is I who have
aroused their anger and *I* will answer for it. Your lot will be
only the fame of having inspired me . . . Who is Artemis,
after all? The cruel-hearted goddess of the chase. She runs
through the forest with her pack of hunting-dogs, shoots
from her bow and hides herself from the gaze of mortal
men. She is incapable of love, poor thing that she is. Why do
people build temples to her? Why do they bring tribute and
make sacrifices to her? As a woman, she's not worth your
little finger . . .

CLEMENTINA. Stop it! You're making me faint with terror at
your blasphemy!

HEROSTRATUS. No I'm not, Clementina – you're enjoying it. I
can see it and sense it: the blood has rushed to your face and
you're dizzy with excitement. Just think: the years will pass,
your skin will wrinkle, your hair will turn grey, but people
will still look at you and say: 'There is the woman who
outshone a goddess in beauty. She was loved as no other
woman on earth was loved . . .' Poems and plays will be
written about you. The best actresses in the world will make
up their faces to look like yours, and your very name –
Clementina – will become a symbol of beauty and greatness.
An enviable fate, I would say.

CLEMENTINA. What do you want, Herostratus?

HEROSTRATUS. Tomorrow, when I am taken out to be
executed, I shall shout the name of Clementina for all to
hear. I shall say that I fell in love with you and, knowing my
love could never be returned, I hurled defiance at the gods.
I shall say that no Greek should dare to bow down before a
mythical figure like Artemis when there lives and breathes
among us such a real, flesh-and-blood marvel as you. May I
say that?

CLEMENTINA (*thrilled and aroused, huskily*). You may.

HEROSTRATUS (*briskly*). Right, that's agreed then. We have the
makings of a deal. What is your price?

CLEMENTINA. Price? What price?

HEROSTRATUS. I am paying for my fame with my life. What
will you pay me?

CLEMENTINA. I will pay you with gold.

HEROSTRATUS. What use is gold to me? Condemned men lose
interest in mere money.

CLEMENTINA. What do you want instead? To escape?

HEROSTRATUS. If I escape, who will set you on the path to
immortality?

CLEMENTINA. I'm confused – I don't see what you want.

HEROSTRATUS. You said just now that there is one emotion no
less powerful than fame: love. I have always been mistrustful
of love, but perhaps I was wrong to do so. (*Firmly:*) I want to
make love to you, Clementina!

CLEMENTINA (*shocked*). What?! Have you gone out of your
mind?

HEROSTRATUS. Possibly. But that's my price.

CLEMENTINA. You fool! I am the consort of the Ruler of
Ephesus and you talk to me as if I were a common
prostitute!

HEROSTRATUS (*in an affected tone of false, servile contrition*).
Oh forgive me, my lady, I didn't mean to offend your noble
person. I've lived all my life among rough, common folk, so
how could I have learned good manners? After all, I'm only

a bankrupt shopkeeper, my lady, and as you have so rightly remarked, I think like a shopkeeper. I thought that since I was being bought, I could name my price.

CLEMENTINA. Stop it . . ! Be sensible, Herostratus. Don't forget that I am the wife of Tissafernes and I have a great deal of influence over him. Do you want me to make him postpone your execution?

HEROSTRATUS. Yes, I do – but I want to make love to you into the bargain. A postponement can only prolong my waiting for a few extra days, but to have made love to you will make the agony bearable.

CLEMENTINA. What can making love to me mean to you? Half an hour ago you weren't even thinking about me; I might not have existed for all you cared.

HEROSTRATUS. I fell in love with you at first sight.

CLEMENTINA. Liar! You've thought up some plan and you're just pretending to love me.

HEROSTRATUS. I'm not pretending, Clementina, I'm simply throwing myself into a new role. Tomorrow the whole city will learn that I'm a man driven mad by love for you – let me believe that, too. Make love to me, Clementina.

CLEMENTINA. A prison cell is hardly the place for making love.

HEROSTRATUS. It's not my fault that criminals aren't given separate bedrooms!

The MAN OF THE THEATRE *gets up from where he has been sitting and approaches* CLEMENTINA.

MAN OF THE THEATRE. Forgive me, Clementina, but I must speak. I can see you're beginning to give in to Herostratus. Be firm, I beg of you. He's nothing but a blackmailer. Who knows how he may exploit your favours to him?

HEROSTRATUS (*angrily*). You promised not to interfere!

CLEMENTINA (*to the* MAN OF THE THEATRE). But I want him to cry my name aloud before he is executed! Am I not worthy of that?

MAN OF THE THEATRE. That's not for me to judge, Clementina. Your beauty is incessantly praised by poets and chroniclers – why do you need to stoop to deception?

HEROSTRATUS. Remember, Clementina – I can always name some *other* woman on the scaffold . . .

CLEMENTINA (*alarmed*). *Another* woman?

HEROSTRATUS. Do you suppose there aren't enough prominent women in Ephesus who would like to be glorified in this way?

CLEMENTINA. You wouldn't dare!

HEROSTRATUS. Look at me, Clementina . . . Is there *anything* I wouldn't do if driven to it?

MAN OF THE THEATRE. Clementina, don't be crazy! You're a woman of nobility and dignity. You can't buy true fame at *that* sort of price . . .

CLEMENTINA. And what if I like him? What if I've almost fallen in love with him?

HEROSTRATUS. Well said, Clementina!

MAN OF THE THEATRE. You – in love? You've fallen in love with Herostratus? (*Glumly:*) In that case, go ahead – do what you like . . .

Enter JAILER

JAILER. Time's up! You've had your little talk. There are other people waiting outside . . . (*Recognises* CLEMENTINA.) O gods! Can it be? Am I seeing things?

CLEMENTINA. You see nothing, jailer.

JAILER. But I see you, my lady!

CLEMENTINA (*imperiously*). No, you see nothing, jailer. And if you don't keep your mouth shut, you'll pay for it with your head. Understood?

JAILER (*terrified*). I understand, my lady.

CLEMENTINA. Then get out! (*To the* MAN OF THE THEATRE:) And you get out too! I'm bored with your moral lectures.

Exit JAILER

HEROSTRATUS (*embraces and kisses* CLEMENTINA, *then turns to the* MAN OF THE THEATRE). You heard what she said! Well, what are you hanging around for? Snuff the candles and get out! (*As* CLEMENTINA *starts to undress,*

HEROSTRATUS *points to the audience.*) And tell them to get out too!

MAN OF THE THEATRE (*extinguishes the candelabrum, comes forward and says sadly to the audience*). I am obliged to announce that there will now be an interval!

PART TWO

Scene One

The MAN OF THE THEATRE *appears on the fore-stage.*

MAN OF THE THEATRE. How simple it is, when one turns over
the pages of history, to order all the dates and events into
their proper sequence and to explain who was right and who
was wrong. Everything seems so clear-cut and
comprehensible. But it is salutary to stop for a minute or two
and turn oneself into a contemporary of those past events,
because then you realise at once how much more tangled
and complicated everything really was . . .

For twenty days the heap of ashes has been glowing in the
heart of the city of Ephesus; for twenty days Herostratus, the
self-confessed arsonist, has been allowed to stay alive. How
has that happened?

*The lights go up on stage to reveal a courtroom. In one corner, behind a
low barrier, are the rows of benches for the jury.* CLEON *is seated in
a throne-like chair on a raised central dais.*

We are now in the city courtroom of Ephesus. On the days
when the court is in session, the public seats are full of
people, passions rage, plaintiff and defendant vie with one
another in eloquence, while the impartial judge and jurors
hear them out before casting a black or a white stone into the
urn. Where is your black stone, Cleon?

Noise of a crowd off-stage. The door is flung open and two CITIZENS
drag the THIRD CITIZEN *into the courtroom. His hands are bound,
his tunic torn, his face and arms bruised.*

CLEON. What has happened, citizens?

FIRST CITIZEN (*pointing to* THIRD CITIZEN). This man was
trying to set fire to the municipal theatre.

SECOND CITIZEN. We caught him just as he was smearing the walls with pitch.

THIRD CITIZEN. Untie my hands, you fools! Idiots! You're going to regret this! When the hour strikes, we'll slit your throats!

CLEON (*gazing intently at the* THIRD CITIZEN). I've seen you somewhere before. Wasn't it you who broke into Herostratus' prison cell twenty days ago?

FIRST CITIZEN. Yes, he was with us.

THIRD CITIZEN. I was a fool! Herostratus is a son of the gods! He'll soon come out and join us, and we'll rip Ephesus apart like slitting open an old pillow. We'll set up a new order of things here! And *you* will be dancing on a roasting-griddle over the great bonfire that we're going to light in the city square . . .

CLEON. You will be executed tomorrow!

THIRD CITIZEN. Save your breath, Cleon – no one believes your threats any more. You said the same thing to Herostratus on the day after he burned down the temple. But what can you do, feeble mortal, against a demigod? Long live Herostratus!

CLEON (*to* FIRST CITIZEN). Take him away. Put him in prison under an armed guard of soldiers from the garrison. His trial is hereby set for tomorrow.

THIRD CITIZEN. Do you think you'll live that long, Archon?

FIRST CITIZEN *leads* THIRD CITIZEN *out.*

SECOND CITIZEN (*approaches* CLEON). Listen, Cleon . . .

CLEON (*interrupting*). I know what you're going to say, stonemason: I didn't keep my word. But it is not my fault. Although I am Chief Magistrate, Tissafernes rules the city and he has ordered that the trial of Herostratus shall not take place until the envoy returns from Delphi. We must have patience and wait.

SECOND CITIZEN. We know all that, Archon. I have come with a request: please give orders admitting me to the prison to see Herostratus . . .

CLEON. Your plan is not approved, stonemason. Under the laws of Ephesus, whoever kills a criminal before execution will himself be executed.

SECOND CITIZEN. I know that, but I still beg you: order them to let me in!

CLEON. No!

SECOND CITIZEN. I alone will be responsible.

CLEON (*firmly*). No! The law must be observed . . .

SECOND CITIZEN. Has Herostratus observed our laws? He acts, and we wait. When we come to our senses, I fear it may be too late.

CLEON. Herostratus is in prison, under secure guard. How then can he act?

SECOND CITIZEN. Every day all the rogues of Ephesus get drunk at Dionysios' tavern on Herostratus' money . . .

CLEON. I shall order them to be dispersed from there with whips!

SECOND CITIZEN. They'll go somewhere else. There are many of them, Archon. They do nothing but drink and sing the praises of their benefactor, Herostratus. Yesterday in the market a fortune-telling woman shouted that Herostratus was the son of Zeus, and many people took her seriously, believing she was inspired by the gods.

CLEON. I shall have that fortune-teller arrested . . .

SECOND CITIZEN. Even if you do, Archon, you are still being hoodwinked. Herostratus is taking action – by bribery and simply by staying alive . . . Order them to let me into the prison!

CLEON. No! Don't try to persuade me, stonemason. I will not change my decision.

SECOND CITIZEN. Very well, then . . . But consult your conscience, Archon, and if you change your mind, send for me. I shall be ready . . . (*Exit.*)

MAN OF THE THEATRE. I had no idea that events in Ephesus would move so fast . . .

CLEON. Twenty days have passed since the fire. That's not very long.

MAN OF THE THEATRE. Who are they, these supporters of Herostratus?

CLEON. They can hardly be called supporters. Wretched, insignificant people who are attracted by Herostratus' impudence . . . You've just seen one of them – that pathetic barber. He read something that Herostratus had written and decided that he could get away with the same thing . . .

MAN OF THE THEATRE. Have you read that papyrus written by Herostratus?

CLEON. Of course. The court has to know everything about the accused.

MAN OF THE THEATRE. Did it contain some kind of political programme?

CLEON (*contemptuously*). No. Herostratus is no thinker and no politician. He's a semi-literate man who never finished his schooling, but thinks he's a superman. (*Quotes:*)
    'Do what you will, fearing neither the gods nor mankind!
    Thus will you gain for yourself everlasting glory and
        honour!'
That is all the political theory he has managed to think up.

MAN OF THE THEATRE (*repeats thoughtfully*). 'Do what you will, fearing neither the gods nor mankind . . .' Don't dismiss those words too lightly, Cleon. They contain a terrible, magnetic force. Believe me, I've lived slightly over two thousand years longer than you have, and I've seen how semi-literates like him have been able to turn the heads of millions. You are witnessing the birth of a disease that in time will bring disaster to the whole human race. My generation paid with its blood to save the world from this very plague.

CLEON. I don't know . . . I'm not a historian and not a prophet. I'm an ordinary human being and I live in the present. I'm not responsible for what may happen in a thousand years' time.

MAN OF THE THEATRE. Don't talk like that, Cleon. Every person bears some responsibility for what happens in their time and after them – and how much the more so if they are endowed with power and authority.

CLEON. Why did you have to come to us at this time? In the future, where you come from, surely people don't just remember Ephesus because of Herostratus, do they? Ephesus is a beautiful and prosperous city, inhabited by good, law-abiding citizens, whereas that abominable man is an exception . . . He is a freak phenomenon in the long and honourable life of this city, like snow in summer, like a drought in mid-winter. I rack my brains trying to think how to blot out the memory of him. It must all be forgotten – the hour of his birth and the day of his death . . . Curse him! He never existed!

MAN OF THE THEATRE. That is your chief miscalculation, Cleon. He was born; he does exist; and unfortunately he will be born again . . . You see, Cleon, in that distant future in which I live, the world will be a prey to many problems. Wars will be fought and cities built, men will fly to the moon and dive to the bottom of the ocean. But from time to time *he* will appear on earth again – a reincarnation of Herostratus. Once more he will proclaim: 'Do what you will, fearing neither the gods nor mankind!' And all over the planet fires will rage, blood will flow and the innocent will perish. And people will ask in bewilderment: 'Where has this scourge come from?' Yet it has an ancestry going back over two thousand years! And it began here – in Ephesus. That is why I have come to you, Archon. That is why I say to you: 'Do not try to lull your memory asleep by consigning this man to oblivion. Arm it instead with anger, for memory is man's best weapon against evil!'

CLEON (*despondently*). I was not made to be a fighter. I am a bad warrior, but an honest judge. I have never killed anyone, I have served the law – and that is why my name is respected in Ephesus . . . But now I have taken to carrying this knife . . . (*Produces a sheath-knife from the folds of his robe.*) If the messenger from Delphi brings news that Herostratus is to be freed, if the gods pardon his felony, then I shall take leave of this life . . .

MAN OF THE THEATRE. That will solve nothing, Archon! Give me that knife. People need you – alive!

CLEON. What meaning has a judge's life if lawlessness rules in the city?

MAN OF THE THEATRE. Even so – give me the knife.

CLEON (*hands over the knife*). Take it . . . It was only an impulse in a moment of despair.

MAN OF THE THEATRE. Have courage, Cleon. Truth and right are on your side.

CLEON. If only you knew how hard it is to get at the truth. Everyone seems to be conspiring to prevent justice being done. (*Suddenly, angrily and resolutely:*) But as long as I am alive, I am the judge! (*Shouts:*) Jailer! Come forward! (*To the* MAN OF THE THEATRE:) I swear this rogue is finally going to tell me the truth!

Enter JAILER

JAILER. Did you call me, O godlike Archon?

CLEON. Yes. But this will be our final talk. If you imagine you can play me up as you did last time, I shall order you to be put in irons and subjected to torture.

JAILER. Why are you angry with me, Cleon? I haven't told you one word of a lie. Would I dare to deceive a man like you?

CLEON. Be quiet! Answer my questions . . . You have been entrusted with the task of guarding a dangerous criminal; are you carrying out this duty honestly and in accordance with your instructions?

JAILER. I never take my eyes off the brute. Day and night I watch his every movement.

CLEON. In that case, how was he able to acquire a considerable sum of money? Why is it that copies of a papyrus written by him are circulating in the city?

JAILER. I don't know, Cleon. How can a mere jailer know about such things?

CLEON. Who has been to see Herostratus?

JAILER. You have.

CLEON. Don't try and play the idiot! I know I have. Who *else* has visited Herostratus in prison?

JAILER. No one, Archon – I swear it by the shades of my ancestors. I wouldn't let so much as a fly into his cell . . .

CLEON. You won't tell me? Very well; when I have you put on the rack, you will tell me.

JAILER *(falling to his knees)*. Spare me, Cleon!

CLEON. Then who else came to see Herostratus?

JAILER. Chrysippus the money-lender.

CLEON. I thought so. Who else?

JAILER. No one else.

CLEON. Don't lie! Remember – this is your last chance to avoid torture.

JAILER. I dare not tell even you, Cleon.

CLEON. In other words, you have decided to choose torture.

JAILER *(in despair)*. Have mercy on me, great and good Archon! If I don't tell you who else came to see Herostratus, torture awaits me. If I tell you – death awaits me! What is a wretched jailer to do?

CLEMENTINA *enters the courtroom, having heard the* JAILER's *last remark.*

CLEMENTINA. This man is in a truly difficult position, Cleon. One can sympathise with him . . .

CLEON *(getting up to greet her)*. The consort of the Ruler of Ephesus does this court a great honour by her visit.

CLEMENTINA. I was passing by and thought I would find out what progress has been made in the investigation of the case of Herostratus. *(Pointing to the* JAILER:) Who is this man?

CLEON. The jailer who is guarding Herostratus. However, it seems that the city has been paying him his wages for nothing. Thanks to him, several unauthorised persons have already gained access to Herostratus' cell, and among them, apparently, is a certain prominent personage . . .

CLEMENTINA. Have you discovered the name of that personage?

CLEON. Not yet.

CLEMENTINA. Do you expect to find it out?

CLEON. Of course. Under torture. He will tell me everything . . .

JAILER *(terrified, to* CLEMENTINA). No, my lady! No! I will never tell her name, even if they tear me to pieces!! Have no fear, Clementina!

CLEMENTINA *(hisses, to* JAILER). You fool!!

Awkward pause.

You can release this man, Cleon. You have learned what you wanted to know.

CLEON *(staring thoughtfully at* CLEMENTINA). Yes, I think I have. *(To* JAILER:) You may go!

JAILER *starts to go.*

No, wait. Stay in the small ante-chamber outside the door; you will be under guard. I may still have need of you.

Exit JAILER.

So, Clementina, why did you go to see Herostratus?

CLEMENTINA. Am I now being formally questioned?

CLEON. Yes.

CLEMENTINA. Are you sure you have the right to interrogate the wife of the Ruler of Ephesus?

CLEON. The consort of the Ruler is a citizeness of Ephesus and is subject to all the laws of the city.

CLEMENTINA *(angrily)*. I warn you, Cleon – it will do you no good to make an enemy of me . . . *(Smiles)* I am used to being addressed with servility.

CLEON. I shall try to be servile, my lady . . . Why, O gracious one, did you visit Herostratus?

CLEMENTINA. Out of curiosity.

CLEON. Did your husband know about it?

CLEMENTINA. That is none of your business!

CLEON. Everything concerning this criminal is my business. So Tissafernes knew about this visit of yours, did he?

CLEMENTINA. No . . . I could have told him, though.

CLEON. But you didn't. Why not?

CLEMENTINA. The opportunity didn't arise.

CLEON. You mean you and your husband haven't seen each other in the last three weeks?

CLEMENTINA. I don't like your sarcastic tone, Cleon! I am free to talk to my husband when I like and about what I like.

CLEON. And yet so far you haven't mentioned it to him. I suppose you had your reasons for that, didn't you, Clementina?

CLEMENTINA. Listen, Cleon – you're wasting your time playing hide-and-seek with me. I came to the court of my own accord to tell you about my conversation with Herostratus. Do you remember that occasion in the palace, when I said I didn't believe your assertion that Herostratus had burned down the temple out of vanity? I surmised that he had done it out of despair at his unrequited love for some woman. Well, believe it or not, I was right . . . That wretched man really has lost his head over a woman.

CLEON. Are you that woman?

CLEMENTINA. You've guessed it.

CLEON. I had already guessed it then, when we were in the palace. You changed your mind too quickly when you suddenly decided to support Erita . . . Well, when did Herostratus discover this?

CLEMENTINA. Discover what?

CLEON. That he was in love with you!

CLEMENTINA. I've already told you, Cleon – I don't care for your sarcastic tone. You have no right to disbelieve me.

CLEON. I know you too well and I have also made quite a thorough study of Herostratus' character. He would never dream up such a fairy-story on his own – it was *you* who suggested it to him. A lovelorn youth who goes off his head – not a bad tale to impress a panel of sentimental jurors. To be the fascinating charmer for whose sake a distraught lover burns down a temple – why, that's enough to make any woman immortally famous. A beautiful invention of yours, Clementina . . . Knowing Herostratus, though, he would not

have agreed to it without demanding something in return . . .
And what was that, Clementina?

CLEMENTINA. How dare you talk to me like that? I am your
ruler here – and you are my servant!

CLEON. I am a servant of this city, Clementina, and I
acknowledge one master – Ephesus, whom I shall continue to
serve faithfully and loyally. Now – what bargain did you
strike with Herostratus? How are you proposing to repay that
scoundrel for the fame he is supposed to bring you?

CLEMENTINA. I refuse to answer!

CLEON. You will answer, Clementina – I swear it by the gods.
And the jailer will give me the answer, too.

CLEMENTINA. I've had enough of talking to you. I shall go at
once to Tissafernes and he will use his power to punish you
for your insulting remarks to his wife. (*Turns to go.*)

CLEON. Stop, Clementina! By the authority vested in me by the
people's assembly of Ephesus, I forbid you to leave this
courthouse!

CLEMENTINA. What?!

CLEON. You will remain in this building until I have discovered
the nature and extent of your complicity in the plot that
Herostratus is weaving. (*Shouts:*) The lady Clementina is not
to be let out of the courthouse!

MAN OF THE THEATRE. Bravo, Archon!

CLEMENTINA. You will bitterly regret this, Cleon. By the gods,
how you will regret it . . . (*Exit.*)

CLEON. So be it! There's no turning back now – come what may.
Citizens of Ephesus, you can trust the word of your judge.
He has never deceived you before and will not deceive you
now. (*Shouts:*) Come in, Chrysippus, I'm expecting you!

Enter CHRYSIPPUS, *bowing respectfully.*

CHRYSIPPUS. I greet you, O wisest and most just of magistrates,
may peace be upon your house, may the gods show favour to
you . . .

CLEON (*interrupting*). Stop this flow of eloquence, you old
swindler!

CHRYSIPPUS. How have I angered you, Cleon?

CLEON. Didn't you guess what it was, when you were served with a subpoena?

CHRYSIPPUS. What could I have guessed from the formal wording of a writ? Except, perhaps, that there must have been some misunderstanding . . . It is usually Chrysippus who serves writs on his debtors, but no one has ever served one on Chrysippus before.

CLEON. Chrysippus the money-lender, you are charged with entering into a criminal conspiracy with the prisoner Herostratus and with distributing his writings about the city, contrary to law and for purposes of gain.

CHRYSIPPUS (in mock astonishment). Is that all? . . . But worthy Cleon, that was simply the normal sale of an author's writings! Since when has commerce been regarded as a crime in Ephesus?

CLEON. What you did has been a crime since the people's assembly of Ephesus and Tissafernes, Ruler of Ephesus, promulgated a law forbidding not only the name of the arsonist to be mentioned again, but also forbidding the retailing of any act, saying or writing that might redound to the fame or reputation of that felon.

CHRYSIPPUS. Quite correct. But the law was not passed until a week after the fire, whereas my men were selling the memoirs of Herostratus on the second day after it . . . As soon as the ban was issued, I destroyed all my remaining copies of the papyrus.

CLEON. Liar! The papyruses are being sold in the market to this day – and what's more, at a greatly increased price.

CHRYSIPPUS. I swear by all the gods that I have nothing to do with that . . . Just think, Cleon: why should I take the risk? I deal in leather, fish, grain, timber . . . Why move into a completely different line of business, selling scrolls – and at the risk of my life, what's more? Anyhow, who's going to buy them now? According to the new law, the buyer of a Herostratus papyrus is punished no less severely than the seller.

CLEON. You have studied the law carefully, I see. Even so, you are breaking it.

CHRYSIPPUS. What oath can I swear to make you believe me?

CLEON. I don't want your oaths. Give me the keys!

CHRYSIPPUS. What keys?

CLEON. The keys to your warehouse. We will have it searched.

CHRYSIPPUS (*hastily producing a bunch of keys*). Here they are, Cleon. Make your search!

CLEON (*brushing the keys aside*). The papyruses are obviously not in your warehouse. So where are they? Where are the scrolls hidden? In your shop? In your house?

CHRYSIPPUS. I swear, Archon, that you are mistaken.

CLEON. Where are they hidden, Chrysippus? I will find them anyway, and then your guilt will be doubled . . . Spare yourself from the consequences!

CHRYSIPPUS. Spare my wife and daughter, Archon! (*Sobs.*)

CLEON. Ah, I have it! You've hidden them in the women's quarters. You thought they were quite safe there – no outsider would dare to cross the threshold of the women's half of the house. Have I guessed rightly . . ? Well? Why won't you say something? I can order those rooms to be searched, you know . . .

CHRYSIPPUS. Do you want to disgrace an old man, Cleon?

CLEON. I want to hear at least one word of the truth. (*Shouts:*) Guards! Send a party to search the house of Chrysippus the money-lender. Examine it carefully, especially the women's rooms!

CHRYSIPPUS (*frightened*). Stop, Cleon. I am prepared to make a voluntary confession . . . I hope it's not too late for that.

CLEON. Speak!

CHRYSIPPUS. Some copies of Herostratus' papyrus are indeed hidden in the women's quarters of my house. There are fifteen of them.

CLEON. Is that so?

CHRYSIPPUS. They were ordered by one purchaser.

CLEON. Fifteen papyruses – for one purchaser? Why does he want so many?

CHRYSIPPUS. How should I know? He pays – it's my business to deliver the goods.

CLEON. Who is he?

CHRYSIPPUS. A distinguished person, whose name I've promised to keep secret.

CLEON. Whoever he may be, I must know his name.

CHRYSIPPUS. But I deserve *some* consideration, seeing that I've made a voluntary confession.

CLEON. The court will take account of your repentance. Tell me his name!

CHRYSIPPUS. What will become of the wretched purchaser if I tell you?

CLEON. He will be arrested and imprisoned.

CHRYSIPPUS. Really?! And will nothing make you alter that decision, Cleon?

CLEON. Nothing!

CHRYSIPPUS. Word of an Archon?

CLEON. I swear it!

Enter TISSAFERNES.

CHRYSIPPUS (*seeing* TISSAFERNES, *with malicious relish*). You are fortunate, Cleon. The purchaser himself has just entered the courtroom. All you have to do now is lock him up in jail. Turn round!

CLEON *turns round and sees* TISSAFERNES.

Pause.

CLEON (*confused, bowing respectfully*). I am happy to greet the Ruler of Ephesus! (*To* CHRYSIPPUS:) You may go . . . I will speak to you later . . .

CHRYSIPPUS (*smiling*). Certainly, Archon, certainly . . . Don't forget the oath you have just sworn.

CLEON (*angrily*). Go!

Exit CHRYSIPPUS, *with a polite bow to* TISSAFERNES.

TISSAFERNES. It's terribly hot in the city today, the sun is beating down unmercifully. Driving to see you, I was quite soaked with sweat . . . How do you manage to keep working in this heat?

CLEON. A public servant must do his job in all weathers.

TISSAFERNES. That is true, but do not overdo your zeal . . . You're not a young man any longer, Cleon, you must look after your health.

CLEON. I appreciate the Ruler's concern for me.

TISSAFERNES. It is my duty to take care of my servants.

CLEON. Allow me, O Ruler, to put one question to you: why are you buying the writings of Herostratus?

TISSAFERNES. *I* am buying them? *I* . . ? It's a lie (*Catching CLEON's unwavering stare, gives in at once:*) Yes, yes, you're right, I am buying them . . . I suppose that old swindler Chrysippus has been whining to you about them. I'll show him!

CLEON. Why are you doing it, O Ruler?

TISSAFERNES. Oh, you know . . . out of sheer curiosity. I thought I would like to keep a copy in my library.

CLEON. But you ordered *fifteen* copies.

TISSAFERNES. Did he tell you that too? (*Indignantly:*) Really! You can't rely on anyone . . ! You see, Cleon, the king of Macedonia asked me to send him the memoirs of Herostratus, and then the ruler of Syracuse wanted one . . . well, and several even more eminent people. It is interesting, after all, to know what that bandit has written. It contains some curious ideas . . .

CLEON. You are breaking the law!

TISSAFERNES. Of course . . . but I issued the decree myself. Therefore, according to you, it is not I who govern the laws but the laws that govern me! Anyway, it's a trivial matter, and not worth getting incensed about, my dear Archon . . .

CLEON. But it sets a bad example.

TISSAFERNES. It cannot really be an example to anyone, because I am doing it in secret . . . Only your unsleeping eye is aware of it. Anyway – I repeat: it is a trivial matter and

your fears are baseless . . . (*To the* MAN OF THE THEATRE:)
Give me a quotation that will make me sound convincing . . .

MAN OF THE THEATRE. From Sophocles: 'He who trembles at
baseless fears deserves to face real fears.'

TISSAFERNES. Precisely! Sophocles was right . . . (*Looks around.*)
But where is Clementina? I was told she was here.

CLEON (*in an official tone*). I have placed your wife under arrest,
O Ruler!

TISSAFERNES (*after a pause*). It is extremely hot in the city today,
Cleon. It is impossible to work in such heat, your brain is
obviously softening.

CLEON. My brain is working well, Tissafernes. Your wife has
been arrested. She is accused of visiting Herostratus and
entering into a secret conspiracy with him.

TISSAFERNES (*nervously*). Think, Cleon, think . . . When you say
what you think, think what you're saying!

CLEON. I will answer for every word I have spoken, Tissafernes.

TISSAFERNES (*nervously*). Just don't make a mistake, Cleon. I will
not forgive even you for making such a mistake. (*To the* MAN
OF THE THEATRE:) Go away! You may not hear this . . .

(*To* CLEON:) Have you any proof, any witnesses?

CLEON. Clementina does not deny that she visited Herostratus.
The jailer is waiting in the courthouse and he will confirm
it . . .

TISSAFERNES. Call Clementina!

CLEON. Very well. (*Exit, returning at once with* CLEMENTINA.)

TISSAFERNES. My dear Clementina, our respected Archon has
been telling me the strangest stories.

CLEMENTINA. He spoke to me somewhat strangely, too, if you
call it strange to be rude to me.

TISSAFERNES. Did you speak rudely to my wife?

CLEON. I spoke as a judge speaks.

TISSAFERNES (*to* CLEMENTINA). Did you go and see
Herostratus?

CLEMENTINA. No!

TISSAFERNES (*to* CLEON). And you maintain that she did go and see him?

CLEON. I do!

TISSAFERNES. One of you, therefore, is lying. A lie must be punished. I swear by all the gods of the Greeks and of the Persians that the liar shall be punished!

CLEON (*shouts*). Bring in the jailer!

TISSAFERNES. We shall hear what the jailer has to say. If my friend has deceived me, he is no longer my friend; if my wife has deceived me – then she is no longer my wife!

CLEMENTINA. Fine words. We will have them entered in the palace records . . .

Enter the MAN OF THE THEATRE.

CLEON (*rushing towards him*). Well? Where is the jailer?

MAN OF THE THEATRE. He has been killed.

Pause.

TISSAFERNES *looks suspiciously at* CLEON *and at* CLEMENTINA.

CLEON. Who had him murdered? (*Looking at* CLEMENTINA *and at* TISSAFERNES:) You – or you?

CLEMENTINA. Or perhaps it was you, Archon? (*Takes* TISSAFERNES' *arm.*) Come along, my dear. He is so suspicious he has gone mad . . .

Exeunt both.

CLEON (*in despair, stretching out his hand to the* MAN OF THE THEATRE). Give me back my knife, man! I beg you, give me back my knife . . .

Scene Two

'Jailer! Jailer!' – *this cry from* HEROSTRATUS *can be heard all the time as one by one the candelabra are lit which illuminate the prison cell. The cell is now considerably better furnished than it was in the first and third scenes: there is a couch, and beside it a low table, on which are some empty plates and a drinking-cup. In one corner of the cell is a large painted vase.*

HEROSTRATUS (*pacing nervously up and down the cell*). Jailer! . . . Jailer! . . . Where are you, damn you?! . . . Idle bastard! . . . Hey, will somebody kindly come in here? . . . Jailer!

Enter CLEON.

CLEON. Why are you shouting?

HEROSTRATUS. I'm shouting because this isn't a prison, it's a pig-sty! This is the second day running that no one has come to my cell. You'd better give orders to have your jailers well and truly thrashed, Archon – they're not earning their pay. Prisoners are supposed to be given food and drink and to have their piss-pots emptied, but that idle slacker has been dodging his duties . . . (*Shouts:*) Hey, jailer!

CLEON. Don't shout, he won't come.

HEROSTRATUS. Why not?

CLEON. He's been killed.

HEROSTRATUS. Killed? . . . So that's it, is it? . . . By whom?

CLEON. We don't know yet.

HEROSTRATUS. Pity, he was quite a decent fellow.

CLEON. Especially to you, it seems.

HEROSTRATUS. And why not? Who likes jailers, except their prisoners? (*Goes over to the table to drink, but finds the cup empty.*) Damn! No one has brought me a drop of water for two days. It's time to appoint a new jailer, Archon.

CLEON. He has been appointed.

HEROSTRATUS. Where is he?

CLEON. Standing before you.

HEROSTRATUS. You're joking!

CLEON. I wouldn't stoop to joke with you.

HEROSTRATUS (*looks at* CLEON *in amazement*). Ye gods! . . . Well, Herostratus – how about that?! You really *are* someone, it seems: they've given you the Chief Magistrate himself as your jailer! . . . I didn't expect *this* . . . Ha, ha, ha . . . wonders will never cease!

CLEON (*angrily*). Why are you so pleased?

HEROSTRATUS. Why? In my wildest dreams I never imagined that the honourable Cleon, Chief Magistrate of Ephesus, would guard me and carry out my piss-pot!

CLEON (*furiously*). You will carry out your own piss-pot, you villain!

HEROSTRATUS (*helpless with laughter*). Even so, you will have to walk alongside and smell it . . . Oh, it's too much – I'm going to die laughing!!

CLEON. Shut up!

HEROSTRATUS (*still laughing*). Poor old Cleon! Why have you been demoted to such a humiliating job? How did you displease the people of Ephesus?

CLEON. I myself asked to be appointed your jailer, Herostratus.

HEROSTRATUS (*abruptly stops laughing*). You did? . . . That's strange. Well, it makes no difference to me. Now that you're the jailer, be a good fellow and bring me something to eat and drink . . . I'm hungry!

Without a word, CLEON *turns around and exits.*

HEROSTRATUS (*shouts after him*). And bring me two days' worth of rations, the prison owes it to me. And be sharp about it! (*Laughs.*) Funny things happen in Ephesus, I must say! (*Sits down on the couch.*)

Enter the MAN OF THE THEATRE, *who, as usual, takes his seat in a corner of the stage.*

(*Sees* MAN OF THE THEATRE, *takes on a grim look.*) Why have *you* come?

MAN OF THE THEATRE. Does my presence disturb you?

HEROSTRATUS. I'm disturbed by the fact that you're always poking your nose in where you're not wanted.

MAN OF THE THEATRE. I never interfere; I'm only following the logic of events.

HEROSTRATUS (*irritably*). I'm fed up with you and your logic. Why can't you leave me alone? The ruler has decreed: 'Forget Herostratus!' So forget me, will you?

MAN OF THE THEATRE. Aha – you're reconciled to being consigned to oblivion, is that it? No, that won't work . . . To forget means to forgive.

HEROSTRATUS. What's all this about 'forgiving' . . . O gods, I have had my fill of people passing moral judgment on me. I never thought the trial would be postponed for two thousand years . . .

MAN OF THE THEATRE. That judgment will be all the more severe, Herostratus.

For a while the MAN OF THE THEATRE *and* HEROSTRATUS *stare at each other with dislike. Enter* CLEON *with a bowl of food and a jug.*

HEROSTRATUS (*grinning, to the* MAN OF THE THEATRE). There's another great thinker for you. Our descendants will probably laugh themselves silly when they read about poor old Cleon in the history books . . . (*To* CLEON:) Well, what muck have the cooks dished up today?

CLEON (*his voice rising to a shriek*). Get up! Stand to attention! A prisoner has to stand up when a warder comes into the cell, doesn't he?! Right, then! (*Swings his arm back to throw the contents of the bowl into* HEROSTRATUS' *face.*)

HEROSTRATUS (*jumping up from the couch in alarm*). Hey, Cleon! What are you doing? Careful, now!

CLEON. Be quiet! Otherwise I'll chuck all this in your impudent face. You're getting no food until you've cleaned up this cell. I want it spotlessly clean in one minute from now!

HEROSTRATUS (*hurriedly*). All right, all right! Why get so worked up? (*Clears up rubbish, apple cores, fruit skins, etc. from the floor.*)

CLEON. What's that you've got there?

HEROSTRATUS. This? (*Shows him fruit peelings.*) That's orange peel, that's banana skin.

CLEON. Pretty good dessert for a prisoner! Many people in Ephesus would envy you. (*Inspects the drinking-cup.*) I see you've had wine, too.

HEROSTRATUS (*with a smile*). It was brought to me out of compassion, Cleon, pure compassion. What's so terrible about giving a condemned man a bit of decent food and drink?

CLEON. Your time in the condemned cell has lasted too long, Herostratus. (*Notices the vase.*) And what's that?

HEROSTRATUS. A vase.

CLEON. A richly painted vase in a prison cell? H'mm! If that jailer were to come alive again at this moment, I'd kill him all over again! (*Examines the vase.*) Who's portrait is painted on this vase?

HEROSTRATUS. Don't you recognise it? Strange . . .

CLEON (*looking from the vase to* HEROSTRATUS *and back again*). Who dared paint your portrait?

HEROSTRATUS. The artist Varantius. He said I had remarkable features. I agree with him. (*Examining the vase.*) He hasn't got the eyes very well, but that can be put right. The painting isn't finished yet . . .

CLEON. Varantius will pay dearly for his audacity. As Archon of Ephesus . . .

HEROSTRATUS (*interrupting*). Ex-Archon.

CLEON. As a citizen of Ephesus I shall sue him for illegally glorifying a self-confessed criminal! Or he can sue me for smashing his vase!! (*Picks up the vase in fury and smashes it to fragments.*)

HEROSTRATUS (*sadly*). Why do you dislike me so much, Cleon?

CLEON. I hate you!

HEROSTRATUS. What a pity! It seems the earth is too small a place for you and me to live on it together . . .

For a second they stare at each other with hatred, then HEROSTRATUS *turns away, sits down at the table and begins to eat his bowl of stew.*

CLEON (*in a tone of authority*). When you've finished eating, you will wash out your bowl and wash the cell floor. I will no longer tolerate this disorder. You will be whipped for every speck of dust that I find . . .

HEROSTRATUS. It's the visitors who make the mess, not me.

CLEON. There will be no more visitors! Understand? This is a prison, not a theatre.

Enter TISSAFERNES.

TISSAFERNES. You are absolutely right, Cleon, but sometimes one has to make an exception . . .

Seeing TISSAFERNES, CLEON *and* HEROSTRATUS *bow respectfully.*

CLEON (*gloomily*). The Ruler of Ephesus can visit whom he likes and when he thinks fit.

TISSAFERNES. I think so too. Surely the master of the city ought to know how dangerous criminals are kept? (*Goes up to* CLEON.) Cleon, I wanted to talk to you . . . Listen, I'm extremely sorry about what has happened. I meant to give you a mild reprimand, not to dismiss you from the office of Archon.

CLEON. The people's assembly took the decision, and I accepted it.

TISSAFERNES (*in a conciliatory tone*). Don't be evasive, Cleon. You know perfectly well that all you had to do was to apologise, and everything would have been forgotten . . . You must curb your pride, my friend, when you're in the wrong!

CLEON. I have nothing to apologise for, O Ruler . . . Circumstances proved stronger than me, that was all . . .

TISSAFERNES. What a pity you persist so obstinately in your delusion. You must agree that a man who has no confidence in his rulers cannot hold the office of Archon.

CLEON. Indeed, I do agree! That is why I resigned.

TISSAFERNES. That is your right. But why did you want to become a humble jailer? What is it – a challenge, a mere caprice? Such touchy behaviour is what one expects from an insecure, nervous young man, not from you. It's undignified, my friend – most undignified!

CLEON. I was thinking least of all about my dignity. What matters to me is to serve my people. At this moment Ephesus is in danger; the danger comes from that man over there

(*Gestures towards* HEROSTRATUS.) – therefore my place is here.

TISSAFERNES. You exaggerate the danger represented by that miserable wretch. What is he? A gadfly, no more, that will be swatted with one blow.

CLEON. I thought so, too, Tissafernes, but I see now that I was mistaken . . .

TISSAFERNES. Why?

CLEON. Because Rulers do not come to visit a mere gadfly.

TISSAFERNES (*embarrassed*). You don't think I came here to see *him*, do you? What nonsense . . . (*Catching* CLEON's *eye, gives in at once.*) Well, yes, yes . . . I did come here to talk to Herostratus! And what of it? Why should I have to justify what I do?

CLEON. I am not asking you to do that, O Ruler.

TISSAFERNES. And I should think so too! . . . I'm tired of that perpetual look of reproach in your eyes, Cleon . . . There is a limit to everything. (*Angrily:*) Get out of here!

CLEON (*offended*). You never used to talk to me like that before!

TISSAFERNES. Then you were the Chief Magistrate. Now you're a mere jailer. You had better get used to your new position . . . Go! When I need you, I'll call you.

Exit CLEON.

HEROSTRATUS (*cheerfully*). Bravo, Tissafernes, bravo! Serve him right! It's time that arrogant man was put in his place.

TISSAFERNES (*grimly*). Least of all do I need *your* approval.

HEROSTRATUS. Why start our talk in that tone of voice? I have been expecting you to come for a long time, and you have to insult me as soon as you open your mouth.

TISSAFERNES. You've been expecting me to come?

HEROSTRATUS. Of course! For every hour that I've been shut up here I've been expecting you, Tissafernes. I sensed that you wanted to meet me, and I prayed to the gods to strengthen you in your wish.

TISSAFERNES. I should leave the gods out of it, Herostratus.

Your relationship with them is ambiguous, to say the least
. . . As for me, it's true that I have wanted to have a chat with
you about this and that . . .

HEROSTRATUS. That is a great honour.

TISSAFERNES. Indeed it is! I rarely show such graciousness even
to my own courtiers.

HEROSTRATUS. I truly appreciate your kindness, O Ruler.

TISSAFERNES. Good. Now let's get to the point. The whole city
is saying that you are in love with Clementina . . .

HEROSTRATUS (*hurriedly*). Don't believe it, my lord!

TISSAFERNES. I am not pressing you for a hasty answer.
Although the matter concerns my wife, that doesn't mean
you should be afraid of telling me the truth . . .

HEROSTRATUS. I am telling you the truth, Tissafernes! I have
never felt anything resembling love for Clementina.

TISSAFERNES (*slightly offended*). Oh, really? Everybody says . . .

HEROSTRATUS. People will say anything. They get bored
without something to gossip about.

TISSAFERNES. There would be nothing strange about it if you
did love her. Clementina is young and intelligent, she's the
most beautiful woman in the city . . . Any man could be
forgiven for falling in love with her.

HEROSTRATUS. I agree with you, O Ruler, but her charms have
not affected me. I don't know why. No doubt I am too
coarse-natured to experience genuine feelings . . .

TISSAFERNES (*growing nervous*). Strange, strange . . . I was
convinced that you set fire to the temple out of unrequited
love, in a state of noble distraction, so to speak . . .

HEROSTRATUS. Nothing of the sort, Tissafernes! I simply
wanted to immortalise my name. A stupid act of vanity, no
more . . .

TISSAFERNES (*thoughtfully*). H'mm, yes. A pity . . .

HEROSTRATUS. Alas . . .

TISSAFERNES. Sad . . .

HEROSTRATUS. Unfortunately . . .

TISSAFERNES (*with a sigh*). In that case, it really was nothing but gossip, was it?

HEROSTRATUS. Of course it was, O Ruler. And I even know how the story was started . . . The fact is – Clementina is in love with me . . .

Pause. The MAN OF THE THEATRE *opens his mouth in amazement and mutters something like:* 'Well, I'm damned! Did you ever hear such a thing!'

TISSAFERNES (*to* HEROSTRATUS). What was that? Would you mind saying that again?

HEROSTRATUS. I said that Clementina was in love with me.

TISSAFERNES. That's a lie!

HEROSTRATUS. Would I dare lie to you, O Ruler? It is true, Tissafernes.

TISSAFERNES. What proof have you?

HEROSTRATUS. What proof is needed of the act of love, except that it took place?

TISSAFERNES. Do you mean to say that Clementina came here to see you?

HEROSTRATUS. Well, I didn't go to the palace to see her . . .

TISSAFERNES (*furious*). Be quiet! Answer my question!

HEROSTRATUS. I am answering it . . . Clementina came here, told me of her feelings, threw her arms around me . . .

TISSAFERNES. Silence!

HEROSTRATUS. I cannot answer your questions in silence, Tissafernes. If you don't like what you hear, why did you ask me? . . . How strange! I felt sure you knew all about it.

TISSAFERNES. How could I know about it, idiot?!

HEROSTRATUS. But in that case, why did you have the jailer killed?

Pause. Again the MAN OF THE THEATRE *mumbles something in astonishment.*

TISSAFERNES (*in a low voice*). How did you know that?

HEROSTRATUS. I guessed it. When I was told the jailer had

been murdered, I wondered who might find him a nuisance and want him out of the way.

TISSAFERNES. You're not stupid, Herostratus. Yes, I ordered him to be killed . . . I wanted no witnesses to my family disgrace. But I didn't think things had gone so far . . .

HEROSTRATUS. You did right to remove him.

TISSAFERNES. That leaves you as the only other witness.

HEROSTRATUS. I'm not a witness – I'm an accomplice.

TISSAFERNES. Even so, you will have to go. You will die today!

HEROSTRATUS. Wait, Tissafernes – don't be in such a hurry. It will be easier to kill me than the jailer, but he is silent after death, whereas I will speak . . . My love-making with your wife has already been described in a new papyrus that I have written, and the scroll is hidden in a safe place, with friends. If I die today, then tomorrow the Ephesians will read how Clementina caressed and made love to Herostratus . . .

TISSAFERNES. Who will believe your scribblings? A madman like you is liable to invent all sorts of nonsense.

HEROSTRATUS. My story contains several spicy details which will leave no doubt that the author is telling the truth . . . A birthmark on her left breast, a little scar on her right buttock . . . The sort of things that can't be invented, but must have been seen . . .

TISSAFERNES (*crushed*). Yes, you're not lying.

HEROSTRATUS. I'm a decent man, Tissafernes. It's not in my nature to boast about my conquests of women. It just happened.

TISSAFERNES. Well, in that case, she must die too!

HEROSTRATUS. Won't there be rather too many deaths, O Ruler? And what would you gain? Sympathy? Never! No one sympathises with deceived husbands, they laugh at them. The Ruler of Ephesus – with horns on his head! The Ephesians won't like that – and nor will the King of Persia. Think of what it will do to your authority, Tissafernes!

Deep in thought, TISSAFERNES *goes over to the couch, sits down and starts to eat the stew in silence.*

TISSAFERNES (*still deep in thought*). What filth they give you to eat here!

HEROSTRATUS. That's one of Cleon's dirty tricks. They used to feed me better.

TISSAFERNES. When I'm worried I must eat.

HEROSTRATUS (*hospitably*). Be my guest! Eat your fill!

TISSAFERNES (*pushing the bowl aside*). Well, what do you advise me to do?

HEROSTRATUS. Do you really need my advice, O Ruler?

TISSAFERNES. Of course I do. Since you've so carefully arranged this whole affair, I presume you've already decided how it is to be resolved. I'm listening, Herostratus.

HEROSTRATUS. I am too insignificant to offer you advice.

TISSAFERNES (*irritably*). Stop pretending! If you were Tissafernes, what would you do?

HEROSTRATUS. Ah, if I were Tissafernes, I would act with great cunning: I wouldn't execute Herostratus, but I wouldn't pardon him either. I would give him his freedom – but in such a way that he was totally dependent on me.

TISSAFERNES. Vague. too vague. In any case, I'm not the one who is planning to execute you – it is your fellow-citizens. Today or tomorrow the envoy will return from Delphi and will announce the will of the gods. I am certain that the gods will want you to die.

HEROSTRATUS (*gets up, walks up and down the cell*). Listen, Tissafernes, and I will tell you how I stopped believing in the power of the gods. Don't be afraid, there's nothing blasphemous in my story . . . Well, it happened a couple of years ago. My business was going badly, I was ruined, but I hadn't lost hope. I dreamed of making a lot of money – and quickly. That's the way inveterate gamblers think, and I've always been one. I decided to make one big killing at cock-fighting. I borrowed five hundred drachmas from a money-lender and bought a fighting cock from Rhodes. It was a fantastic bird – red, with a beak like an eagle's and spurs that any of your knights might envy. For a whole month I trained my rooster to fight and win, and fed him on garlic. Finally, when I reckoned that he was as tough and aggressive as any

Scythian, I went to the market to see Theodorus, a rich man
who keeps the best fighting cocks in Ephesus, and bet him
that my red brute would beat any one of his birds. He
accepted, and chose a black cock to fight my red fellow. The
stake was a thousand drachmas, which I also borrowed from
a money-lender who was convinced that my bird would win
. . . The entire market crowded round to watch the fight. My
red one was twice the size of his black opponent, and when
Theodorus saw this he turned pale and said: 'Your cock,
Herostratus, is obviously much stronger than mine. Will you
allow me to ask the gods to protect my little black one?'
I laughed and said: 'Go ahead! It won't do him any good!'
. . . Well, the fight began. The red bird went for the black
cock so hard that feathers started to fly . . . After they'd been
fighting for five minutes, the black one began to weaken and
I saw that before much longer my red fellow was going to rip
his opponent to pieces. But at that moment Theodorus
pulled his bird out of the ring and said: 'Herostratus, will
you allow me to pray to the gods once more to protect my
little blackie?' – 'Pray away!' said I. We bathed our fighting-
birds' wounds. Theodorus mumbled something over his
black cock and threw him back into the ring. And what do
you think, Tissafernes? That black bird started fighting as
though new strength had been poured into him, as though
my redhead hadn't been hammering him with his beak at all.
But my fellow was not planning to give in – I tell you he was
'a wonder-bird, a Heracles among fighting cocks! He flew at
the black one again like a whirlwind, and although he'd
already lost an eye in the fight, he went for the other so hard
that it began to squawk like a hen and rolled over on its side.
Once again Theodorus stopped and asked permission to pray
to the gods for help. I generously agreed, because I could see
that the black bird was at death's door. Theodorus prayed
over his bird, and then the fight started again. It was like a
miracle: once more the black cock seemed to have been
brought back to life. Where could it have got so much
strength from? It flung itself at my exhausted red bird,
knocked him down, ripped open his chest with its spurs and
stabbed him right in the heart with its beak . . . My poor old
fellow just gave up the ghost . . . I threw Theodorus his
thousand drachmas, ran out into the street, raised my hands
to heaven and shouted: 'Forgive me, O gods, for having no
faith in your power! You have performed a miracle to punish

me for my disbelief.' Just then, though, an old slave came up to me, laughing, and he said: 'You fool! What have the gods got to do with it? You're blind. Every time the fight was stopped for Theodorus to pray over his bird, his servants cunningly replaced the dying black cock with another, fresh one . . .' I wept with fury at having been cheated, and then I laughed – because I had discovered a great truth: human cunning, impudence and effrontery are stronger than the gods! That truth cost me a thousand drachmas, Tissafernes, and I am passing it on to you for nothing . . .

TISSAFERNES (*thoughtfully*). Interesting . . . But I still don't understand what your advice to me is . . .

HEROSTRATUS. Change the cocks, Tissafernes! The envoy from Delphi is soon going to announce the will of the gods, which may or may not suit you: but what will really suit you, Tissafernes, is that I should stay alive and serve you.

TISSAFERNES. Are you sure?

HEROSTRATUS. Of course! There is unrest in Ephesus, as you well know. The Greeks do not care for the Persians; they only pretend to obey you, the king's satrap, but in fact they're just waiting for the moment when they can throw you out of your palace. Put me in charge of them as their overseer! By now I can call on a good thousand faithful supporters who will go through fire and water for me. We will dissolve the People's Assembly, abolish the election of judges and trial by jury. You will establish the kind of order that *you* want in Ephesus, and I will see to it that you are obeyed. People will start to respect and fear Herostratus – after all, the gods themselves will have forgiven his act of effrontery. They may even start thinking that Herostratus is one of the gods himself. How about that? They say a fortune-teller in the market shouted that I was the son of Zeus . . .

TISSAFERNES (*with a snigger*). How much did you pay her?

HEROSTRATUS. I changed the cocks, Tissafernes! And I'll go on doing it until the opposition falls down dead.

TISSAFERNES. And what will the priests say?

HEROSTRATUS. The priests will say nothing. They're in disgrace anyway: where are the avenging thunderbolts of Zeus? Where are the arrows from the sacred bow of Artemis? But *I*, please note, am alive and well. It means one of two things: either there are no gods at all, or I am a god myself!

TISSAFERNES. Not bad, not bad at all . . . But how is our personal matter to be resolved?

HEROSTRATUS. What personal matter, Tissafernes? Your wife is faithful to you, and any gossip-mongers who say otherwise will have their tongues cut out by me on the city square . . . Think carefully about my proposal, O Ruler. You're a foreigner among Greeks, and you're old . . .

TISSAFERNES. Now Herostratus – don't forget yourself!

HEROSTRATUS. Forgive me, Tissafernes. But years are years; you're not the man you were thirty years ago. What you need now is a firm hand in the city, and for that you won't find anyone better than me.

TISSAFERNES. I must think about it. (*Slowly eats some more stew, then puts aside the spoon and lets his head droop.*)

HEROSTRATUS. What's the matter, Tissafernes? There are tears in your eyes . . .

TISSAFERNES. It's the stew . . . they put in too much onion and too much pepper . . .

HEROSTRATUS (*laughing*). I hadn't noticed . . .

TISSAFERNES. Be quiet, Herostratus! You can't understand how sad it is to grow old . . . You see, I never wanted to be a Ruler; in my heart I'm still just a fisherman. I should be sitting at the water's edge with my rod and line, instead of which I have to live in a palace and rule over thousands of people who hate me. I love my wife very much, Herostratus, but I'm an old man now and I have no right to demand that she should feel physical love for me in return. I've been expecting her to be unfaithful to me sooner or later, but I thought it would cause pain to no one but me; now it has come, and it has turned into a political problem . . . I don't want to be the Ruler of Ephesus. I want to spend my last days living for myself, not for history. But who ever asks us what we want? . . . (*Firmly and decisively.*) I can't release you, Herostratus. The people wouldn't stand for it and it would cause serious trouble. However, if it so happened that you somehow escaped from prison . . .

HEROSTRATUS. That might have been possible before, but now that I'm being guarded by Cleon . . .

TISSAFERNES. That's exactly what I mean . . . you can't bargain with him.

HEROSTRATUS. So what am I to do?

TISSAFERNES. I'm thinking, I'm thinking . . . (*Eats some more stew.*) What do you use to cut your bread with, Herostratus?

HEROSTRATUS. I don't cut it, I have to break it with my hands.

TISSAFERNES. Oh dear, that won't do at all – your hands are probably dirty. Most unhygienic . . . (*Produces a dagger from under his cloak.*) There – take it. It's very sharp and sits well in the hand . . .

HEROSTRATUS (*taking the dagger and hiding it in his tunic*). Thank you, O Ruler! You are wise and magnanimous . . .

MAN OF THE THEATRE (*indignantly*). What are you doing, Tissafernes?

TISSAFERNES (*irritably*). I didn't ask for your opinion! Leave us alone and don't interfere.

The MAN OF THE THEATRE *resumes his seat in silence.*

Well, it's time for me to go. (*Shouts:*) Cleon!

Enter CLEON.

I have had an entertaining talk with this rogue. From now on you must not take your eyes off him, and on the appointed day I expect you to deliver him to the courthouse in one piece.

CLEON. I shall, O Ruler . . . When are you expecting the messenger from Delphi?

TISSAFERNES. He is on his way back, and if nothing happens to him . . .

CLEON (*suspiciously*). What could happen to him?

TISSAFERNES. All sorts of things . . . a storm at sea . . . pirates . . . ships often sink . . .

CLEON. What do you mean by that, O Ruler?

TISSAFERNES. We are all in the hands of the gods, Cleon. (*Exit.*)

CLEON (*to* HEROSTRATUS). What have you been plotting with Tissafernes? Answer me!

HEROSTRATUS. Plotting? He is the Ruler and I am a mere gadfly, a gnat, a midge. What sort of plot could there be between two such unequal creatures?

CLEON. What were you talking about?

HEROSTRATUS. The weather . . .

CLEON. This is no time for jokes. Herostratus. I sense that a plot is being hatched in Ephesus. Answer me, or else . . .

HEROSTRATUS. Don't try to frighten me. I'm not afraid of anything now. Anyway, who are you? I don't have to answer your questions now. A jailer should know his place and not ask about things he's not meant to know.

CLEON. Listen, Herostratus – I'm speaking to you in a final hope that there is some spark of conscience left in you. You're a Greek and an Ephesian. I implore you not to bring any more destruction and death to our city! What were you and Tissafernes whispering about? In the name of all Ephesians I beg you not to help him in his sinister plans . . . Do you want me to get down on my knees? Stop whatever you're up to, Herostratus! The very worst of criminals can expect leniency if . . .

HEROSTRATUS (*angrily*). Be quiet, you failed judge! You realise that the power of the state can't touch me now, so you're hoping to move me to pity, is that it? Well, it won't work! Get out!

CLEON (*to* MAN OF THE THEATRE). What were they plotting?

HEROSTRATUS *draws his dagger and starts to creep up on* CLEON *from behind.*

MAN OF THE THEATRE (*jumping to his feet*). Cleon, turn round! (CLEON *turns round;* HEROSTRATUS *freezes, the dagger clutched in his hand.*)

HEROSTRATUS (*livid with fury, to* MAN OF THE THEATRE). You promised never to interfere!

MAN OF THE THEATRE. Sorry, it was beyond my powers of restraint.

HEROSTRATUS (*to* CLEON). I am now about to leave this prison, and if you don't try to prevent me I'll allow you to stay alive.

CLEON. I won't let you out, Herostratus!

HEROSTRATUS. In that case you're finished. (*Advances on* CLEON, *who retreats to the edge of the stage.*)

MAN OF THE THEATRE (*handing* CLEON *his knife*). Your knife, Archon.

HEROSTRATUS (*dancing with anger*). You *cannot* interfere!!

MAN OF THE THEATRE (*to* CLEON). Take the knife, Archon! You have no choice. If I had lived two thousand years ago, I would have done so myself . . .

CLEON *takes the knife from the* MAN OF THE THEATRE.

HEROSTRATUS (*frightened*). You won't kill me, Cleon! A man who kills a felon before his trial will himself be executed!

CLEON. I know that, Herostratus. (*Advances on him.*)

The light in the cell is extinguished. Sounds of a struggle are heard, then cease; the silence is gradually broken by the noise of falling stones, the blows of sledgehammers. Then mens' voices start singing, quietly at first, then more and more loudly and confidently.

The lights go up again on stage. Head bowed, CLEON *stands over the corpse of* HEROSTRATUS.

(To MAN OF THE THEATRE.·) I have killed a man for the first time in my life . . .

MAN OF THE THEATRE. All you did was to carry out the inevitable sentence of the court.

CLEON (*in despair*). I . . . killed him!

MAN OF THE THEATRE. The fight has begun!!

The sounds of falling masonry and singing grow louder.

MAN OF THE THEATRE. What is that?

CLEON. They are rebuilding the temple of Artemis . . .

MAN OF THE THEATRE. Who are?

CLEON. They are . . . the Ephesians . . .

MAN OF THE THEATRE. What are their names? Tell me at least one of their names . . . It's important for us to know . . . Well?

CLEON (*lifelessly*). I don't remember . . .

MAN OF THE THEATRE. Remember, Cleon! It's not fair that they should always be anonymous. Remember! . . .

Off-stage, the crash of masonry, the whining of saws and the notes of the song swell and then fade.

THREE GIRLS IN BLUE ■ LUDMILA PETRUSHEVSKAYA

Translated by LIANE AUKIN and MICHAEL GLENNY

Often compared with both Chekhov and Gogol, Petrushevskaya, the USSR's leading woman playwright, is known for the humanity and truth to life of her characters. *Three Girls in Blue* follows the realistically confused doings of its three women protagonists and is full of insight into their apparently inconsequential lives. The British premiere was on Radio 3 in April 1988.

Characters

IRA	a young woman; aged 30–32.
PAVLIK	her son; aged 5.
MARIA PHILIPPOVNA	IRA's mother; aged 56.
FYODOROVNA	an elderly woman who owns the dacha and lives in half of it; aged 72.
SVETLANA	a young woman; a nurse-practitioner, aged 30–32.
MAXIM	her son; aged 8.
LEOKADIA	SVETLANA's mother-in-law; aged 70.
TATYANA	a young woman; aged 27–29.
ANTON	her son; aged 7.
VALERA	her husband; aged 30.
NIKOLAI IVANOVICH	a friend of IRA's; aged 44.
YOUNG MAN	aged 24.
AIRPORT OFFICIAL	
WOMAN PASSENGER	
MAN PASSENGER	
ELKA	FYODOROVNA's cat.

The action takes place in a dacha at Romanovka, a commuter village in the country outside Moscow; in Moscow; and at Koktebel, a resort on the Black Sea.

Three Girls in Blue was first performed in English in a version prepared by Liane Aukin from a literal translation by Boris Issarov for BBC Radio 3 on 5 April 1988 with the following cast:

IRA	Frances Barber
PAVLIK	Lawrence Cooper
MARIA PHILIPPOVNA	Ann Mitchell
FYODOROVNA	Elizabeth Spriggs
SVETLANA	Maureen O'Brien
MAXIM	Richard Pearce
LEOKADIA	Eva Stuart
TATYANA	Caroline Gruber
ANTON	Leo Docherty
VALERA	Kim Wall
NIKOLAI	Anthony Jackson
YOUNG MAN	Stephen Rushbrook
AIRPORT OFFICIAL	Peter Craze
WOMAN PASSENGER	Joan Walker

Directed by Jane Morgan

ACT ONE

PAVLIK'S VOICE. Mum, how much is one from two . . ? Mum, shall I tell you a fairy-story? Once upon a time there were two brothers. One was in the middle, one was older and one was very little. He was teeny, weeny. One day he went fishing. So he took a pail with him and caught a fish. On the way home the fish started to croak, so he cut it up and made a fishcake.

Scene One

The verandah of a dacha. One door leads into a room, the other leads outside. IRA is preparing lemonade.

IRA (*calls out*). How are you feeling, Pavlik?

PAVLIK'S VOICE. Bit better.

> *Enter* FYODOROVNA. *She wears an aged dressing-gown and yellow rubber boots. In her arms is her cat,* ELKA.

FYODOROVNA. Have you seen her kitten? It's gone. Did you feed it?

IRA. No, I didn't. I told you.

FYODOROVNA. Been gone three days now. Maybe it's your lad, Pavlik, who's gone and done him in. (*Looks into the room.*) Look at him, the lazy layabout! Get up! Stir your stumps . . ! Why's he lying there looking such a misery?

IRA. That boy has a temperature of 39.3.

FYODOROVNA. Caught a cold, has he? It's no good me saying anything to them. They wouldn't listen. Sat in the river, they were, for hours on end. Now it's you who's all upset and in a bother. But there's no telling boys, is there? I went into the raspberry-canes yesterday – fruit lying all over the ground.

Found my hammer lying on the doorstep. Now who d'you s'pose pinched that? I'll bet they've killed that kitten. Been gone since Thursday. That's three days. I thought Elka was keeping him up in the loft, so I drag myself up there to have a look, and there she is, miaowing and looking for him herself. *(To the cat:)* Where's your little one gone, eh, Elka? What? *(Cat miaows.)* 'Miaow?' No, it wasn't miaow, it was them naughty boys. I've got my eye on them.

IRA. We weren't here on Thursday. We went to Moscow to have baths.

FYODOROVNA. You took him to his gran's to give him his bath, and straight after that bath he was sat in the river like he was trying to wash his sins away. And he needs to – got enough sins on his conscience! Mind you, I never wanted you staying here in the first place. Three boys all charging around the place, it's bound to end in trouble. They'll burn the house down next, like as not. They lured that kitten away and done it in. I noticed long ago they had their eye on it. Either they tempted him down from the loft with a saucer of milk or by waving a bit of paper to attract him.

IRA. I've told you already, Fyodorovna – we weren't here on Thursday.

FYODOROVNA. 'Course, it could've been Jack, next door's dog. Bet that dog's gone and torn him to pieces. If you can call it a dog. More like a wolf. The kitten took fright, the boys chased him, so he runs off next door. I'm going to find out.

IRA. Maybe it was Maxim or Anton.

FYODOROVNA. 'Maybe' won't bring back the kitten. It was them all right! They ganged up and did it. Like those Ruchkins opposite. Young Igor Ruchkin bought himself a rifle. Well, he starts shooting stray dogs. And he killed my dog Yuzik. Just playing in the field, was Yuzik – what harm was he doing to anyone? I didn't say anything, just picked up old Yuzik and buried him. No point trying to talk to people like that. Everyone here in Romanovka knows about them. Only a couple of weeks later that Lenka Ruchkin got pissed and drowned. Rushed down the hill, dived head first into the river where it's only two feet deep. I ask you – what's the point in talking to them?

IRA. Pavlik has a high temperature and Maxim and Anton are

screaming and shouting under his window like a pair of
banshees.

FYODOROVNA. I've planted balsam under that window! I'll tell
them off all right! There's celandine in that bed, too.

IRA. I tell those two over and over again: keep to your end of the
house! They just turn round and say to me: it's not your
house. And that's it.

FYODOROVNA. Ah, if you've got enough cheek you can get
away with anything in this life. See that house on the top of
the hill? The one that looks like a two-storey army hut?
That's where the Blums live. All the Blums. I don't know
how many times the downstairs Blumses have been to court
to get old man Valka Blum out of the house. He lived in one
room and nailed up the door into the next room, the room
where Isabella Blum died. She used to work for me at the
kindergarten. Taught music. She was terrible at it. Couldn't
hardly stay on her feet. She'd stagger in, try to get her breath
back, and then sit and cry into the soup because there was no
serviettes to wipe her mouth with. She'd say: I used to play at
concerts, but now I can't even manage 'The Sun over the
Homeland' without making mistakes, believe me,
Fyodorovna, she'd say. She didn't need to tell me, I'm not
deaf. I heard her sing, and if hearing is believing she wasn't
lying. There was a famine in that year. 1947. And one of my
teachers couldn't help herself – started pinching things. I had
to keep a sharp eye on them all, I can tell you. She had a
daughter who'd been bedridden since childhood, that's why
she stole. Well, she was nicking apples from the kids. And
bread. Our kindergarten was on special rations for under-
nourished kids, you see. Anyway, there she is stuffing all she
can into her stocking and keeping the stocking in her locker.
My cleaner, she said to me, Yegorova's got apples and things
in her stocking, so we emptied Yegorova's stocking and put
wooden blocks in instead. So she took the stocking home like
that. And that evening they had blocks of wood for their
supper. Next day she left. And that was the time Isabella
Blum was dying in hospital. I used to visit her there. I buried
her. Straight away Valka Blum broke down the door into her
room and moved in with his family. He had three kids, did
Valka. No one could prove anything to the police. It was all
in the family, you see – he was a Blum, they were all Blums.
To this day Nina Osipovna Blum – she's the one who's a

doctor – she won't forgive him. Only the other day they were queuing for their pension – he was in front, signing – and she shouts at him in the corridor: 'The way you carry on, you reckon you can get away with anything in life!' And he says to her: 'What do I want to get away with? I'm seventy years old!' (*To the cat:*) And you've gone and lost your baby, eh? When she had that litter, all the kittens were there all right, but she started bringing them down from the loft, first one, then another – and now there's not one left! She's lost all her kittens. And there's that dog Jack, backwards and forwards, in and out, never stops – like the waves at the seaside. I tell you, last winter I had three cats in this house – and this summer it's just Elka.

IRA. 'It's not your house'?! Whose is it, I'd like to know? Theirs? They barge in here and pay nothing, but I have to rent my room! I'll inherit my share of this place just as they will. I have a right to this half of the house.

FYODOROVNA. Yes, old Vera's still alive, even though she's on her last legs. But I warned you it'd be expensive, and you still wanted to take it on.

IRA. I had no choice. I was longing to come out here.

FYODOROVNA. You're always longing for something. But I've got to think of the people in my own family who'll inherit. Little Seryozha needs new shoes. Will *she* buy them? Will she hell. No, it's me, Gran, who has to fork out from my pension. The pension's fifty a month, then there's the insurance. The gas. The electric . . . I bought him a warm black winter coat, a yellow ski suit, knitted gloves, Vietnamese trainers. I bought him a briefcase and I gave him money towards his school books. And all out of my fifty roubles a month. Now Vadim wants some hiking boots and a rabbit-fur hat for the winter. You think *she* cares? No. She wants a Zhiguli car. That's all *she* cares about . . . I did have two thousand put away, what mother had left me, but Seryozha, one of my lodgers, pinched it last year. I wondered why he was always spending so much time up in the loft. Then when he'd gone, I went up there and looked in the place behind the chimney-stack where I'd hidden the money . . . Fifteen years it'd been there – and it was gone, all two thousand of it!

During FYODOROVNA's *soliloquy,* IRA *has taken her son his*

drink, has come back, taken out a thermometer, taken her son's
temperature and wound up an alarm clock.

FYODOROVNA. And the two thousand was only my share –
altogether it was six thousand what mother left us, to me, my
sister and my brother. So that dirty thief Seryozha got his
sticky hands on *six thousand*! I went into Moscow to where he
lived. And before I'd even gone inside I saw it in the street –
they'd bought a Zhiguli. With my six thousand. I didn't start
telling him off – what good would it do? – I just said: 'How
d'you like my Zhiguli – suit you all right, does it?' Well,
Seryozha's father went as red as a lobster and mumbled, said
he didn't know what I was talking about. Then Seryozha
himself turned up. Smiling all the time and rubbing his
hands on his trousers 'cos they were sweating, and didn't
dare look me in the eye, not once. He'd bought that car with
three old people's nest-eggs. How can I ever pay back my
brother and sister? My brother wanted to come over from
Dorogomilovka, where he lives, and fix an indoor toilet for
me. And he'd promised to help my son Vadim buy a Zhiguli:
said he'd give him the seven thousand, and that included the
two thousand what I was keeping for him – and it'd been
pinched! My sister come, brought two kilos of meat and a
whole lot of bones for Yuzik – and that Ruchkin tearaway
had killed the poor dog. She brought me some material for a
dress, a five-litre jar of tomatoes and ten packets of soup.
They're still there – never touched 'em. And poor Yuzik's
gone! Yuzik's mother was a real sheepdog, heaven knows
what his father was. His mother, the sheepdog, used to run
around everywhere 'cos I never did keep her tied up, and last
spring Igor Ruchkin shot her. One day in March I found her
in one of the huts in the Pioneers' summer camp, and there
she was with five little fat puppies. I fed her on bread and
milk, like I eat myself, since I lost my teeth. And Igor
Ruchkin shot her. Three days later I went and took one of
her puppies home with me. They'd already started to crawl,
even though they were still blind – they crawled 'cos they
were starving hungry, poor little mites. Well, that puppy was
Yuzik.

The alarm-clock rings, startling FYODOROVNA. *The cat jumps out*
of her arms and runs off. Exit IRA *to the adjoining room to attend to*
PAVLIK.

FYODOROVNA. Ira, how much do you earn a month?

IRA'S VOICE. A hundred and twenty roubles.

FYODOROVNA. Then how did you reckon you could pay me so much rent? 240 roubles is a lot of money.

IRA (*enters, with thermometer*). So what, then?

FYODOROVNA. What?

IRA. How much should I pay?

FYODOROVNA (*hastily*). Oh, that's all settled now. All I'm wondering is, how do you manage?

IRA. I surprise myself.

FYODOROVNA. Maybe I can get you a lodger from the rest-home. Eh? A woman did come here and ask. Spends all day in the rest-home up the hill. She'd only sleep here. She's got a bloke in the rest-home she comes to see.

IRA. I can manage for the time being.

FYODOROVNA. I could always let her come if you say so. She and her husband can sleep in a bed on the verandah. Twenty-four days would mean twenty-four roubles for you. Or he may not be her husband, for all I know.

IRA. Don't bother. I'm only just feeling free of my mother who lived with us. If there's one thing I don't want, it's a lodger.

FYODOROVNA. So I said to her I'd ask you, but I couldn't be sure what you'd say. What's twenty-four roubles nowadays, anyway? I'm sure she'd pay more.

IRA. What's a hundred and twenty-four roubles nowadays?!

FYODOROVNA. I also told her you didn't want her thirty-six roubles, your divan isn't big enough for two. You never know – you might want to have a lie-down on it for an hour or so when the kids were out. I told her you had a kid and there were two others as well. Three boys – it's like a whole platoon! And that was that. Then she asked me whether I couldn't find room on my plot for her bee-hives. She's got three bee-hives.

IRA. Fancy that!

FYODOROVNA. I ask you – bee-hives! First she wants a bed,

then it's her husband, then bee-hives! . . . You got a husband?

IRA. Divorced.

FYODOROVNA. Pays you alimony, does he?

IRA. Yes. Twenty-five roubles.

FYODOROVNA. Shocking. Well, that's the way of it . . . Valka Blum, he proposed to me the other day. He gets a pension of seventy-two roubles. He's got his three grown-up children in two rooms. Me, I've got half a house. He's seventy, and I'm seventy-two. And I can still water my apple-trees – thirty buckets a day. Maria Vasilievna Blum did the matchmaking. Wore my yellow shoes, put my teeth in, put on my blue raincoat and my blue shawl with the roses on it. She gave it me – my daughter-in-law, that is. Only present she ever gave me. It's in my chest-of-drawers, I'll show it you one day . . . Here I just wear any old thing, but I've got a Persian lamb coat, you know – been hanging in my daughter-in-law's cupboard since God knows when, along with a pair of shoes and a beaver-lamb tippet. One of these days I'll come to see you in Moscow and I'll look like a pantomime princess. I'm keeping it all for a rainy day. My daughter-in-law's mother's always boasting: 'How much have you got in your savings account?' So I say: 'What about you? Five figures, I expect?' And she says: 'No point in hiding it – around that and some more.' She wears diamond earrings to work, she's a cashier in one of them new supermarkets. One day two Georgians came up to her, one of 'em says: 'Look, my mother badly needs a pair of earrings just like yours.' Next day when she came to work – no earrings . . . Anyway, what do I want Valka Blum for? Men. Don't even like them. Why should I want to look after an old wreck like him? I didn't even love my husband.

Enter SVETLANA, TATYANA *and* VALERA.

VALERA. And here's the old lady herself! Hullo, bábushka.

FYODOROVNA (*not listening*). I just didn't love him, you see. Soon as I'd had my Vadim I left and went straight back to my mum. I dunno where my old man's buried, even.

VALERA. Gi's a kiss, baba Alya!

FYODOROVNA (*trying to ward off his embrace*). Don't!

VALERA. How you doing, old girl? (*Puts a bottle on the table.*)

FYODOROVNA (*wipes the corners of her mouth with two fingers*). I see you've got company. I'll be off.

SVETLANA (*thin as a rake, speaks in a bass voice*). Join us, Fyodorovna. We'll have a party.

TATYANA (*giggling*). Do yourself a favour, gran, and sit down – you can't go now!

VALERA (*mock-pompously*). Kindly take a seat.

FYODOROVNA. Well, the yid got hanged for company, I s'pose. I'll just get a spoon, my special dessert spoon. Be right back. (*Exit.*)

VALERA. H'mm!

All sit down, except VALERA. IRA *gets up and shuts the door to the adjoining room.*

VALERA. We're not so much friends as relations. All from the same farrow, as they say.

TATYANA (*giggles*). The things you say!

SVETLANA. What's a farrow, anyway?

VALERA. What's a farrow?! (*Raises his clenched fist.*) It's when a sow has piglets. Called farrowing. A farrow of piglets.

TATYANA. We're all sitting around waiting and you're going on about pigs. (*Giggles.*)

IRA *gets up, fetches cups and a loaf of bread and slices the bread.*

SVETLANA. Tatyana, we forgot – we've got some cheese. Mine's wrapped in cellophane, yours is in paper.

TATYANA (*giggles*). You get it then!

Exit SVETLANA. IRA *goes off into the next room, shutting the door firmly behind her.*

TATYANA (*to* VALERA). You took my purse again!

VALERA. I had to buy a bottle, didn't I?

TATYANA. I don't intend to keep you in food and drink.

VALERA. A fool is a fool is a fool.

TATYANA. I'm *not* a fool.

VALERA. These matters can only be settled over a bottle.

TATYANA. And supposing I won't agree?

VALERA. Shut up! Anything can be settled over a bottle. And who begged me to come? You. So I go out and buy some booze. All for *your* sakes, you cows.

TATYANA. You took my purse! Bastard!

VALERA. Have you ever stopped to think what it means for a man to be permanently skint?

TATYANA. Eight years with you and it's nothing but debts and alimony, dirty deals and once-in-a-lifetime bargains.

VALERA. How can a man live when he gets a hundred and thirty a month minus thirty-five roubles alimony?

TATYANA. You and your drink. that's what gets you into this mess.

VALERA (*hisses*). I'll sort you out later!

TATYANA. You've spawned kids.

VALERA (*indignantly*). Who has? Me?

TATYANA. Yes, you. Like it says in the Bible: Isaac begat Jacob.

VALERA. Listen! Each time a baby's born, the man dies a bit. And it's the same each time it happens. No man wants that. There's even a novel called 'You Only Live Twice'. Got it?

TATYANA. Why are you talking all this rubbish! Waste of time coming here, if that's all you're going to do.

VALERA (*laughs*). Right.

TATYANA *giggles as* IRA *enters carrying a chamber-pot.*

IRA. Back in a minute.

VALERA. Empty it in our loo. Feel free.

Exit IRA.

TATYANA. It's always the same: soon as you want something to eat or drink it's my purse that goes to the shops.

VALERA. Enjoy rubbing my nose in it, don't you?!

TATYANA. I should kick you out and sue for alimony.

VALERA. Good luck, sunshine! Know what you'd get? Sod all. I've worked it all out. Wages – 143 roubles. Thirty-three percent of that . . . three into a hundred and forty-three . . . that's forty-seven roubles and a few kopecks.

TATYANA. Forty-seven roubles and sixty-six kopecks.

VALERA (*maliciously*). And then divide it by two! You forgot that! Twenty-three roubles and a bit. And that's *monthly*! You're getting more out of me the way things are now.

TATYANA. It's twenty-five.

VALERA. Right.

TATYANA. I'm sick of it. I pay the rent and the electric. You eat. You sleep.

VALERA. Going to charge me for sleeping now, are you?

Pause.

TATYANA (*blinking back tears*). And what about your washing? I send it out to the laundry.

VALERA (*cheerfully*). Let's do an all-in deal – a rouble a day. But that includes nights. (*Uncorks the bottle.*)

VALERA *pours out into the cups, which they clink and toss down. Enter* SVETLANA *with cheese.*

SVETLANA. My old Leokadia is sitting in our room. She's convinced it's going to rain and if she lies down the water will pour in and she'll drown.

VALERA *offers a drink to* SVETLANA, *who first covers her cup with her hand, then gives in.* TATYANA *giggles.* SVETLANA *drinks.*

TATYANA. Call that a roof? One winter, and it's more like a sieve.

SVETLANA (*wipes her mouth with the back of her hand and nibbles a piece of cheese*). It's you who let the house get into this state. Rotten right through. It's your fault.

TATYANA. Listen to that. Let me tell you, without us to keep an eye on it, this house'd be a pile of rubble. Any house rots without an owner. We've kept it from falling down. Valera's at it day and night. The buckets of earth he's put on the roof.

SVETLANA. That's as maybe, but it's still you who let the roof rot.

TATYANA. It was not. We just happened to be living here. It's obvious. If you lived in a house that wasn't yours, you'd be doing sums in your head too. The roof'll cost four hundred to mend. We could rent something in the village for two whole summers for that kind of money! Four hundred! (*Giggles*.)

SVETLANA. You're using it, you ought to pay for it.

TATYANA. You're using it now, *you* pay.

SVETLANA. It was you made the holes in it.

TATYANA. We didn't dance on it, did we? It's just time that's done it – you know, old age. If you'd been living here, would *you* have paid?

VALERA. Her pay? That's a laugh.

TATYANA. You wouldn't fix someone else's roof, now would you?

SVETLANA. My old Leokadia's sitting in that room, hunched up under an umbrella, waiting to be drowned.

VALERA. She your mother, this old biddy?

SVETLANA. My mother-in-law. A legacy from my husband, her son. She was living with us when he died, so she stayed on for old times' sake. Anyway, since I do mainly night shifts, it means Maxim isn't alone at night. In my situation you can't be too choosy about your relatives.

VALERA. Who's Maxim?

TATYANA. Her son.

VALERA. Oh yes, that young lad . . . Was it him who had a fight with our Anton?

TATYANA. I work days, she's on nights. When she gets a shift on one of my days off, I sit with the boys. I tell you, we'd be better off doing a stretch in Siberia.

VALERA. Well, it's good that Anton has his friend with him. Otherwise he'd be getting into trouble with those Ruchkins . . . Hey, heard this one? 'Who's got whiskers and stripes?'

SVETLANA. Well, who has?

VALERA. Your mattress, of course!

TATYANA *giggles in embarrassment.*

SVETLANA. Hooligans, those Ruchkins.

VALERA. And the Blums are a gang of tearaways, too. The ones who live upstairs. Those kids are only seven or eight and they're already smoking.

SVETLANA (*to* TATYANA). I must say, I never thought you'd sweet-talk me into coming to this hell-hole.

TATYANA. Well, it's good enough for me . . . Could be worse. You just try and rent a dacha round here. They're all owned by Gosplan. There's the river, a forest, the airport. And you're getting it for nothing.

VALERA. Just like Gosplan!

SVETLANA. What's the good if the roof leaks? Suppose it decides to rain all summer?

VALERA. You'll get the rain for free, too.

TATYANA. She's right, Valera. There's no getting away from it – we've got to cover the roof with roofing felt.

VALERA. Roofing felt? Manual work turns me off. And brain-work makes me feel sick.

TATYANA. Perhaps we could thatch it.

VALERA. You dum-dum – where can you get thatch at this time of year? It's early summer – all last year's straw's been used up.

SVETLANA. What shall we do with the kids if the roof starts to leak?

VALERA. Sheet-metal workers, now – they make a fortune. The ones who put a car's bodywork together again after an overhaul. Think I'll go and try my hand at it.

TATYANA. Oh, of course – the Zhiguli car factory's just *waiting* for you to go and offer your services.

VALERA. Watch your mouth, you!

TATYANA. Call yourself a husband? If it starts raining, your own son's going to catch pneumonia.

VALERA. He should've done exercises to toughen him up, but you wouldn't let him!

Two boys – ANTON *and* MAXIM – *appear in the doorway.*

MAXIM. Aunty Ira's locked herself in our toilet.

VALERA. Out of here, you kids. Push off and play outside. Don't hang around here. Go and climb a tree. Your wounded comrade's out there! Your wounded comrade's up that tree! And you're going to rescue him, okay? Now. Move.

The boys exchange glances and disappear.

VALERA. Kids love me. And dogs. And drunks.

TATYANA. They can tell one of their own a mile off.

VALERA. I'll set them a training programme. Soon knock 'em into shape. I'll come down here regularly to see to it.

TATYANA. I'll believe that when I see it.

SVETLANA. I must've been mad to come here! As if it wasn't enough for me to crawl around after your Anton on all fours: 'Anton, your lunch is ready.' 'Anton, wash your hands, dear.' All the time he's playing me like a fish, and then he goes and buggers off.

TATYANA. You don't have to call him. He'll come soon enough when he's hungry.

SVETLANA. Oh, thanks – that's fine for him, but it's *me* who has to reheat the food. What am I supposed to be? A cook as well as a child-minder?

TATYANA. He can heat it himself. He's not a baby. He heats up his food at home. Got his key on a string round his neck, comes home from school and cooks his own tea.

SVETLANA. No, I'm not going to let him near a gas-stove. Even with grown-ups it can blow up in your face, and what's more it means kids get the chance to play with matches . . . But one thing's for sure – I can't live here without a roof.

VALERA. Hang on a minute. Let's have another drink, Svetlana, so's we can get to know each other properly. My name's Valera – well, you knew that already. (*Takes her hand and shakes it.*) I'm a useful bloke to have about. All we need is to lay our hands on the roofing material.

VALERA *pours out and they all drink. Enter* IRA.

VALERA. Ira! You're too uptight, want to watch that.

TATYANA. Ah, the long-awaited one. Come over here, Ira, and sit down.

SVETLANA. But we're cousins! Let's drink to it.

IRA. No, I'm sorry. I must see to my boy. He's not well.

TATYANA. We're all cousins . . . three cousins . . . twice removed . . .

VALERA. Time for another drink. The family that drinks together, sinks together.

SVETLANA. We had the same great-grandmother and great-grandfather.

IRA. I don't know as far back as that. I do remember an uncle by marriage called Philip Nikolayevich.

TATYANA. I can't remember any of my family. They all stayed behind in the village.

VALERA. Pity you can't remember. We could all go to your village and stay with them. For free.

TATYANA. We'd have to take presents. Parcels and rucksacks full of second-hand clothes.

VALERA. Oh, come on – no one wants dead relatives' cast-offs any more.

TATYANA. Nowadays they take little crimplene two-pieces for the kids.

IRA. I took my husband's surname. But my maiden name was Chantseva.

SVETLANA. Same with me. My married name's Vygolovskaya, but my dad's surname is Sysóyev. Mum's was Katagoshcheva.

IRA. My father was called Chantsev, but he's been dead for years. Mother married again, so she took my stepfather's name – Schilling.

VALERA. English?

IRA. He was a russified German.

TATYANA. My mum and dad had the same surname – they were

both Kuznetsovs. So both grandads and grandmas were all Kuznetsovs too!

VALERA. They were namesakes, but not related, please note. Now *my* surname is quite something – I'll spell it out for you: Kozlos Brodov! Kozlos! (*Pause.*) Brodov.

SVETLANA. With a hyphen?

VALERA. No. Why should it be?

TATYANA. And I'm Kuznetsova!

VALERA. So our young Anton is Kozlosbrodov!

TATYANA. We'll change it. We'll grease some pen-pusher's palm with ten roubles and change it one of these days.

VALERA. You watch your tongue! So . . . I propose a toast to the family. I don't mean all our biological relatives, I mean those here present!

Enter FYODOROVNA, *wearing a blue silk raincoat, a blue shawl patterned with roses, yellow shoes and flashing a double set of gleaming false teeth. She is holding a dessert spoon.*

FYODOROVNA. Welcome, all! I've made you a salad . . . Just what was growing in the garden. Washed it in the water-butt. So get some vitamins in you! It's a cress salad.

VALERA. You deserve a drink, Panteleimonovna. (*Pours some into her spoon.*)

FYODOROVNA (*drinks, pulls a face and eats some of the salad*). No, I'm Fyodorovna. My husband was Panteleimonovich. His father was a merchant of the second guild, owned a mill and two bakeries. There was twelve of them in his family. I married Vladimir. Then there was Anna, Dimitry, Ivan, Nadezhda, Vera, Lyubov, and their mother Sophie. The rest I've forgotten. Vera's the only one still living. In Drezna, in an old people's home. Bless her. So you lot are all sort of their grandchildren, but who's from who I dunno. Vladimir was a pilot in the air force, but I've no idea where he's buried. We were divorced. Now your mum, Ira, she'd remember more.

VALERA. So you're all cuckoos in old Vera's nest. I expect she had some kids of her own, didn't she?

FYODOROVNA. Outlived the lot. What became of her children's children, I've no idea.

SVETLANA. Were there a lot of them?

FYODOROVNA. Well, there's you three from three of them, but no one knows whether there are any grandchildren from the other nine.

VALERA. So this house isn't anyone's in particular, it belongs to all of you.

SVETLANA. There could be as many as twenty other grandchildren, our cousins.

FYODOROVNA. I doubt it. We had one child each . . . same as you've done. I had Vadim, then went back home to my mum. I just happened to get married to my old man, didn't love him. When Vadim was born I didn't look after him all that well, either. I remember when our next-door neighbour's house caught fire. I grabbed Vadim out of his cot, wrapped him in a blanket, ran outside and laid him on the ground and went off to carry buckets of water. By morning their place was burnt to the ground. Our fence was burnt down too, but luckily it didn't touch the house. Suddenly I remembered – where's my Vadim? He'd been lying there on the ground all night. I wasn't one for sitting around in those days! Now my Vadim's got a son. Sergei. He's very bright, good at school.

VALERA. Come and visit, do they?

FYODOROVNA. Not them! In the old days there was often a big difference in the kid's ages in one family. As much as twenty years between the oldest and the youngest. You lot could have kids for another fifteen years yet.

VALERA. Over my dead body!

SVETLANA. I wouldn't want to tie a stepfather down with another kid.

IRA. Suppose something happens to me before Pavlik is strong enough to look after himself? You just pray and pray you'll live long enough.

VALERA. You want to toughen him up. Wash his ears, neck and face in cold water every morning. That's what I want to do with our Anton.

TATYANA. Idiot! Who'd do that to him in winter?

VALERA. If it wasn't for *her*, I'd have made him really tough by now. Cold weather. Open windows. Cold showers . . .

SVETLANA. If it's showers they need, we've got the perfect place here. I'm not on duty today . . . so Tanya and I can put plastic sheeting over their beds . . . We'll never get the place properly dry . . . Thank you, Tatyana *dear*, for luring me here to be a free baby-sitter for your Anton while you go off to work and take life easy. So what about this roof, then?! What's more I've as much right to live in this dacha as you have. I don't need your permission . . .

VALERA. Last drinks, people. (*Pours out all round.*)

Exit IRA *to the adjoining room.*

VALERA. Look, Fyodorovna, have you got any of that medicine made from marigolds steeped in vodka?

FYODOROVNA (*guardedly*). What's it for?

VALERA. For a sore throat.

FYODOROVNA. No, Valera, for sore throats I use a gargle made with burdock. Shall I go and pick some for you?

VALERA. How about some of that lemon extract that the cosmonauts use – eleutherococcus?

FYODOROVNA. No, Valera. What's *that* for?

VALERA. It's for improving poor muscle-tone. Haven't you got any sort of cordial?

FYODOROVNA. Made with spirit?

VALERA. Of course.

FYODOROVNA. Matter of fact I have, but you wouldn't like it. It's made with iodine.

VALERA. Something a bit sweeter?

FYODOROVNA. I'll go and have a look. (*Exit.*)

Enter IRA.

IRA (*firmly*). Whatever you may think, I have a right to live in the other half of the house too. My mother's got the papers to prove it. So don't imagine I'm just making it up. Just because you moved in here first doesn't mean I have to pay a rent of 240 roubles a month.

SVETLANA (*quickly*). Nobody said anything! We'll swop rooms.

TATYANA. We'll move in here, you go over there – simple.

VALERA. What did I tell you? The only way to sort out a problem is over a bottle. And everybody's happy.

IRA (*getting worked up*). Fyodorovna phoned my mother and said there was no one living in your half of the house and that an empty house goes to pot. So down I come, spring clean everything, white-wash the window-frames in the room, clean the windows . . . I arrive a week later with all my things, with a fridge, with the kid, in a van, and what do I find? You've moved into the rooms I cleaned and painted. Marvellous. (*She sits down, exhausted.*)

VALERA. What's done's done, can't be undone. It's the law of the jungle.

IRA. You've played a disgusting trick on me.

VALERA. Women! They're all fools. Don't know when they're well off . . . Right, now! On your feet, girls. Clean the place up and hand it over to Ira. They haven't made too much of a mess there. You move over into the other half, Ira, and I'll cart your fridge over in the wheelbarrow.

IRA. I haven't the strength to move now. I suggest we all stay here on equal terms. Split the rent between us. Eighty roubles each. Otherwise, you're living rent free in *my* part of the house.

VALERA. Fine. We'll each put eighty roubles in the kitty. What do we get out of it?

IRA. Why should I pay at all when you're living here?

VALERA. All right, suppose only *we* pay. What are the arrangements then?

IRA. I stay here – you stay there.

SVETLANA. No. You don't understand. We'll pay the lot and move in here.

IRA. Oh, great. Me and my sick child in a room with a leaking roof.

TATYANA. All right, let's do it like this then: we'll mend the roof – Valera can do it – meanwhile you let our kids and the old lady stay under your bit of the roof.

IRA. Out on the verandah?

SVETLANA. In the room, in the room. It's cold out here.

IRA. What about me and Pavlik? His temperature's thirty-nine point six!

SVETLANA. What do we always do, we medics, in a case like this? We use blankets to put up a screen round him . . . We swab the room down with chloride of lime.

IRA. But it's not raining.

TATYANA. Seen that sky? It'll be sheeting down any minute.

SVETLANA. So we'll put up screens. The most important thing for him at the moment is warmth. He'll get that from our body-heat around him.

IRA. We split the expenses into three. Eighty each.

TATYANA. But you heard what I said just now, didn't you? It's going to cost 400 to mend the roof. Driving a hard bargain, aren't you? You pay 80 and we pay 280 each?

VALERA. Other people would charge 600 to do the roof. But because it's in the family . . .

IRA. You've lost me . . . You pay 200 each . . . But I have to pay 240, plus having *how* many people in my one room?

SVETLANA. There's only one roof and it's yours as well as ours.

IRA. Why is it mine?

SVETLANA. It's over your room, isn't it?

IRA. My bit doesn't leak!

VALERA. This is getting us nowhere. Listen, girls – how about us each putting a rouble into the kitty before the boozer shuts? Tatyana and me've already put in four roubles for this vodka.

IRA. I haven't got any money. Anyway, you won't even let me use your lav.

VALERA. That's because you're too proud to ask, Ira! Your pride'll be your undoing.

TATYANA. Valera built that lav himself eight years ago, didn't you love? You're a tenant here, aren't you? The landlady's bound to provide you with one.

IRA. Fyodorovna hasn't got one herself. She says go out to the hen-house. And there's a nasty-minded cockerel out there . . .

VALERA. You mean Vaska? Don't worry, he knows where to put his pecker and where not to.

IRA. I'm afraid of him. (*Sits down, hanging her head.*)

VALERA. Come on, girls! We're wasting time. The shop'll shut.

SVETLANA. The fact is, we've got to live together and make the best of it.

IRA. I know for a fact your two boys beat up Pavlik and held him in the water with his pants off. That's what made him ill.

SVETLANA. I'm going to bring them in here and we'll soon find out who pulled whose pants off. I'll be right back. (*Exit with rapid, purposeful stride, red-faced.*)

Enter FYODOROVNA, *carrying a medicine-bottle full of a dark liquid.*

FYODOROVNA. Here we are. It's sweet, Valera, like you wanted.

VALERA (*takes the bottle*). Aha! A hundred and fifty grammes.

FYODOROVNA. Infusion of poison-ivy root. (*Hands him her dessert spoon.*)

VALERA. Ta. (*With an air of mock seriousness:*) Sodium benzoate. Or sodium hydrocarbonate. It's all chemicals nowadays. Ammonia and aniseed drops. I know the stuff. Cough mixture. Why should I want it? No better than sugar syrup. To hell with it.

FYODOROVNA *takes back her spoon.*

VALERA. Hang on . . . (*Sniffs the liquid.*) Some muck. Doesn't smell of anything. Grandma's patent elixir. Oh well, here goes. (*Drinks from the bottle.*)

TATYANA. God – you're a bottomless pit . . .

VALERA (*shuddering with disgust*). Ugh! What the hell is this stuff?

FYODOROVNA. Even kids drink it. It's harmless. Anyway, you

wanted it. There – it says on the label: 'Dose – One dessertspoonful'. (*Snatches the bottle from* VALERA, *pours out a spoonful.*) This is the way to drink it. (*Drinks with relish, then wipes her mouth with the back of her hand.*)

VALERA (*groans*). Pfooo! It's disgusting! Ugh!

FYODOROVNA. It's very good for you. In a moment you'll start coughing up all that nasty phlegm.

VALERA. What's the stuff called?

FYODOROVNA. Ex-pect-or-ant.

VALERA. Holy mother! (*Rushes out of the door.*)

FYODOROVNA. What d'you expect if you drink almost the whole lot all at once?

TATYANA. Hey – you've still got my purse! . . . He'll spend my last two roubles, see if he doesn't.

Exit FYODOROVNA *to see what is the matter with* VALERA.

IRA. Oh Tanya, I can't go on. I'm so lonely. I'm nobody. Nobody needs me. When you came here, I thought we'd make up and be friends. Call yourselves cousins . . .

TATYANA. What about you?

IRA. I'm on my own. I've never had any brothers or sisters. Only my one little son.

TATYANA. But you've got your mum.

IRA. My mother! Huh . . . What a mother . . .

TATYANA. If I had my mum with me all the time I'd get rid of that piss-artist (*Nods towards the door.*) before he could turn round. When she comes to visit me from Sakhalin, it's like every holiday rolled into one. All warm and bright. Real home-sweet-home feeling. When she remarried they got sent there.

IRA. If only! If only it was like that for me!

TATYANA. Mama! 'Mama' 's the first word a person says, and the last.

IRA. My mother hates me. She really hates me.

TATYANA. Leave off, Ira. I don't like that kind of talk. It's got to

be at least half your fault as well. A mum is a mum . . .
Listen, I sussed you out from the start. You come over all
soft but then you sink your claws into anyone who comes
your way.

IRA. Maybe. I do it to stay alive.

TATYANA. So don't come whining to me. Our mothers give
birth to us in pain. They raise us, feed us and everything . . .
do our washing. Everything that we do now. Plus doing a job
as well. All our lives are built on motherly love. I don't think
I could ever be angry with Anton, let alone hate him. I could
kiss every toe on his little feet! I'd kill for him. Honest.

IRA. I could kill for Pavlik, too. So you can understand what it's
like when someone tries to drown your kid.

TATYANA. Oh, cut out the sob-stuff, for God's sake.

IRA. How would you like your Anton to be held under water?

Both women are losing their tempers.

TATYANA. Who told you that load of rubbish? Pavlik, I'll bet.
Stayed in the water till he was blue with cold, then made up
the whole story.

IRA. Two against one.

TATYANA. He's like a little old man, your Pavlik, not like a
proper kid at all. Always got his nose in a book. Too clever
by half. It's goody-goodies and mummy's boys like him who
always cop it from other kids. You'll see.

IRA. I've had enough of you. Go on, clear off out of here.

TATYANA (*slumped in despair*). It's going to rain, that's the trouble
. . . Anton's eight, and he needs a summer in the fresh air.
Had pneumonia last winter 'cos that fool would keep pouring
cold water over him. I'd like to kill him. Anton was ill for
two months, so I had to take two months unpaid leave to
nurse him. Wouldn't put him in hospital. My mother said to
me she'd rather see me die than let him go to hospital. She
lost her first kid – a boy – in hospital. I'd've had an older
brother. Let Anton sleep in your room, Ira!

IRA. When I cried and begged you to let me have your room,
you wouldn't!

TATYANA. But he's a kid, Ira – a kid!

SVETLANA *marches in, eyes blazing.*

SVETLANA. I've got to the bottom of it. It turns out your Pavlik
bit my Maxim on the shoulder. It's left an infected wound! A
lacerated wound! I'm going to see to it that that boy of yours
ends up in a remand home. Worst of all, Maxim was too
frightened to tell me. He knows what my reaction would be.
Maxim's been sickly ever since his father died. Diarrhoea
with blood in it. They suspected dysentery, but it was nothing
of the sort – he had a perforated intestine! I changed to
nights so as to look after him in the daytime.

TATYANA. He'll get better, your Maxim. These things heal by
themselves at that age. Did you know he grabbed hold of my
Anton yesterday and beat his head against a big stone? When
I came yesterday evening, his forehead was all bruised. Don't
suppose you're going to send your little Maxie off to a
remand home, are you? Didn't take *his* saliva for analysis, did
you?

SVETLANA *(in despair)*. I treated his wound – it was an accident.
You know what kids are when they're playing.

TATYANA. Of course – we mustn't forget you're a senior
member of the medical profession, must we.

SVETLANA. And by the way, Maxim said it wasn't him who held
Pavlik under water. Anton did. Maxim was standing on the
bank.

TATYANA. Yeah – and giving the orders.

Enter FYODOROVNA *with* ELKA *the cat; the old lady has
changed back into her everyday clothes.*

FYODOROVNA. She still can't find her kitten. Has anyone seen
it? Driving me mad with her crying. Can't sleep for it.

TATYANA. And Pavlik bit Maxim because Maxim screamed at
him: 'We won't let your mother come here any more – we
won't let her!' so Pavlik bit him. And he did right. I'd bite
someone if I was standing up for my mother.

Pause.

FYODOROVNA. She's got too much milk and it hurts her. That's
why she's yowling. Or she wants a tom. Is that it, Elka?
Miaow!

IRA. Svetlana, please take a look at Pavlik. I'm so worried about him.

SVETLANA (*instantly transformed into her professional self*). I'm sure it's nothing serious. I'll look at him right away.

IRA. There's a clean towel here. You'll find a washbasin in his room. (*Takes a towel from a line where it has been hanging.*)

Exit SVETLANA.

FYODOROVNA. Elka, Elka, Elka, poor little Elka! (*Looks under the table.*)

TATYANA *looks under the table too. Tense with anxiety,* IRA *waits for* SVETLANA. FYODOROVNA *is clearly unwilling to leave.*

TATYANA. Look, Fyodorovna, I've got some soup left over from yesterday evening. The boys didn't eat it all. Anton was probably just stirring his soup with his spoon and slopping it over, as usual. I'm going to make some more today, with some bone stock. You can have half a saucepanful.

FYODOROVNA (*after thinking it over*). It'll do for the cat. I'll bring her bowl.

TATYANA. It's not cat-food! I made it for the kids. Honestly, you treat that cat like she was some great lady. (*Exit.*)

Enter SVETLANA, *holding her wet hands out in front of her.* IRA *rushes to dry her hands with the towel;* SVETLANA *wears a white overall, a stethoscope round her neck.*

IRA. Let me dry your hands.

Exeunt IRA *and* SVETLANA.

PAVLIK'S VOICE. . . . and then the octopus started to twitch and jump and said: 'Oh, let me go, I'm hot.' So he let the octopus go, and the octopus flew up into the air. He did a bit of swimming and some flying too, and then they caught him high up in the sky . . .

For a while the verandah is empty. There is a knock on the outside door. Enter NIKOLAI IVANOVICH, *carrying a hold-all and an umbrella. He wears a very expensive all-wool tracksuit with a big, white plastic zip-fastener and white piping around the edges of the jacket – the successful Soviet bureaucrat's leisure-wear.*

NIKOLAI IVANOVICH. Hallo . . ? Have I come to the right place?

No one answers. Enter SVETLANA *and* IRA.

SVETLANA. Well, he has quite a severe respiratory infection. There's a lot of it about among children at the moment. His temperature will stay high for a while. You should give him sulfadimetoxin. One tablet now, another whole tablet tomorrow morning, then half a tablet twice a day. You have to start the course with a high dose, and he'll need attention, because he'll sweat a lot. When his temperature drops, keep an eye on him, change his clothes frequently and make sure he's dry.

IRA. I haven't got any sulfadimetoxin.

SVETLANA. I haven't got any either.

IRA. Isn't there something else we can give him?

SVETLANA. Personally I only ever use homoeopathic medicine. I suggest lime flowers, honey and lemon. I'll let you have some. Frankly, I haven't much faith in drugs. Only in special cases.

IRA. What am I to do?

NIKOLAI IVANOVICH. Far be it from me to interfere, but for influenza there's an excellent British preparation called Veganin. It'll put him right in three days. I caught 'flu in London, the hotel provided me with some and I brought a supply of it back with me.

SVETLANA. I couldn't recommend it. I don't know it . . . (*Adopts a very 'professional' tone:*) The important thing is to reduce the fever, let him sweat it out and give him diluted lemon juice to drink. Have you got any lemons?

IRA. Yes, I have.

SVETLANA. And I'll bring you some lime flowers. They're last year's, but the lime trees will soon be in bud again. (*Exit.*)

IRA. Well, at least I've got the lemons.

NIKOLAI. At last I've found you. What happened? Why weren't you at the Orient Hotel at eleven? If I hadn't met your postman I'd never have found you. Have you read the newspapers?

IRA. Why? Was there something special?

NIKOLAI IVANOVICH (*clearly hinting at something*). Was there something interesting in that news magazine *The Week*?

IRA. How should I know? (*Embarrassed, she does not look at* NIKOLAI IVANOVICH *but busies herself preparing a lemon drink.*)

NIKOLAI IVANOVICH. Look, I've covered every square metre of this place looking for you. My car's in for repairs. Not that I mind, because the exercise is good for me. This morning I sprinted all the way to meet you – and my copy of *The Week* wasn't there. My mother-in-law gave me a real ticking-off for giving it to you. She collects them all in a binder for my daughter Alyona, so when Alyona gets back and finds a copy missing, there'll be trouble. Right now she's on holiday on the Black Sea, at Koktebel, with her mother. (*Playfully:*) So might I ask what it was about that magazine that caught your eye?

IRA. I don't know.

NIKOLAI IVANOVICH. You must give it back. I haven't come all this way just for fun. My mother-in-law will blow it up out of all proportion. Only yesterday she said to me: 'For once in your life, Nikolai, you travel by train – and immediately a pretty girl tries to get off with you. She's all right, really, my mother-in-law but she does keep rather a beady eye on me.

IRA *has been pouring boiling water into a thermos and spooning in sugar.*

NIKOLAI IVANOVICH. If someone's ill, I do happen to have some oranges with me. (*Takes out a paper bag full of oranges and puts it on the table.*) Mind if I sit down? (*Sits down.*) I combed the whole of Romanovka, looking for my copy of *The Week*. I had only a rough idea of where you lived – you said 'Near the filling-station, name of Chantseva'. The postman told me how to get here. Nuisance about the car. Only a minor thing, but it still meant I had to walk.
This morning I almost sprinted to the Orient Hotel – but no sign of you or my copy of *The Week*! But thank God I've found you, otherwise I'd have had no peace from my mother-in-law. I can hear her now: 'Get that magazine back – I don't care how!' So it's her fault I've been chasing after you. Haven't run such a marathon for years. Especially

chasing a girl. You're about twenty-five, I'd guess – and crazy with it!

IRA. Ah – you're the man on the train! Of course. *The Week* . . . hang on a minute. *(She sorts through a pile of newspapers and hands a copy of the magazine to* NIKOLAI IVANOVICH).

NIKOLAI IVANOVICH. Well, was there anything interesting in it?

IRA. I haven't read it. Didn't have time. So you can go now. Haven't got time for you now, either.

NIKOLAI IVANOVICH *(stands up, puts the magazine on the table).* That's all right. You can read it later. Until my car's fixed – the brakes failed. *(Laughs.)* Crazy girl. Anyway, I've found you at last. And I'm going to keep my eye on you from now on. I can keep my mother-in-law happy now. I'll tell her I managed to pick up another copy at a kiosk.

Carrying the thermos, IRA *goes into the adjoining room.*

Where's your son? *(Glances into the room.)* Well now – what a big lad he is . . . Got a temperature, has he?

IRA'S VOICE. Forty.

NIKOLAI IVANOVICH. Well, could be worse . . . The bug I had in London, now, that really knocked me out. Don't worry, he'll get over it. Sweat it out. That young lady doctor was right. Natural medicines are gaining ground. Still, I'll get that drug for you right away. Just give me time to get my breath back. Thought I'd never see my magazine again! Mother-in-law collects them for my daughter. They both like reading them. Did I tell you I've got a daughter? Lovely girl, too. And *very* mature . . ! You know, finding you was just like a detective story . . .

IRA'S VOICE. Pavlik, please take your Analgin.

PAVLIK'S VOICE *(shouts).* Won't!

NIKOLAI IVANOVICH. Why give him Analgin? Now that stuff Veganin is a compound of three drugs, that's why it's so effective . . . Ah, he's taken it – good lad. You must always do as Mummy tells you. And drink your lemon juice . . . Oh, what a face he pulls . . ! That's it. Well done. Now you'll get better.

Enter IRA.

NIKOLAI IVANOVICH. Look, Mummy, peel him an orange . . . When you didn't show up at eleven, I started to comb the place at once. You see, I was wondering what could have happened to you. We'd made such a precise arrangement, she's a decent girl, I said to myself, something's amiss.

IRA. Not now, please. We'll talk about it later, I'm too worried now. He's got such a high fever.

NIKOLAI IVANOVICH. When will 'later' be? Children are always getting ill. You mustn't weaken the boy's resistance by letting him see you're upset. Life must go on. You're not in mourning, after all. He'll be all right after a bit longer in bed, you'll see. No harm in him knowing you have visitors. He's *quite* happy in there on his own.

IRA. No, please go. I told you – I can't see you now.

NIKOLAI IVANOVICH. You mustn't let yourself go to pieces like this. You're setting him a bad example.

Exit IRA, *closing the door behind her. Enter* SVETLANA, *who opens the door into* PAVLIK's *room. She is holding a bicycle-tyre and inner tube.*

SVETLANA (*indignantly*). *Now* look what I've just found out. Good thing there's an outsider here as well. I'll have you know his dad bought him this bike – it's his only memory of his father! Now tell me, in front of a witness, what did Pavlik slash Maxim's inner tube with and why did he do it? Look, Pavel, you did this with a knife, didn't you? I'll give you knife, you little wretch!

IRA *sharply closes the door.*

SVETLANA (*bursts into tears*). Maxim's crying . . . I can't bear it when a kid's made to cry . . . I don't know what I'll do . . .

NIKOLAI IVANOVICH (*kindly*). Look, don't be upset. Let me have a look . . . (SVETLANA *gives him the inner tube.*) . . . I see . . . well, the inner tube's done for, I'm afraid it's beyond repair. You can throw it away. And the tyre, too.

SVETLANA *nods, wiping away her tears.*

NIKOLAI IVANOVICH. I'll try and find you another one like it by this evening. My daughter's bike is knocking around somehow at home, and it's the same make. She's got a new one, a folding bike. She's this big now. (*Stretches his arm upwards to indicate someone very tall.*)

SVETLANA *nods and sits down.*

My mother-in-law never throws anything away. We got that bike seven years ago.

SVETLANA. Maxim said: 'If I catch Pavlik, I'll beat him up.' I yelled back at him: 'You mustn't do that, he's younger than you!' But I can't be watching him all the time. I've got two of them on my hands already. (*Stretches out her arms and turns her hands over palms-up.*) Look! They're trembling! So, Pavlik (*Turns towards the door.*) you can run away or defend yourself from now on, I won't help you. (*Exit.*)

NIKOLAI IVANOVICH (*hangs the tyre and inner tube around his neck, then opens the door into* PAVLIK's *room*). Boo! You wouldn't run away, would you? Not when you're the son of a mother like yours. You'd face the enemy with whatever came to hand, a log of wood or a stick, wouldn't you? And if you can't find anything – stick out two fingers . . . Oh, do it to me, would you? (*Gives the two-fingered salute, nods and cocks a snook.*) That's right – I deserved it!

Enter IRA. *She closes the door behind her and leans her back against it.*

NIKOLAI IVANOVICH. May I introduce myself? I live up the hill, above the quarry. One of the Gosplan dachas. I commute from Moscow nearly every day. (*Shouts towards the door.*) My name's Nikolai Ivanovich, but please call me Kolya. And what's your mummy's name? Eh?

IRA. Ira.

NIKOLAI IVANOVICH. Pleased to meet you. Any chance of a cup of tea, Ira? I'm parched.

IRA. The water in the thermos is for Pavlik.

NIKOLAI IVANOVICH. Is that the only water there is? What about the kettle? (*Picks up the kettle and shakes it.*) You're right. There's no water in it.

IRA. There's no water because I've had no time to go out to the pump today.

NIKOLAI IVANOVICH. Where are your buckets? I know where the pump is. Having received your orders, I will proceed to carry them out.

Exit NIKOLAI IVANOVICH *with two buckets. In the doorway he almost bumps into* SVETLANA, *who is carrying a jar of honey.*

SVETLANA. Here's some honey. Make a horseshoe-shaped compress and put it round his neck. With children, you mustn't put a compress on the thyroid, it can have a bad effect later . . . And another thing! Your darling Pavlik, even though he's smaller and younger, pushed my Maxim off his bike into that heap of scrap metal round the corner.

IRA. But why is Maxim always ramming people with that bike of his? He knocked down a little girl in the playground yesterday. Her grandma came here in tears. He never stops ramming Pavlik with it.

SVETLANA. It was just in fun. Or an accident. Maxim's not a telltale, doesn't come running to me for nothing. Know what 'Maxim' means in Latin? The best!

IRA. Wrong. Not the best – the biggest. Maximus.

SVETLANA. No, it means the best. I looked it up. The best.

IRA *says nothing.*

SVETLANA. The fact remains Maxim was pushed on to a pile of rusty tins – that's a horrible thing to do. He could get tetanus. Anyway, it burst the tyre, so what might it do to a child? (*Shakes her fist towards the door.*) I'll get you, you little ape. Nasty little monkey. (*To* IRA.) You've spoilt him rotten and one day you'll pay for it. (*Bursts into tears.*) God, when a child hasn't got a father, people think they can do what they like to him.

NIKOLAI IVANOVICH (*enters breathless*). That pump is pretty far away for you members of the weaker sex. (*Puts down the buckets.*) Long time since I carried water in buckets. Takes me back to my young days. Listen, Ira. Is this house your property?

IRA (*angrily*). Yes, it is. Belonged to my grandmother's aunt.

SVETLANA. Huh! Her property?! That's a good one! Tatyana'll have a fit when she hears that. Her house, indeed!

NIKOLAI IVANOVICH. You should get that great-aunt of yours to write a request to have the water-main extended to her property.

IRA. She doesn't live here. She's been in an old people's home at Drezna for the past eight years.

NIKOLAI IVANOVICH. Why couldn't you forge her signature? I'll get the application through for you. I've got a contact on the district council.

SVETLANA. First it'll be the water, then she'll claim the whole place. Her house. Huh! (*Exit.*)

NIKOLAI IVANOVICH. Ira, do put the kettle on. I'm simply dying of thirst. I've been run off my feet trying to find you. My wife and daughter have been away for six weeks. Mother-in-law is staying here at the dacha. I'm in Moscow, mostly living out of tins. After work most of the shops are shut, so I drag myself down here, because at least mother-in-law will cook me fresh food. I've not got a healthy constitution. That's why she and I were taking the local train out here yesterday to find some strawberries, and that's where you bumped into me! My mother-in-law said: 'What a forward girl! Fancy asking a strange man for his magazine! She's obviously got her eye on you, Nikolai.' And she thinks I oughtn't to have given it to you. 'Obviously', she said, 'if you gave it to her, she'll take it as a sign that you fancy her too.' I assured her she'd have the magazine back. So mother-in-law knows we're meeting . . . Why *did* you ask for it? Do you fancy me? Be honest, now.

IRA. For heaven's sake, can't a person ask to read someone's paper these days?

NIKOLAI IVANOVICH. You're great! You really are. And you're gutsy. I love a gutsy girl (*Shouts towards the door:*) Tell me, Pavlik – where's your dad?

IRA. Leave the child out of this. You're going too far.

NIKOLAI IVANOVICH. I think I have my answer. No dad.

IRA. That has nothing to do with anything.

NIKOLAI IVANOVICH. And what does Mummy do?

IRA. I teach Gaelic. I make 120 roubles a month. I'm paid by the hour.

NIKOLAI IVANOVICH. Good for you! There can't be much competition!

IRA. I also know Manx.

NIKOLAI IVANOVICH. It's not exactly my field, but I can always look around and see if I can be of help. If those languages really exist, there must be a certain potential demand.

IRA. Welsh and Cornish as well.

NIKOLAI IVANOVICH. Really? I'm impressed. Young – and clever with it.

IRA. Though Cornish is almost a dead language.

NIKOLAI IVANOVICH. Never mind, we'll see what we can do. Listen, Ira. Come back with me to my dacha and I'll give you some of that Veganin. You'll have to lock Pavlik's door to stop your neighbours from getting at him. And we shouldn't forget to take that bicycle and inner tube. My mother-in-law's spending the evening with a neighbour, so she won't notice if I take a wheel off that old bike and bring it back here.

IRA. They're not neighbours. They're my relations. My second cousins.

NIKOLAI IVANOVICH. Relations, eh? Well, it happens . . .

IRA (*pause; then through the door*). Pavlik, I'm just popping out to fetch you some medicine. I'll lock the door, all right? The pot's under the bed and your lemon drink's in the thermos. Don't spill it. (*To* NIKOLAI IVANOVICH:) His hands are shaking, you see.

NIKOLAI IVANOVICH. Can you peel an orange, young man?

PAVLIK'S VOICE. No!!

NIKOLAI IVANOVICH. Then you peel some for him, Mummy. A whole pile of them. Give him a treat. I can go and get some more. I can get as many as I want. One of the perks of my job. (*Laughs.*) For the time being, at least.

IRA. Pavlik, shall I ask Fyodorovna to come and sit with you?

NIKOLAI IVANOVICH. Look, if I were you I'd put something warm round you. A rug or something.

IRA. I've got a raincoat.

NIKOLAI IVANOVICH. A rug's what we really need. I know these parts. It can get very misty and damp.

IRA. I haven't got a rug.

NIKOLAI IVANOVICH. Have you got a blanket?

IRA. Yes, I have.

NIKOLAI IVANOVICH. That'll do, then.

IRA. Wait a moment. Pavlik's calling me. (*Exit.*)

NIKOLAI IVANOVICH (*through the door*). He'll be all right. We won't be long. Back in half an hour or forty minutes. I'll bring him back my slide projector and some slides. My daughter's away . . . mother-in-law's over at the neighbours . . . then we'll all look at the slides. Changing the guard in London. Took them myself. I'm good at it. (*Holds up his thumb in an 'OK' gesture.*)

IRA (*entering*). It's no good. I can't come with you. He'll start sweating in a minute. I'll have to change his clothes. Fyodorovna can't do it.

NIKOLAI IVANOVICH. Pity . . . damned pity . . . Oh well, mist or not I'll toddle off and get the stuff myself. The patient needs it. Oh, and that inner tube and tyre.

IRA. Shall I get you a blanket?

NIKOLAI IVANOVICH (*bitterly*). What do I want a rug for on my own?

VALERA (*looks in from outside*). Strategic reconnaissance! (*Disappears.*)

NIKOLAI IVANOVICH. With neighbours like this you should keep your door locked. (*Exit.*)

Enter VALERA.

VALERA. You're a dark horse, Ira, and no mistake. (*Produces a bottle and sits down, a smug grin on his face.*)

IRA. Please go – he's just getting off to sleep.

VALERA. When I look at you, you're like a wood floor before it's been sanded smooth. Only the second time I've seen you, and each time I've thought the same thing. Once I was going to a funeral with my sister. By train. She tipped all those pots and jars out of her bag and started smearing, painting and powdering her face. Blow me, she was like a new woman. Mind you, you'd need paint-stripper to get it off her. But what a woman! (*Uncorks the bottle.*)

Enter TATYANA.

VALERA (*hastily*). I came to see her about the roof. I'll explain everything.

TATYANA. Had a few in the grocery, did you?

VALERA. What are you on about? I bought this for you.

TATYANA. You can give me back my purse for starters. Where are my two roubles?

VALERA *hands over the purse.*

TATYANA (*looking in the purse*). Where are they?

VALERA *flicks his fingernail against the bottle.*

That didn't cost two roubles. It costs one fifteen.

VALERA (*righteously*). There's a surcharge if you buy it in a restaurant.

TATYANA. You got it in the restaurant?

VALERA (*would-be seriously*). Now about the roof . . .

TATYANA. Pissed to the eyeballs. Soon they'll haul you off to the cooler and slap a 70-rouble fine on you.

VALERA. Don't be bloody silly! Don't know what you're talking about . . .

TATYANA. Listen, Ira, I've got something to tell you. I've found out it wasn't Anton who pushed your boy under the water. Anton owned up to me. He'd been by himself all that day. It's that Maxim who acts the little boss and orders him about. Anton always tells me everything. I came home from work and he came running to meet me. He didn't say anything, he just put his face in my hands and I could feel my hands were wet from his tears. Anton had asked Maxim to lend him a book – one of yours, by the way, *Mary Poppins*. Maxim had already read it, but he wouldn't give it to Anton. 'You can only have it,' he said, 'if you'll be my slave'. He made him kneel down in front of him. I said to him: 'Maxim you've read this book, and it's about good, kind people.

Hasn't it taught you anything?' It's your book, Ira. Please lend it to Anton.

IRA. Sure, take it. Tell Maxim I said he must pass it on to you.

TATYANA. I think you should know he wasn't going to give it back to you at all! Until you'd got him a new inner tube and tyre for his bike.

VALERA. And don't let him or his mum in here, either.

TATYANA. Exactly . . . Listen, tell your Pavlik to play with Anton. Much better for them to be pals with each other than with that Maxim. And I'll cook for you, instead of for Svetlana. I'd rather cook for you anyway. All you have to do is feed Anton. She won't. She doesn't give a toss. And I'll make it up to you. I'm due for my holiday in November.

VALERA (*portentously*). I get my leave in December. (*Pours out, drinks.*) I'm a Decembrist, I am.

TATYANA. Is that a deal, then?

Enter FYODOROVNA.

FYODOROVNA. I was just telling Svetlana it's going to rain any minute. Tatyana, you'd better get the buckets and basins. It'll be pelting down soon. Now, where are you going to sleep tonight? Go on, there's a couple of buckets in the larder and a tin bath under the front steps.

TATYANA. Ira's letting us sleep in here.

IRA. On the verandah.

Enter NIKOLAI IVANOVICH.

FYODOROVNA. Come on, Valera, up you get. Never mind the state you're in, you're going to give me a hand.

NIKOLAI IVANOVICH. Some medicine was wanted. I've brought it.

IRA. Thanks. No need now. He'll sweat it out, and we're getting ready to go to bed. (*Exit to* PAVLIK's *room.*)

VALERA. Sit down. I'm Valery Gerasimovich. Qualified motor mechanic temporarily employed on car-washing duties. Have a drink.

NIKOLAI IVANOVICH. Someone's ill in this house, you should keep your voice down.

VALERA. You Ira's husband?

NIKOLAI IVANOVICH. Ah, if only!

Pause.

FYODOROVNA. All right, time for bed. You take his feet, Tatyana.

They heave VALERA *to his feet.*

VALERA. Ira! Don't let *them* in here, got it?

TATYANA. Come on, on your feet.

VALERA. Life's like a battle at sea – loser goes to the bottom!

TATYANA. If you won't walk, I don't know what . . .

VALERA. There are two sorts of ifs – if you drink, you die, if you don't drink you die anyway, so drink . . .

TATYANA *picks up the bottle; she and* FYODOROVNA *lead* VALERA *out.*

NIKOLAI IVANOVICH. And I've brought another sort of medicine! (*Puts a bottle of brandy on the table.*)

IRA. Kindly get out!

NIKOLAI IVANOVICH. Now, now. Temper, temper. Look, I've brought a new inner tube and tyre. (*Produces them from a bag.*) I really had to sweat to get them off that bike. And here are those tablets I brought from England. Well?

IRA. God, how many times do I have to tell you? Please go!

NIKOLAI IVANOVICH. It's started to rain. Well, that's all right, I've got an umbrella. You know, I love it when it's raining and you're indoors. Out there it's all wet, and you're all snug and dry in the warm. Gives you a nice, safe feeling. Don't chase me out, don't swear at me. I've been so longing to be with you.

NIKOLAI IVANOVICH *puts the kettle on the gas, lights it and warms his hands.*

NIKOLAI IVANOVICH. The joke was, my mother-in-law hadn't gone out and she was padding around for ages, so I had to lie in wait. Felt like James Bond.

IRA. They'll get soaked before long. Their half of the roof's a mass of holes. So you've got to go, because they'll be coming in here soon. We made an agreement. I said they could sleep in here. Now hurry up and go!

Through the verandah windows FYODOROVNA *can be seen scuttling past with an upturned tin bath over her head.*

NIKOLAI IVANOVICH. Yes, I can sense the great migration is about to start. No more sitting around for you and me, eh? Listen, come to the little bridge in the meadow tomorrow evening. About ten-ish, OK? We'll make a bonfire and I'll bring some skewers of meat and things and cook shashlik. Like shashlik? And some Georgian wine. If only you knew how much I've fallen for you. Your eyes are like a couple of skewers, too, know that?

IRA. Don't just sit there! They'll be here any minute and you look as if you've taken root. And they are the people who won't even let me use their loo. Now I have to put up with *them*, on top of having a sick child. Please go! Quickly! They're coming already.

NIKOLAI IVANOVICH (*sadly*). You know, you frighten me!

IRA *starts busily pushing the table and the chairs towards the walls. Exit* NIKOLAI IVANOVICH. IRA *watches him go, holding out her hand to feel the rain. She shivers. A procession appears, led by* FYODOROVNA, *still with the tin bath held over her head; next comes* VALERA, *his jacket collar turned up, a rucksack on his back and carrying two folded camp beds. Behind him comes* TATYANA, *holding out her raincoat on each side to shelter* ANTON *and* MAXIM; *one of them carries a kettle, the other a saucepan.* SVETLANA *brings up the rear, with one hand holding an umbrella over the aged* LEOKADIA *and carrying a suitcase in the other hand. None of them look at* IRA.

FYODOROVNA. Plenty of room for all of you in my room. Sixteen square metres, all warm and dry.

Exeunt through the door leading off to FYODOROVNA's *quarters.* IRA *shuts and bolts the verandah door, moves the furniture back to its previous positions. She puts out the light and goes into* PAVLIK's *room, leaving the door ajar.*

PAVLIK'S VOICE. Mum, would you like me to tell you another fairy story? One day a grey wolf got into the city hospital. They grabbed him by the tail and brought him to the doctor.

That was where they did operations on all the wolves. They cut out their livers and looked at them in case their dinner had got stuck in them. Then they sewed them up again and it hurt. But the wolf liked it there. They gave him meat and cabbage for his lunch. He was very crafty and ate lots and lots and lots of cabbage, but the wolf had a big, big liver and all his lunch went in it. He was an English wolf and he grew wings. They grew out from *here* – little tiny, thin, thin wings . . .

ACT TWO

Scene One

IRA's flat in Moscow. IRA's mother, MARIA PHILIPPOVNA, *is talking on the telephone.*

MARIA PHILIPPOVNA. Hullo. It's me, Maria . . . Is that you
. . ? Why haven't you rung me for such ages . . ? What . . ?
All right. I'll call you again this evening. (*Hurriedly.*) Be sure
to come to my funeral. That's all. I'll explain when I ring
later. (*Replaces the receiver. Pause for thought, then she dials again.*)
Hullo . . ? Ask Kondrashkova to come to the phone, please
. . . Oh. When will she be back . . ? Are the Yelovskys there
. . ? Or any of the old staff . . ? This is Maria Schilling. Who
is that speaking . . ? This is the first time I've spoken to you
. . . I've just never come across you before. Or rather, you
haven't spoken to me before. So sorry to have bothered you.
Forgive me . . . No, no – not at all! Goodbye . . . (*Replaces the
receiver. For a while she sits, smiling, then dials another number.*)
Hullo . . . Yes . . . I've definitely decided to go into hospital.
No, don't hang up . . . Listen, don't hang up . . . You know
very well why . . . No, no one else is here . . . Ira's renting a
dacha for 240 a month. She borrowed 100 of it from me, for
the advance payment. Now she won't have to give it back to
me . . . Listen, I've finally decided to go in. I don't yet know
what my address will be, but as soon as I know I'll tell you.
I've been dithering over it for six months, now I'm taking a
leap in the dark. If they cut me to ribbons, they cut me to
ribbons . . . She'll actually benefit from it. She'll get a two-
roomed flat . . . And she won't have to pay back the hundred
roubles . . . Don't hang up! Hear me out . . ! I've made up
my mind to go in. Ira needs my help, but what help can *I*
give her? Pavlik's ill all the time, because she lets him catch
cold and doesn't feed him properly. The child needs feeding
up, but she won't. The effort's killing me . . . My admission-
order's already to hand . . . All right, I'll phone you again

from the hospital, provided they don't put me on the operating-table straight away. After that I won't ring. If I don't ring, it'll mean I'm already in the operating theatre. But I'll try and ring before the operation . . . Well, of course, there'll be other patients to prepare for surgery, blood samples to take. But mine's an emergency operation . . . As long as possible. I'll probably hang on for six months or so . . . No, I haven't been to the dacha. Ira doesn't want me there and I don't even know how to get in touch with her . . . Telegram. Yes, but I don't yet know the address of the hospital . . . How can one send it from the hospital? She sometimes brings the boy back for a bath, maybe once a week, but now it's been a whole fortnight . . . They could be dead, for all I know. I'll leave a note for her here, telling her to phone you . . . But if Pavlik gets ill and she's sick too, she might not come back for another week yet. That boy's always so sickly when he's out there . . . And she won't take him swimming, because she's been terrified of water since childhood . . . Well, it's a nice situation I've got myself into. If Pavlik's ill, she wouldn't even show up to bury me. Now that would give people something to think about!

The door opens. Enter IRA *and* PAVLIK. *The boy's head is wrapped in a scarf, topped by a woolly cap.* IRA *leads* PAVLIK *past* MARIA PHILIPPOVNA, *who turns to face them and continues speaking in a very clear and distinct voice until* IRA *and* PAVLIK *have gone into their room and the door is shut behind them.*

Anyway, you now know what's happening. I invite you to my funeral. You may well be the only person to come. Don't bring Mikhail, he doesn't like these things. I want to be buried wearing my navy-blue English tailormade. It's hanging in the wardrobe in a gauze bag. And with my medal. My blue shoes are wrapped in tissue paper in a box below the suit. My blouse and all the other things are in the large pink box under the shoes . . . No, Ira knows nothing about it. She doesn't want to know and never listens to me . . . So I'll call you again before I die. I've put aside the money for my funeral and for a wake – it's in my savings-bank account. I shall have my will notarised in hospital, before the operation. I'm making *you* my sole heir and executor . . ! No, don't go just yet – you'll get to the doctor in plenty of time, and in any case you'll have to wait your turn for ages. I sat in the waiting-room for four hours the day before yesterday. They

were only checking my blood-pressure, which of course had
gone up . . . No, don't do that. Your Mikhail will wait for
you . . . Look, it's summer now. What if he is dressed? He
won't die of heat-stroke – he's not exactly wearing a fur coat
. . . Don't interrupt! I want to be buried in the Vagankovskoe
Cemetery, alongside my mother. The grave's in the name of
Chantseva-Schilling. Plot number 183. Got that . . ? Are you
writing this down . . ? Then make a note of it . . . Well, sit
him in your chair, and I'll talk to him while you go and get a
pencil . . . Put him on the phone . . . Hello, Misha! How are
you . . ? He can't hear . . . Misha! Put on your hearing-aid
. . . Misha! Ah, she's guessed what to do and put it in his ear
. . . Hello! It's me, Maria . . ! Why are you so late in going to
see the doctor? You'll be too late if you don't look out.
Surgery hours are only till three, and you'll have to wait for
four hours . . . He doesn't understand a thing. Senile. Misha,
this is Masha Schilling! . . . What . . ? He's getting feeble-
minded. Doesn't remember. Which doctor are you seeing
. . ? They're taking him to see a urologist. He's speaking at
last. He's very worried about it . . . You're very sprightly for
your age, I'd say. Now I'll make him laugh: Misha! Come
over and see me. I've got a bottle of vodka and we'll split it,
you and I . . ! No good, he's not hearing again. The old
boy's practically stone deaf . . . Hello, it's me. Is that you?
Have you found a pencil? Right. Note this down: Plot
number 183. Philip Nikolaevich Schilling, that's my father,
and Alexandra Nikitichna Schilling, my mother. That's all
. . . What time do you have to be there . . ? Well, there's still
some time. So it's agreed, then – I'll leave everything to you
in my will and you'll bury me . . . No, you fool – *you're* going
to bury me! (*Jokingly.*) No – *you* bury *me*! (*Laughs.*) I'll come
round this evening and take a cup of tea off you . . . No, I
won't go into hospital today, I'll go tomorrow.
After all, I've waited six months already, so what's another day?

IRA (*Enters*). Mama . . .

MARIA PHILIPPOVNA. When you've waited half a year for
    admission, what difference is one day going to make?

IRA. Mama, Pavlik's ill.

MARIA PHILIPPOVNA. Now tell me about yourself. How are
    you coping?

IRA. Mama!

MARIA PHILIPPOVNA. Don't shout, I'm not deaf . . . It's Ira, she's come back unexpectedly . . . No, you mustn't! She'll be leaving again straight away, as she always does. Don't put down the receiver. (*To* IRA:) Do you realise your mother's dying a slow death? . . . (*To the telephone:*) I'm talking to her . . . Yes, all right. I'll try and pop in, if I'm still capable of 'popping in'. I'll tell Ira to look to you for guidance. (*To* IRA:) I'm talking to Nina Nikiforovna. She's ringing because she's worried about me. (*To the telephone:*) I'm just telling her that other people phone me more often than she does. My own daughter, too . . . Listen, I still haven't got around to the most important question: How is Leonid . . ? Oh, my God . . . Run, run, if you can still run. (*Replaces the receiver.*) They're getting very frail.

IRA. Mama, I've brought Pavlik home because he's ill.

MARIA PHILIPPOVNA. Have you stopped to think that I could be ill too? Have you? Why haven't you been near me for two weeks? In my condition, I might have died in that two weeks.

IRA. Just sit with him while I run out to the chemist and the bakery.

MARIA PHILIPPOVNA. I'm going into hospital. I've had my admission-card.

IRA. Why the sudden rush?

MARIA PHILIPPOVNA. It has to be done some time.

IRA. You can wait a little bit longer. I'm tied hand and foot!

MARIA PHILIPPOVNA. I knew it! You haven't brought him here for a bath for two weeks. The child's covered in spots. But if anything were to happen to me, you'd only find out when they broke the door down.

IRA. Oh, don't start that again! You're perfectly fit.

MARIA PHILIPPOVNA (*rummaging in her handbag*). What's this then? Is this an admission-card or isn't it? Why are you so full of malice?

IRA. This says it's just for an examination.

MARIA PHILIPPOVNA. But what are they looking for?

IRA. All right. But please just wait fifteen minutes while I go out for some bread.

MARIA PHILIPPOVNA. The doctors will all have gone home by then.

IRA. 'Course they won't! Which hospital are you going to?

MARIA PHILIPPOVNA. Why do you want to know?

IRA. Mama, don't be so selfish. Look what I've brought: a jar of goat's milk . . . Eggs . . . A jarful of soup for him and you . . . Some rissoles in this saucepan . . . Just feed him and put him to bed. He's exhausted.

MARIA PHILIPPOVNA. It's you who've brought him to this state! He's so skinny . . . Socks full of holes . . . Who do you love better, Pavlik, Mama or Grandma? He's forgotten who I am, or else he's been turned against me. Listen, darling, I'll read you your favourite book, *Mary Poppins*, shall I . . ? Did you bring it with you, Ira?

IRA. I lent it to someone to read.

MARIA PHILIPPOVNA. But it's not your book – it's mine.

IRA. No, it's *mine*. I bought it in Kamenets at the same time as I bought *A Hundred Years of Solitude*.

MARIA PHILIPPOVNA. And where is *A Hundred Years of Solitude*? I haven't seen that for ages either. You just give everything away – and me still alive! You're a weak person! You believe everything people tell you and you'll do whatever they say! You never know where anything is: now it's your books; soon you won't know where your mother's grave is.

IRA. That's enough! What am I s'posed to do – drag Pavlik with me to the chemist? He can't be left on his own. He'll cry . . . All right, then. *I'll* feed him; *I'll* put him to bed; and then when he's asleep I'll run down to the chemist and the bakery.

MARIA PHILIPPOVNA. The impertinence of her! (*Wipes away tears.*) I sit here, worried to death, and she doesn't even bother to phone me. She couldn't care less about Pavlik or me. Oh, just you wait. One day you'll be sorry. I shall die soon and then you'll be sorry.

IRA. We've all got to die sometime!

MARIA PHILIPPOVNA. When are you going to give me back my hundred roubles?

IRA. I told you. In the autumn.

MARIA PHILIPPOVNA. Go and get the money from the boy's father. It's his duty to give you financial support.

IRA. He already does.

MARIA PHILIPPOVNA. Then go and ask that boyfriend of yours.

IRA (*bursts into tears*). Oh God!!

PAVLIK'S VOICE. The impertinence of her.

MARIA PHILIPPOVNA. See what he learns from you?!

IRA. Look, Pavlik, we'll have something to eat, have a wash and a rest, and then we'll go back to the dacha. We'll walk down to the river and into the woods to look for mushrooms.

MARIA PHILIPPOVNA (*to* PAVLIK). Mama spends time and money on everyone else, but she wouldn't bring her own mother a few sweets.

IRA. I'm short of money.

MARIA PHILIPPOVNA. And I'm short of a hundred roubles. And there'll be my funeral to pay for! What with?

IRA. You've got a savings-bank account.

MARIA PHILIPPOVNA. That's meant for something else.

IRA. Aunty Nina will take care of it.

MARIA PHILIPPOVNA. I do not intend to leave the money to you.

IRA. That's just fine by me. (*Exit to* PAVLIK's *room.*)

MARIA PHILIPPOVNA *picks up the telephone receiver, dials a number and waits for the call to be answered.*

MARIA PHILIPPOVNA. Hello . . . May I speak to Kondrashkova, please . . ? Oh, I'm sorry, I obviously misunderstood you when I rang earlier . . . she won't be in today . . . I see . . . Ah, it's you – the same person I spoke to last time. This is Maria Schilling speaking. Please tell Kondrashkova tomorrow that the panic's over. I was going to look for my family, who had vanished. They'd gone out to a dacha where there's no

telephone . . . Please tell Kondrashkova that all's well with
me now . . . I'm simply laughing with happiness . . . (*Wipes
away tears.*) You'll tell her, will you . . ? I won't be here
tomorrow . . . So I won't be able to call her again . . . All the
best to you . . . I've got to run out to the chemist, the little
one's not well. Long life and happiness to you too . . . I'm
just so glad they're back! It seems they were ill, and couldn't
let me know . . .

Enter IRA.

MARIA PHILIPPOVNA. They're all I have in life, you see . . .
You're very kind – what a pity we've never met. I'd introduce
you to my daughter, she's almost got her Ph.D., you know . . .

IRA. Mama!

MARIA PHILIPPOVNA. That's her calling. I must go now.
(*Replaces the receiver.*) What are you shouting for? Go on. Go
out. Do what you want. You can go. Go to your, er . . .
chemist! I'll feed him and put him to bed, my darling! Off
you go and enjoy yourself . . . Oh, by the way, someone rang
for you . . . I made a note of it somewhere, I'll try and find
it . . . Name like Mikhailov, or something . . .

IRA. Nikolsky?

MARIA PHILIPPOVNA. No, I think it was Mikhailov.

IRA. I don't know anyone by that name. I wish you'd write down
any messages for me.

MARIA PHILIPPOVNA. I always think I'll remember, and then I
forget. Just think – I cry all night sometimes because I get
this terrible feeling that Pavlik's dead . . .

IRA. What a horrible thought.

MARIA PHILIPPOVNA. And now here he is! My precious boy!

IRA. I've also brought some sausages. They're in the fridge. And
a packet of buckwheat.

MARIA PHILIPPOVNA. Won't *you* eat with us too? Yes, you will!
You look so pale.

IRA. I'd better run. And as for what's going on at the dacha, it's a
nightmare. The roof leaks in the neighbours' half of the
house.

MARIA PHILIPPOVNA. Did it fall off?

IRA. Rotted. And now it's raining . . .

MARIA PHILIPPOVNA. Rain . . . I wouldn't know; I hardly ever go out. I just sit here and worry about you.

IRA. Anyway, I ended up by inviting them into my part, and then Pavlik gets ill with a temperature between thirty-nine and forty. Can you imagine? And those people are so difficult to get on with . . .

MARIA PHILIPPOVNA. You shouldn't let yourself be such a doormat. You ask them in, but what about me? You should have asked me to come down and stay. Here am I, your mother, all on my own . . .

IRA (*exasperated*). D'you think we want to spend the summer listening to your endless complaining?

MARIA PHILIPPOVNA. Don't you shout at me! You're just neurotic!

PAVLIK'S VOICE. What's neurotic, mum?

MARIA PHILIPPOVNA (*shouts*). *She's* neurotic!

PAVLIK'S VOICE. Neurotic yourself!

IRA. Right, we won't stay for lunch. We'll go – now, and that's that.

MARIA PHILIPPOVNA. That just shows how neurotic you are. Can't even spare a plate of soup for her old mother. Go on, off you go, have your fun. Think I can't see what you want? In a moment Pavlik and I will have a bite to eat, I'll read to him and he'll go to sleep. Don't mind me, I can climb back into harness again . . . And what did you do with *Mary Poppins*? You've given away everything in the house, so the boy has nothing to read . . . I wonder if you even think of yourself as my daughter any longer.

IRA *stalks out, slamming the door.*

Oh, Granny's got such a sore tummy, it aches and aches . . . Could be a hernia . . . or something . . .

Scene Two

IRA's *verandah at the dacha. A key clicks in the lock. Enter* FYODOROVNA, *who switches on the light. She is followed, cautiously, by*

the other tenants of the dacha, carrying bundles and camp-beds:
SVETLANA, TATYANA, MAXIM *and* ANTON. *Last to appear,*
framed majestically in the doorway, is LEOKADIA, *with an open*
umbrella. They all look extremely scruffy and rumpled. The two boys
immediately run off again.

FYODOROVNA. Now look – I'm letting you in here at my own
    risk. You can stay in this part for tonight, and then we'll have
    to see. We can't sleep all hugger-mugger like last night . . . I
    need my sleep. She won't be back till tomorrow evening at
    the earliest. And if Pavlik's still coughing, she may stay and
    take him to the doctor. She said she might. So that'll take
    another day or so.

SVETLANA. We're like refugees.

TATYANA. Or bloody partisans. Like in the war.

FYODOROVNA. Will you want to use her room? It's locked.

SVETLANA. I don't know. Maybe.

FYODOROVNA. I haven't got the key.

SVETLANA. In that case, we won't. We're not going to break it
    open. The kids can sleep on the sofa, and I'm off to do my
    night shift. (*To* TATYANA:) Where will you sleep?

TATYANA. Anton and I are going to sleep on the camp-beds.
    Otherwise Maxim will get up to his tricks. He'll pinch Anton.
    He can sleep on his own tonight.

SVETLANA. But you won't get any sleep. Do you really want to
    stay awake all night? You must sleep, otherwise you get so
    ratty and bad-tempered.

TATYANA. Anton will make a fuss if I'm not near him.

SVETLANA. Nonsense! Children always used to be locked
    indoors on their own all day. My mother went out to work
    and I was alone all day with the cat. And I managed to grow
    up all right.

TATYANA. Well, that's a matter of opinion.

SVETLANA. You're in a filthy mood today.

    Meanwhile they have been sorting out the furniture and bedding, and
    LEOKADIA *has been installed in an armchair.*

FYODOROVNA (*To* LEOKADIA). That's it. You stay there and by the time Ira's back I'll be off to Moscow to arrange my mother's memorial service. It's almost the anniversary. I'll stay the night with my brother, and you can use my room then. It'll only be for one night, but one day at a time, that's what I always say.

SVETLANA. If you ask me, Ira won't be back for some time. I've just got that feeling. It was awkward for her and that Nikolai here.

FYODOROVNA. Just look at that toilet he built for her. That's what I call a man – someone you can rely on.

TATYANA *giggles.*

FYODOROVNA. And all she'd do was give him dirty looks. She's already got a boyfriend in Moscow, you see. He's at the university, she was saying.

TATYANA. Well, at least we've got a new loo.

FYODOROVNA. Shows you what a pair of beautiful eyes will do.

SVETLANA. Her – beautiful eyes? Put her in a sauna, give her a good wash and then they might be beautiful.

TATYANA. Her eyes are big all right.

SVETLANA. But have you noticed? She never laughs.

FYODOROVNA. What's she got to laugh about?

SVETLANA. Not even when she watches a film or something?

TATYANA. She doesn't laugh because she's got a tooth missing. I broke a tooth once and I didn't laugh for a month. If I couldn't help it, I covered my mouth with my sleeve. (*Demonstrates, putting her sleeve in front of her mouth.*)

SVETLANA. Life's not a bundle of fun for us, either, but we laugh.

FYODOROVNA. Good-looking bloke that Nikolai. And how he found a carpenter to build that toilet I'll never know. I've been trying six months to get Volodya to do a job for me. Says he's never got time. Six months I nagged him to come and make me some fence-posts and knock them in. Thirty-five posts at five roubles a piece – plus his usual bottle of vodka – that would have made him nearly 200! Then my son Vadim showed up. I could see his socks were full of holes, so

I bought him two new pairs. *She* never buys him anything.
Sends him to show off his holes to his mother. When I saw
him, honestly, I could've wept . . . Anyway, he starts poking
around – 'Where's my bike, then?' And when he finds it –
'Why's it all rusty?' What does he expect, when it's been lying
under the house for five years? Makes me weep, he does.
Always *demanding* something. But he's a designer – famous,
too. And she's an inspector or something. Swarthy, she is.
Coal-black hair and eyebrows. Like all her family. Descended
from black beetles . . . They've bought themselves a car, so
they can drive out every summer to a plot they bought in the
country. Built a shack on it. Never come and see me, though,
because he knows I don't like the way he married her after
only knowing her two weeks. He used to have such a nice
girl. He went out with her for three years, but no – he has to
marry this one. 'She from Kazan?' I asked him, 'cos she
looked so like a Tartar. 'No, from Ryazan', says he . . .
Vadim thinks this place is his, but he makes me pay for
everything – insurance, repairs, paint. And what am I
supposed to live on? Well, I'm not telling him about the new
toilet. They'll find out soon enough. Soon as Vadim sees it,
he'll say I shouldn't charge less than 320 – no, 350 roubles
rent for this half of the house . . .

SVETLANA. Yes, Nikolai had it done in three days. Say what you
like, he's a real man.

TATYANA. Yes, he looks the sort who gets things done.

SVETLANA. I've got this neighbour, Shura. She comes to me and
says: 'Look, Svetlana, for God's sake introduce me to some
man – any man, I don't care who he is.' Thought I'd
introduce her to some of my patients. Her husband and
three-year-old son were killed when the taxi they were in
crashed, and she survived . . .

TATYANA. Yes, and introduce *me* to some of your patients, too!
Valera's so soaked in booze he can't get up to anything these
days.

SVETLANA. By the way, I wish your Anton wouldn't keep going
on about 'daddy this' and 'daddy that' in front of Maxim –
it's always 'my daddy's coming' or 'my daddy'll do it'.
Maxim finds it hurtful, having lost his own dad. You might
drop a hint to Anton – after all, he's big enough to
understand.

TATYANA (*stretching and yawning*). Yes, it's quite a long time since our 'daddy' came down here. Anton misses him. Time we went home for a bath.

FYODOROVNA (*raising her finger*). Ah – hear that? It's Elka, bringing all those toms here. They were humping around in the loft all last night.

TATYANA. I was wondering what it was making all that row.

FYODOROVNA. They're all after my Elka. She's already forgotten about her kitten. I counted seven of those toms lurking in the strawberry-bed. I don't like sex myself – not men and women, not cats either . . . always after a bit of the other.

Scene Three

The kitchen of NIKOLAI IVANOVICH's *flat in Moscow.* IRA *and* NIKOLAI, *in dressing-gowns, are sitting at the table.*

NIKOLAI IVANOVICH. Go on, eat. Have some pineapple. It's tinned in its own juice. What else is there? Nescafé. Nothing else in the house, I'm afraid. Oh yes, there is! Shall I spread you some caviar on a slice of bread? (*Spreads it.*)

IRA. Pavlik hasn't had caviar for years.

NIKOLAI IVANOVICH. I'll give you some to take home. Drop of port? It's the real stuff – from Portugal. And there's real jasmine tea. And some that's rose-scented. This is ridiculous. Nothing edible in the place. Not even any eggs. Good thing you thought of bringing some bread.

IRA. I made the excuse of going out to buy bread. Went to the bakery, and then I rang you from a phone-box.

NIKOLAI IVANOVICH. How're you feeling? Head better?

IRA. I've forgotten I've even got a head.

NIKOLAI IVANOVICH *laughs a self-satisfied laugh.*

IRA. Is this her dressing-gown?

NIKOLAI IVANOVICH *nods.*

IRA. And her shower-cap in the bathroom?

NIKOLAI IVANOVICH. She's got three of them.

IRA. There was perfume there as well. I used some. And I saw a manicure-set. All gleaming and tidy.

NIKOLAI IVANOVICH. Have another slice of bread and caviar. Have two. Have another drink. It's my mother-in-law who scrubs this place from top to bottom. 'Nikolai', she'll say to me. 'I'll stay at the dacha all week. I'll be coming back to Moscow on Friday.' That's her way of warning me. No awkward meetings. You know what I mean.

IRA. I know what you mean.

NIKOLAI IVANOVICH. Oh, that evening when we walked in the forest until three in the morning and you said to me: 'Take me. Here. Under this fir tree.' I'll never forget the way you said that. I'm your faithful hound. Woof, woof . . ! The place was spotless that Friday, there was nothing for mother-in-law to do. That's because I'm never here these days. I'm tearing down to the country every day, like a lunatic. There was a bit of dusting for her to do, but I think she suspected something. Woof, woof! Go on, stroke me.

IRA. What's the time?

NIKOLAI IVANOVICH. It's only three. In five hours I'll be flying off on an official trip. Now I'll have something to remember while I'm away. (*Stretches.*) Enough for a week.

IRA. I must go home now.

NIKOLAI IVANOVICH. Oh, come on – must you? We'll have something to eat first, then another little lie-down . . . don't go.

IRA. Are you crazy? I've already been away from home since eight . . . But mother's used to it by now. In the past I used to go off on the loose for three or four days at a time . . . By now she'll have put the chain on the door to make sure she hears me when I get back. Tomorrow she'll ring round all her cronies and tell them how I've been out on the tiles. (*Sarcastically:*) She loves me very much.

NIKOLAI IVANOVICH. No, my mother-in-law's quite tolerant. She puts up with me. Since the time I walked out on them – oh yes, I did! – I can do no wrong. She never suspects anything. I'm not married any more. I tried to start a new life with another woman . . . Even bought a nice two-roomed co-operative. But then my daughter Alyona came to me and said: 'Daddy, we can't live without you.' She's my prime responsibility. She's fifteen. In time, that co-op will belong to my daughter. So it turned out for the best. Shall I show you her photo?

IRA. No.

NIKOLAI IVANOVICH. That's her picture on the wall opposite you. You're looking at her. (*Laughs.*) I've got pictures of her everywhere.

IRA. I was fifteen when my mother first found out I was getting up to no good.

NIKOLAI IVANOVICH. You were obviously quite a dish in those days – and you still are! Well, my Alyona's fifteen. Sweet little tits, lovely little bottom! Lucky the man who gets her . . .

IRA. It was then I started running away from home. I slept at railway stations, in the all-night telegraph office, anything rather than go home. God, she was so horrible to me!

NIKOLAI IVANOVICH. You poor thing. Let's go back to bed, my sweet, and I'll comfort you . . . (*Pause.*) Let's go.

IRA. Sometimes there wasn't even anywhere to sit down in railway stations at night. And it's cold in winter. There they all sit, freezing. How people can just sit there in that cold. Kids, too, sitting or sleeping. Such pale little things. I could have killed all those grown-ups for doing that to those kids.

NIKOLAI IVANOVICH. And I expect some men tried to pick you up.

IRA. What?

NIKOLAI IVANOVICH. Weren't there any dirty old men who tried to get off with you?

IRA. Then one morning I went home again and said to my mother: 'You can now celebrate. I'm a woman.' She was frying potatoes. All she said was: 'I've known that for a long time.' And burst into tears.

NIKOLAI IVANOVICH. Who was he? Tell me exactly what happened.

IRA. I . . . I can't remember. I just said it to annoy my mother.

NIKOLAI IVANOVICH. You poor thing! Come on, drink up . . .
No, knock it all back . . . that's better.

IRA. My mother was so furious she cried into the potatoes, and I
just stood there and laughed.

NIKOLAI IVANOVICH. Funny thing – I don't think I've ever
seen you laugh. Let's see you smile!

IRA. No, I don't feel like it.

Pause.

NIKOLAI IVANOVICH. Tell me how it happened that first time.

IRA. I told you, I don't remember. Don't pressure me.

NIKOLAI IVANOVICH. You can't do that to your faithful old
hound, or I might bite you. Grrr! One day, you know, I went
on a bender in the port of Nakhodka, with some old
scrubber called Lubka. I had exactly 25 roubles in my wallet.
I'll always remember that figure. God, she was an old bag.
Anyway, when I woke up next morning I said to her: 'Lubka,
where's my 25 roubles?' And she said: 'Get out, while you're
still in one piece'. And I was feeling like death, I can tell you.
I stumbled along the street, crying, till I got to a phone-box
and called an ambulance. The police came instead. When I
showed my trade union card to the copper – it was all I had
– he literally couldn't believe his eyes. At that time I had
three books in print . . . Well, more like brochures, really.
Descriptions of new manufacturing techniques. He literally
clutched his head. 'We've been looking for you', he said, 'for
nearly three weeks. Your family reported you missing.'

IRA. Look, I've got to go. It's been fun, but Pavlik's at home, my
mother's sick and she'll have to get up to let me in. She's not
well, yet she's refusing to go into hospital for an examination.

NIKOLAI IVANOVICH. No, I'm not letting you go. For one
thing you're tired. We'll go and lie down. And your mother
won't be waiting up for you, she'll have gone to bed. You'll
feel fine in the morning. I'll wake you at seven and drop you
at home on my way to the airport. All in one fell swoop.
We've got to make the most of our time, 'cos there's not
much of it left.

IRA. When you next come down to the dacha, come mushroom
picking in the forest with Pavlik and me.

NIKOLAI IVANOVICH. That's more my mother-in-law's speciality. I'm not very fond of mushrooms. They don't agree with me.

IRA. Pavlik and I just love it. Early morning, dew on the grass. Mist. About four in the morning. Beautiful.

NIKOLAI IVANOVICH. By the way, how's your new loo? All right, is it? Tolerable? Have you tried it out yet?

IRA. Everybody's crazy about it.

NIKOLAI IVANOVICH (*laughs with pleasure; then, seriously:*). I told them to fit a special lock, a type of latch, so that Pavlik can use it easily. Don't give the key to anyone else.

IRA. We never lock it anyway.

NIKOLAI IVANOVICH. Oh, but you should. The others'll foul it up. Know what the loos are like in Germany? All clean and shiny. You could sit there all day! And there's even an embroidered bag for newspapers hanging from a hook.

IRA. Fyodorovna's in charge of the loo. She's already been to Zelenograd and bought a seat.

NIKOLAI IVANOVICH. No, you must take a firm line with the lock. They wouldn't let you use theirs, would they?

IRA. Yes, theirs is absolutely revolting – it's so awful, you can hardly bear to go in there.

NIKOLAI IVANOVICH (*getting worked up*). Remember, Ira, that loo is my personal gift to you.

IRA. I do remember it – every day, and more than once!

NIKOLAI IVANOVICH. Oh yes, before I forget – do you have any other domestic problems?

IRA. I don't think so. I gave them the bicycle tyre and inner tube. You've built me a lovely loo. And that's all my problems solved! Oh yes . . . Look, I don't suppose you could help them mend the roof, could you? Otherwise their half of the house may collapse.

NIKOLAI IVANOVICH. That I can't promise. (*Cheerfully.*) However, when the house becomes yours – fine. After all, why should I put myself out over communal property? They might decide to grab the whole place and leave you out in

the cold. Tell you what – when they've let the place finally go
to rack and ruin . . . you can buy it off them for half price.
I'll help you with all the legal paper-work. It's a highly
desirable property in a marvellous position.

IRA. First I'll have to wait till my great-aunt Vera dies. She's only
seventy-four.

NIKOLAI IVANOVICH. Never mind. She'll die before too long.
We all turn up our toes in the end, as my old dad used to
say. And sure enough he went. Mother too. And I was left on
my own.

IRA. Now I really must go. I wasn't expecting it, but you've
turned out to be a good man (*Kisses his hand.*)

NIKOLAI IVANOVICH. Oh, come now, Ira . . .

IRA. Take care. I'm off. Where are you going tomorrow?

NIKOLAI IVANOVICH. Business trip.

IRA. I mustn't keep you any longer.

NIKOLAI IVANOVICH (*grabs* IRA *by the hand*). Ira darling, Ira my
angel! Please stay another couple of hours! I'll miss you so
much! My night moth! That's what I'll call you from now on
– my moth. Please stay. I'll take you home at seven in the
morning.

IRA. No, take me home now. I haven't got the money for a taxi,
don't you see?

NIKOLAI IVANOVICH. I'll take you! I'll toot the horn outside
your house. I'll miss the plane. And we'll snatch another day
together, my little night moth. I'll phone you from the
airport, send a taxi for you, we'll go to a sauna, then to some
restaurant out of town. What do you say?

IRA. Well . . . no. I've got the washing to do tomorrow. She never
does it. And the shopping, enough for a whole week. Mother
will make such a scene if I don't turn up till the morning.

NIKOLAI IVANOVICH. I have a mother-in-law . . . But I'm a
free agent, dammit! I've got a stamp in my passport that
shows I'm divorced. Didn't you realise that?

IRA. Just take me home. Now.

NIKOLAI IVANOVICH. But we've *agreed*, Ira darling. Seven o'clock sharp! Now let's go to bed. Are you tired?

IRA. Good thing you've got a car.

NIKOLAI IVANOVICH (*very seriously*). I must get a new model. I *must*. See what I mean? *You*, Ira!

IRA. There's something you must understand too.

NIKOLAI IVANOVICH. What are you getting at?

IRA. I had a boyfriend once, some while back. We used to meet every Friday. That was the day he kept for me. I'd phone and he'd say: 'As usual', or 'Sorry I can't make it today, call me next week'. So it was always me who had to ring him. There was one good thing about him: he lived conveniently near a metro station. Even so, I missed the last train every time, and on my wages I couldn't afford taxis. At first I felt too shy to ask him for the fare, and then I thought – why the hell not? So I asked for the money. And it all fell into place: I was worth the price of a taxi. I was a taxi! But soon the whole thing fizzled out. Either he couldn't spare the money, or I got fed up with taking the initiative. I know it's stupid, but all day I've kept thinking: I must get you to give me five roubles for the taxi-fare!

NIKOLAI IVANOVICH. What else did he give you? I'm jealous!

IRA. End of story. I'm going.

NIKOLAI IVANOVICH. Of course I'd give you five roubles. Without a second thought. I'd see you to a cab, put you in and take you home in it. That's the proper thing to do. I've always been like that.

IRA. A girlfriend of mine is always telling me how her husband kisses her feet.

NIKOLAI IVANOVICH. Give me your foot. Yes. Now.

IRA. That's overdoing it. Anyway, you're not my husband.

NIKOLAI IVANOVICH. To me, you're my wife. Do you love me?

IRA. I love Pavlik.

NIKOLAI IVANOVICH. You're a woman, that's your right.

IRA. To love her child is the most important thing in the world for a woman. Her child is everything to a woman. Family and love – it's all in that relationship.

NIKOLAI IVANOVICH. In time, your Pavlik will be loved by a girl. But *you* ought to love a man. A man ought to be your hobby, my little moth.

IRA. Come on, take me home. I must get *some* sleep. Mother never lets me sleep on in the morning. She sends Pavlik into my room to pat me on the head so that I don't sleep too long! Once he actually hit me on the head with a spoon.

NIKOLAI IVANOVICH. All the more reason to get your sleep here, and then I'll drop you off at home on my way to the airport.

IRA. I'll walk.

NIKOLAI IVANOVICH. Look, it's time you got yourself sorted out. If you don't have your own car, then be sure you have enough for a taxi. You must start seeing further than the end of your nose. Look, let me take you in hand. I'll help you find a place in our system. You speak languages – that's a big plus-point. Ninka, my assistant at the ministry – she's not exactly a high-flyer, but she's already been to Czechoslovakia a couple of times.

IRA. With you?

NIKOLAI IVANOVICH. What – feeling jealous already? I've got a common-law wife, Rimma, to do that. Don't be jealous, little bird. I love you. I have a right to a little joy in my life.

IRA. I've got a headache.

NIKOLAI IVANOVICH. We'll soon fix that. Up you get, Ira.

IRA. OK, I'll go. Just give me five roubles.

NIKOLAI IVANOVICH. Six! I'll give you six! But don't leave me. You're my only joy! What sort of a life do I have? I knock myself out running round in circles, like a squirrel in a cage. My ex-wife had her bit on the side for three years. My daughter Alyona already smokes, the local girls out at the dacha have already tried to beat her up because she looked twice at one of the boys. We only just managed to stop them. Kids grow up so fast . . . (*Relapses into reflective silence.*)

IRA. I've got a splitting headache.

NIKOLAI IVANOVICH. My poor little moth! You should have diamonds, a car, your own flat away from your mother – just look at yourself. You're gorgeous! You should change all those things you're wearing, and what's underneath them. You deserve gold, platinum (*In a transport of delight.*) God, and when I think what cows some women are! (*Laughs.*)

IRA. I won't let you go on this trip. I'm not going to let you out of my sight.

Exeunt.

PAVLIK'S VOICE. Mummy, the stars seem to be changing shape. First they're big, then they're small. Let me tell you a fairy-story. The moon flew into a hospital to have a tooth out. The tooth had broken, it was just dangling on a bit of skin, so they pulled it out and gave her a false tooth. She flew in at my window and whispered about the tooth into my ear. She says there are lovely birds flying in the sky – sparrows, crows, woodpeckers, rooks. And she says she can fly very, very fast, faster than the birds. And she has a tiny little tail. And she can run very fast, too. And she crawls a bit, sometimes, too. And she can use scissors, because she's got hands, only she doesn't like doing it when she's sad.

Scene Four

Koktebel, a resort on the Black Sea. IRA *is in a telephone-box, furiously dialling and re-dialling a number.*

LIFEGUARD'S VOICE. All swimmers return to the safety-zone!

IRA (*coming out of the phone-box; furiously*). How can it be engaged all this time? Has she hanged herself on the cord, or what?

A YOUNG MAN, *wearing shorts and a cheap cloth cap with a yellow plastic peak, shuts the thick book he has been reading and goes nonchalantly into the phone-box.*

YOUNG MAN (*dials, then speaks*). Hello! Mum? How are you? We're here, in Koktebel . . . Yes, we have! We're fixed up nicely . . . Little Sasha, Natasha and I have been studying ants on the doorstep! They've seen the sea, they're absolutely crazy about it. They filled their sunhats with pebbles and lugged them all the way home . . . Not bad: we've found a

decent place to stay and it's not too crowded – not high
season yet. There's one snack-bar and one restaurant open.
We tried to get in, but it's not up to much. They're going to
open a milk-bar soon, where there'll be kasha and cream
cheese. Just what's needed for the kids. So far we've bought
bread, milk and tinned food. And you'll never believe this –
rose-petal jam! Strawberries are seven roubles a kilo in the
market. Just imagine! We bought a hundred grammes each
for the kids. They fairly wolfed them down . . ! Three to a
room, so I sleep outside under an awning. Luxury . . ! What
. . ? Loads of fresh sea air and a great view of the mountains
. . . Can you send us some warm things as soon as poss.:
sweaters, jackets and trousers for the kids . . . And my green
jacket . . . Send them poste restante. I don't know our
landlady's address. Anyway, she has thirty-five lodgers in her
house . . ! A parcel might go astray . . . What do I want an
umbrella for here? OK, send it if you like. Everything's just
great here . . ! Must stop, I'm out of money . . . You OK . . ?
'Bye . . . (*Hangs up and comes out of the phone-box. Nods as he
counts the money in his palm*).

IRA *goes back into the box. When she speaks, she keeps her voice
down, so that the* YOUNG MAN *won't hear her, but in this she is
unsuccessful. She dials, and a look of relief comes over her face when
her mother answers.*

IRA. Hello! Mama . . ? Thank God. I haven't got many coins. I'm
calling (*Dropping her voice.*) from the dacha . . ! From the daa-
acha! I told you before – the roof's leaking . . ! The roof, for
God's sake! (*Lowers her voice again.*) And it's pouring with rain
here. Everything's soaking wet . . . It's not raining in
Moscow? Funny. We're soaked through. I have to keep
emptying the buckets . . ! (*Lowers her voice.*) Buck-ets . . ! Yes. I
need to stay on for a bit longer. How's Pavlik? Only tell me
quickly . . . Right, give him some hot milk with soda last
thing at night. . . . No, I can't get back today, but I'll give
you a call some time tomorrow. So don't use the phone.

MARIA PHILIPPOVNA'S VOICE. Where's that bread you went
out to get two days ago? You were going to bring it! But you
didn't, and now we haven't got any bread. I can't leave
Pavlik, and I'm supposed to be going into hospital today.
Like a fool I lifted Pavlik up, and now I'm in pain.

IRA. You must take care, mama. (*Lowers her voice.*) There's a queue of people outside this phone-box. I'll call you tomorrow. Bye-bye, kisses. Call Aunty Nina and ask her to babysit. Lie to her. Tell her I've run away to the South with my lover. She'll be round like a shot. Must go. (*Lowers her voice.*) It's the roof, the leak. OK, Mama?

Exit YOUNG MAN, *nodding to himself. Enter* NIKOLAI IVANOVICH, *wearing a pair of yellow shorts, the same sort of plastic-peaked cap as the* YOUNG MAN *and dark glasses.*

IRA. Oh, my money's run out. (*Hangs up.*)

IRA *and* NIKOLAI IVANOVICH *sit down on a bench.* NIKOLAI IVANOVICH *looks round uneasily.*

IRA. So tell me how you spent a whole day and a night without me.

NIKOLAI IVANOVICH. I didn't get a wink of sleep last night.

IRA. That shows you were missing me. Congratulations.

NIKOLAI IVANOVICH. Not called for. Alyona, it turns out, is a very light sleeper. Three of us in one room. You can imagine what it's like. And this is called having a holiday?! I can't move a finger without Alyona waking up: 'Daddy, you're snoring. You're snoring like a pig.' Look, I've only got a few minutes. They're doing inhalations. Something to clear the sinuses.

IRA. I slept well. First time for years. And I was in the water for most of the day. Did you see me from the beach? I swam to the bit where you were sunbathing.

NIKOLAI IVANOVICH. Yes, I saw you.

IRA. Did you like the bikini I bought?

NIKOLAI IVANOVICH. I was sitting with my back to you.

IRA. I noticed you turned round to avoid me . . . There's nothing decent to eat in this place, you know. How do people with kids manage?

NIKOLAI IVANOVICH. Imagine the problems Rimma's having with Alyona. I wonder why on earth I chose to come here on a business trip.

IRA. But I'm having the time of my life! I went for another swim last night. Then I waited and waited for you . . . I left the key under the mat. Why didn't you come?

NIKOLAI IVANOVICH. I had to stay at home.

IRA. Wouldn't it be wonderful to bring Pavlik here? I was an idiot. I could have picked him up, still half asleep, and brought him with me – just grabbed some clean clothes and taken him. When I went into our room to get my passport . . . And I didn't even kiss the top of his head as he slept. Didn't want to wake him, I suppose. I can't believe I didn't even think to kiss him.

NIKOLAI IVANOVICH. So what do you plan to do now?

IRA. I'm going to that little bay round the headland. Coming with me?

NIKOLAI IVANOVICH. Look, could you give me your key for an hour and a half or so?

IRA. My key?

NIKOLAI IVANOVICH. Why d'you think I arranged to come down here on a business trip? The flesh is weak, and that includes Rimma. I'll put the key back under the mat. All right?

IRA (*gives him the key*). When am I going to see you?

NIKOLAI IVANOVICH. I have to make a phone-call at ten tomorrow morning. So come here. Provided *they* don't decide to come along too. If they do, you'd better keep clear.

IRA. If they do come, when *will* I see you?

NIKOLAI IVANOVICH. I'll make arrangements and let you know. Right – their inhalation-session must be over by now. Trouble is, Alyona seems to have a bit of a chill and is coughing. It's a nightmare. (*Exit.*)

Scene Five

Evening at the dacha in Romanovka. Wearing her ancient, threadbare dressing-gown with its holes under each armpit, FYODOROVNA *is fiddling with a large rusty key, in an attempt to open the door into* IRA's *room. Eventually she opens it.* SVETLANA, *supporting* LEOKADIA, *prepares to go into the room; in her free hand she is carrying a chair.*

FYODOROVNA. There. Lucky I found this key. Otherwise I can see you two will freeze to death. (*Opens the door.*)

SVETLANA *leads* LEOKADIA *into* IRA's *room.*

SVETLANA (*re-entering*). She'll be warmer in there. When Ira gets back I'll tell her right to her face: while you were away having your little fling, we had to do something to stop the kids catching cold. You can like it or lump it, I'll say.

FYDOROVNA. Don't worry, she won't be back for a while yet. Her Pavlik's poorly.

SVETLANA. At last I can get a proper night's sleep. I've waited long enough. During the day the kids won't let me rest and at night the patients keep me awake . . . How quiet it is today. Maxim on his own just loafs around with nothing to do. Why can't it be like this all the time? He even sat down to read a book. That's my dream – to have a quiet, clean child who doesn't fight all day.

FYODOROVNA. When someone's alone, who's there to fight with? He should follow my example. I feel so sorry for your old lady. Sits there quiet as a mouse, eyes wide open, and never even asks for anything.

Meanwhile the two women are carrying camp-beds, mattresses and bed-linen into IRA's *room.*

SVETLANA. She has everything brought to her. She doesn't have to ask.

FYODOROVNA. She's grieving for her son, I expect.

SVETLANA. She'd do better taking an interest in her grandson while I'm busting a gut to make ends meet.

FYODOROVNA. She couldn't be running after him at her age. She lives in another world.

SVETLANA. I've got no time for her. Never had one word of affection or encouragement out of her. She simply takes everything as her due. My husband, her son, was a lieutenant-colonel . . .

FYODOROVNA. Quite a high-up, then . . .

SVETLANA. And she was a general's wife. Always the great lady . . .

FYODOROVNA. I can tell that. She never asks for anything –

looks, but doesn't ask. It's a pleasure to look after someone like that.

SVETLANA. She's been like that since her son died.

FYODOROVNA. That's what I mean. She misses him.

SVETLANA. There's nothing special about loving your own child. Loving other people's kids, that's the real test. (*Thumps her chest with her fist.*)

FYODOROVNA. Ah, but who can do that these days?

SVETLANA. I know Maxim won't look after me in my old age.

FYODOROVNA. You're right. He won't.

SVETLANA (*trotting back and forth with bedding, etc.*). Should've had a daughter.

FYODOROVNA. My Vadim doesn't look after me. And nor does his wife, the dark one. She's a miner's daughter. Rough lot.

SVETLANA. We give them all we've got and they give us nothing back. Why is it like that?

FYODOROVNA. God knows. I want nothing from no one. Never even ask God for anything. I live here alone all winter, and every night I wash my feet before I go to bed. When they come to bury me I want to have clean heels. Don't know why I believe in God, 'cos I've got no sins on my conscience. Last year I went into town to arrange for a requiem service for my mother. Some old biddy in the church started shouting at me. Had a job getting away from her, only shut her up by shoving some money into her hand. Gave me quite a turn. So this year I've been wondering – to go or not to go. I always remember my old mum, but where else than church can you light a candle?

SVETLANA. I hate churchy people. They're no better than us, but they think they are.

FYODOROVNA. I like a bit of class, though.

SVETLANA. They're all snobs. I hate 'em.

FYODOROVNA. I've always liked a better class of person. A real gentleman or lady never bothers anyone. Always thinks of themselves last. Never uses bad language.

SVETLANA. You just try living with people like that. Any minute you may do the wrong thing or give a wrong look. I went through all that. My husband was one of them. Me, I'd shout first and think second. Then I'd get a conscience about it and say I was wrong, but not before. (*Calls:*) You all right, mother? (*Pause.*) She never answers.

FYODOROVNA. No, she's nodding.

SVETLANA. She's so worn out, she can only say thank you like that – the way they do it on parade. Been raining for a fortnight now and I've been humping her around like a cat with a kitten. She's dirtied everything she's got to wear. Good thing I don't love her, or I'd go off my rocker when I come to bury her. Can't bear even to think about it. As it is, when she does die I'll have good memories of her.

FYODOROVNA. Well-bred people always leave a good memory of them and it lasts forever. I remember my mother like that, and shall till my dying day. And my younger brother too. He died of a heart attack, and she went soon after him. Couldn't bear to go on.

SVETLANA. That one in there'll outlast all of us. It's in the blood.

FYODOROVNA (*sighs*). Well, we'll all be better off in the next world. I'm going to go and have a little nap. You stay here, and if Ira comes you can move in with me. By then I'll have made up my mind about going to the church . . . How long are you going to suffer like this, Svetlana?

SVETLANA (*laughs*). All my life!

Scene Six

Koktebel. The same telephone-box; IRA *is in it, dialling a number.*

LIFEGUARD'S VOICE. Hey, you on the lilo. Back to the swimming zone!

IRA. Hello . . . Mama? I'm very short of coins. Quickly – how is Pavlik?

MARIA PHILIPPOVNA (*on the other side of the stage, in a spotlight*). Hello. How are you?

IRA. How are *you?*

MARIA PHILIPPOVNA's *voice is dull and expressionless.*

MARIA PHILIPPOVNA. Pavlik's so-so. And I'm so-so.

IRA. Mama, we still have this trouble with the roof.

Pause.

MARIA PHILIPPOVNA. Don't tell me now. Don't interrupt. I've *got* to go into hospital today. I can't move. Didn't sleep at all last night. Terrible pain. Can you hear me?

IRA. Yes.

MARIA PHILIPPOVNA (*in the same expressionless tone*). I'm in pain, Ira.

IRA. How's Pavlik?

MARIA PHILIPPOVNA. I told you. So-so. Coughed all night. You must come back at once. Pavlik's going to be on his own. Lyuba's gone to see her grandchildren. Misha's not well, Nina Nikiforovna isn't answering the phone . . . I've rung everybody I could think of . . . But there's no one . . . None of them can come. You'll *have* to come. I've already packed my suitcase, Pavlik will be alone. I've fed him for the last time. It's a good thing you rang. At least I can go and die with a clear conscience. Goodbye for the last time.

IRA (*despairingly*). All right. I'll come, but first I've got to borrow some money for the fare. It's raining here . . . The trains aren't running. The track's flooded. The normal timetable's been suspended. Do you understand? Because of a technical fault.

MARIA PHILIPPOVNA. Whose fault . . ? Come back before it's too late.

IRA. Just don't leave Pavlik on his own, mother – I implore you. Wait till I get there.

MARIA PHILIPPOVNA. No more ifs and buts – *come back.*

The spotlight on MARIA PHILIPPOVNA *goes out abruptly.*

IRA. I've run out of coins! I'm relying on you. Kisses.

IRA *comes out of the telephone-box, and collapses on the bench in a state of near-shock. Enter* NIKOLAI IVANOVICH, *glancing around furtively.*

NIKOLAI IVANOVICH. Trouble, I'm afraid.

IRA (*happy to see him*). Darling!

NIKOLAI IVANOVICH (*teeth gritted, hardly moving his lips*). Not now. Not now.

IRA. God, how I've missed you! I love you more than I can say. You're the only joy of my life!

NIKOLAI IVANOVICH. No, you don't love me.

IRA. I do. It's weird. Yesterday on the beach I found myself gazing at you in admiration.

NIKOLAI IVANOVICH. That's just what you shouldn't have been doing!

IRA (*ecstatically*). I'm not asking you for anything. I'm simply obsessed by you.

NIKOLAI IVANOVICH. There's always a cure for that.

IRA. No there isn't!

NIKOLAI IVANOVICH. If you really love me, you'll leave here immediately. That's what I came to tell you.

IRA. Leave? Why?

NIKOLAI IVANOVICH. Because I'm asking you to.

IRA. You don't have to kick me out like that. I'm leaving anyway, but in my own time.

NIKOLAI IVANOVICH. No, now! Alyona and Rimma picked you out of the crowd on the beach today. Alyona's been in floods of tears. What a performance . . ! I do all I can for you, run every risk to see you, and all you can do is stare at me on the beach for all to see.

IRA. Aren't I allowed to look at you?

NIKOLAI IVANOVICH. No, you're not.

IRA. All right, I won't . . . Look, I want to ask you one favour . . .

NIKOLAI IVANOVICH (*perfunctorily*). How's your son? Better?

IRA. So-so.

NIKOLAI IVANOVICH. And your mother?

IRA. Same old performance.

NIKOLAI IVANOVICH. In that case, give me your key.

IRA. What, again?!

NIKOLAI IVANOVICH. I want you on a plane and out of here. And don't come back!

IRA. If it isn't my mother shouting at me, it's you.

NIKOLAI IVANOVICH. Try and understand. Alyona is a highly-strung child, and she's reacting very badly to having seen you. She can be violent.

IRA. She's fifteen.

NIKOLAI IVANOVICH. She's still a child!

IRA. So what. I was a child too.

NIKOLAI IVANOVICH. At her age you were already a little tart – you told me so.

IRA. Kolya, darling . . .

NIKOLAI IVANOVICH. To put it bluntly, Ira – kindly get out of here.

IRA. Wait till she gets a little bun in the oven, then you'll see how much of a child she is.

NIKOLAI IVANOVICH. I'll knock the bastard's block off, whoever he may be! The point is, that's none of your business. You know how much my family means to me. You just interfere. You shouldn't have come here in the first place.

IRA. I've as much right to be here as anyone else.

NIKOLAI IVANOVICH. You're cheapening yourself. You've lost control. Just look at yourself. What have you become? I'm ashamed to say it.

IRA. There's nothing shameful about being in love.

NIKOLAI IVANOVICH. But you're behaving shamefully! Just stop pressuring me and needling me.

IRA. I'll go wherever I like.

NIKOLAI IVANOVICH. You had no right to be on that beach, anyway. You don't have the right pass. Just who d'you think you are?

IRA. What, isn't there room at the seaside for both of us?

NIKOLAI IVANOVICH. No. Not for you.

IRA. But you don't own the place.

NIKOLAI IVANOVICH. There are rules and they have to be obeyed.

IRA. I like it here and I shall stay here.

NIKOLAI IVANOVICH. In that case, *we* will go. We'll have to cancel everything, waste our accommodation vouchers, treatment at the spa booked in advance – everything. Take them back to the dacha outside Moscow! Is that what you want? Have you no human feelings?

IRA. Aren't you afraid she'll see me at the dacha too? Because I'm going to be there all summer. There's only one river and everyone bathes in it.

NIKOLAI IVANOVICH. You're right. So the best thing is for you to go. Here, take these forty roubles (*Gets out his wallet, slowly counts out the money, lays aside forty roubles and puts the rest back.*) There you are!

IRA doesn't pick up the money. NIKOLAI IVANOVICH *puts the money on the bench beside her.* IRA *gets up, goes into the telephone-box and dials a number.* NIKOLAI IVANOVICH *starts to go, then hesitantly picks up the money.*

NIKOLAI IVANOVICH. People like you should be hounded from the face of this earth.

He starts to go again, but comes back.

Have you any idea what Alyona might do to herself because of all this?

IRA. Yes, I know. (*Turns away from him.*)

NIKOLAI IVANOVICH *slowly walks off. Unexpectedly, he wipes away a tear with the back of his hand. Exit, with the air of a deeply wronged man.*

IRA (*in the phone-box*). Hello . . ! Is that you, Pavlik . . ? Listen, sweetheart, I want to talk to Granny. Only call her quickly, because I haven't got much money for the phone . . . But first, quick, tell me – how are you . . ? A bit better? Lovely. (*Smiles.*) All right, baby. Now be a good boy and let me talk to Granny . . . She's gone out? Fine. At least that means she

can walk. Are you on your own . . ? Good boy! Well done!
What did she say . . ? Ah, she's gone to the hospital . . . Yes,
of course I'm coming home . . . I just wanted to ring you
first to see how you were . . . Pavlik, have you got any water
. . ? What d'you mean you don't know . . ? Is there any in
the kettle . . ? Oh yes, you can't lift it up. Well, use the tap
then . . . You turn the tap on, you take a glass . . . No, of
course you can – I'm allowing you to get it out of the tap
now. Have you got any bread . . ? (*Bites her lower lip to stop
herself crying.*) Right, then open the fridge. You can do that,
can't you . . ? No, you're allowed to use the tap now. Open
the fridge, look carefully inside to see what's there and I'll
tell you what you can eat . . . Run and have a look, and then
I'll call you back in a few minutes. Kisses . . . Hurry, now.

IRA *comes out, because the* YOUNG MAN *of the day before is
waiting to use the telephone. He looks dishevelled and is carrying a
shopping-bag. The* YOUNG MAN *goes into the telephone-box and
dials.*

YOUNG MAN (*after a short pause*). Mama! (*Laughs.*) It's me. Listen,
we've got a bit of a problem. We let Sashka stay in the water
a bit too long . . . Yes. But we can't find a thermometer here
. . . I'm sure it's nothing serious. Look, have you sent off that
parcel of warm things yet . . ? Oh good. Then can you put in
the contents of the medicine-chest as well, please? We didn't
reckon on needing them . . . Yes, everything, including some
mustard-plasters . . . I doubt it. So go to the Moscow-
Feodosia train. Somebody will probably take it for you and
bring it down here. I'll meet the train at this end . . . (*Laughs.*)
How can we tell, when we can't find a thermometer . . ! You
are a funny old thing. I'll call you again this evening. Don't
use the phone then, because there are huge queues at the
phone-boxes in the evening. Kisses. (*Hangs up and comes out of
the telephone-box.*)

IRA (*rushes up to him*). Look, would you like to buy a raincoat for
your wife? Give-away price – forty roubles. It cost ninety, and
it's practically new. Made in Germany.

YOUNG MAN (*smiling*). No, but thanks all the same . . . We don't
need it. We're getting a parcel of warm things from home.

IRA. I'm absolutely broke. Take it for your wife. I need the fare
for the flight to Moscow and I have to get myself to the
airport.

YOUNG MAN (*smiling*). The fact is, we can't afford it. We can only just manage as it is . . .

IRA. Please don't go. I must just make one more phone call and then we can talk about it. (*Goes into the telephone-box and dials.*)

YOUNG MAN (*smiling*). You don't understand – there's nothing to talk about. We don't have that sort of money to spare.

IRA (*From the telephone-box*). I'll send it back to you as soon as I arrive . . . Oh God, it's engaged!

YOUNG MAN. It's not up to me, anyway. My wife looks after our money.

IRA. It *can't* be engaged! (*Dials again and again.*) Engaged! Oh Pavlik, didn't you put the receiver back properly?

YOUNG MAN. You see . . . (*Smiling.*) My wife never lets me have any money. Funny thing is, people often come up to me in the street and ask for money or try to sell me things.

IRA (*feverishly dialling*). That means you must have a kind face . . . Engaged! Pavlik hasn't put the receiver back. What am I to do? (*Comes out of the telephone-box.*)

YOUNG MAN. Sorry, I must go (*Smiling.*) I have to buy some milk . . .

IRA (*smiling in desperation*). So let's go and see your wife.

YOUNG MAN. Look, I'm sorry. I must get that milk – it's urgent. I mustn't lose my place in the queue, and the kids aren't well.

IRA. Fine. We'll queue for the milk together, and then go and see your wife.

YOUNG MAN. I'm awfully sorry, but things are in chaos back at our digs. My wife hasn't slept all night, so don't be frightened if she's a bit upset. The kids aren't well . . . try not to upset her . . . the kids, you see . . .

IRA. Of course, I understand. I have a child of my own, for heaven's sake. (*Falters. She is trying very hard not to cry.*) How long can someone go without food and with only water? Five days . . ?

Exeunt.

PAVLIK'S VOICE. While I was sleeping the moon came to see me, flying on wings. She had black eyes, but I wasn't frightened. She had a blue body and a big pink hook, it was pink at the very end and all shiny. She was very beautiful and flapped her wings. She didn't say anything to me. I told her all my troubles. She said to me: 'I don't fly in Moscow'. She doesn't fly in Moscow at all, she said. She used to fly in Moscow, she said. She's really good at flying, and one day she flew in to see us. Then I told her about myself, and how I sometimes talk to myself at night. 'That's all right, my dear, you'll never do anyone any harm by talking', the moon said to me with her little hook. She said she takes talkative people home with her and goes for walks with them. She told me she had some dinner left. And she'd bought some meat . . .

This monologue should be relayed with breaks and interference, as though coming through by radio. It should be intercut with the following dialogue, which the audience only hears:

ANNOUNCER'S VOICE. The departure of the flight from Simferópol to Moscow is delayed until further notice.

AIRPORT OFFICIAL'S VOICE. I've told you – the flight is fully booked . . .

IRA'S VOICE. But he hasn't got any bread!

AIRPORT OFFICIAL'S VOICE. You shouldn't have left him. I can't help you. I can't issue tickets if there are no seats. I can give you some bread if you like. Next, please.

WOMAN'S VOICE. We have to go to a funeral. You were told to move aside, miss. I have a telegram to prove it, we're going to a funeral.

IRA'S VOICE. But I might get there too late!

AIRPORT OFFICIAL'S VOICE. Look here – I can't turn other passengers off the plane just so that you can fly . . . Next, please.

WOMAN'S VOICE. Look, miss, get up off the floor, it's dirty. Stand over there.

MAN'S VOICE. People like her are always trying to jump the queue.

AIRPORT OFFICIAL'S VOICE. Kindly keep this space clear, and

come up to the desk one at a time . . . Will you please stop crawling after me on your knees?! Yes, I'm talking to you, young woman! I don't want to see his photograph. I've got a photo of my own son – want me to show it to you? Anyway, Moscow is not taking any incoming flights for the time being.

Scene Seven

The verandah of the dacha. TATYANA, SVETLANA *and* FYODOROVNA *are having tea. There is a mountain of unwashed crockery on the table.*

SVETLANA. . . . She kept saying: 'Nobody needs me, nobody needs me'. But we need her, only not here. I keep thinking: if only she doesn't come back.

FYODOROVNA. Let her come back, but when the weather's cleared up. Then you can move back into your own half of the house.

SVETLANA. We're better off without her whatever the weather. I keep thinking about her all the time.

TATYANA. If she comes back, we'll have to get out of her rooms.

FYODOROVNA. I can always let her stay in my room. But from now on I'm not letting this place for less than 320 roubles for the season.

SVETLANA. If we go back to our rooms, that means having to use our filthy old bog again – thanks a lot!

FYODOROVNA. That's up to you. But don't say I didn't warn you.

TATYANA (*giggling*). But you can't raise the rent till next year.

FYODOROVNA. She'll have to get her share, 'cos it's her toilet. *You* didn't put it in, did you?

TATYANA. That's rich – *we* have to pay extra for what she earned lying on her back.

SVETLANA. At 160 each that's no joke.

TATYANA. Hang on – there's three of you but only two of us.

SVETLANA. If you mean Leokadia, what about Valera?

TATYANA (*giggling*). Be a squash with three of us.

SVETLANA. That's your problem.

TATYANA. Two of us, three of you . . .Three plus two is five . . . Five into three hundred and twenty . . . (*Thinks.*) Six times five is thirty . . . carry two . . . Four times five is twenty . . .

FYODOROVNA. That's 128 from you and 192 from them. Plus the electric.

SVETLANA. Maxim's almost never indoors.

TATYANA. And what about me? I only spend the odd night here.

SVETLANA. So what? I'm out working every night.

TATYANA. I'd rather go to some holiday camp much farther away from Moscow – otherwise it's nothing but endless shopping, train journeys, greasy saucepans . . . It's like being lashed to a treadmill.

SVETLANA. What about me? Who sits with your Anton?

TATYANA. You don't. Maxim sits with him and punches him.

SVETLANA. My Maxim's not going to grow up a cissy. I'm not going to let him get like *certain* kids I could mention. (*Nods towards* IRA's *room*). I'm not going to let him die young like his father. That's why I do gymnastics with him. And if your Anton doesn't like it, that's his problem.

Enter IRA *and* PAVLIK. PAVLIK *is holding a kitten in his arms.*

IRA. Ah, you're all here.

Tableau.

IRA. We've found your kitten, Fyodorovna. (*Takes the kitten from* PAVLIK.)

Enter MAXIM *and* ANTON, *who stare fascinated at the kitten and stroke it.* PAVLIK *also strokes it. He has a scarf round his head, topped by a woolly hat. He is wearing a checked shirt, long stockings with holes at the knees, shorts held up by braces – the standard dress for children in Soviet kindergartens.* MAXIM *wears shorts and a smart T-shirt adorned with a slogan.* ANTON *is also in shorts and T-shirt, but his T-shirt is plain.*

IRA. It was extraordinary. We were walking here from the station and there was the kitten sitting at the corner in the middle of the road. A dog was just going to pounce on him. He was so brave. He arched his back like this (*She demonstrates.*) and wouldn't budge. (*Holds the kitten in one hand and a hold-all in the other.*)

PAVLIK *takes the hold-all from her.*

Pavlik chased the dog off, and we tried to catch the kitten, but it ran away. We started looking for it in a clump of weeds, and then we discovered it had gone under the fence and out the other side. And there it was, drinking milk from a saucer and this nice woman was stroking it. (*Laughs.*)

Amazed at this change in IRA – *she is actually laughing* – TATYANA *nudges* SVETLANA *and nods towards* IRA.

IRA. She'd been looking after him all the time since he went lost – he'd simply run away to her place, three doors down the road. What he must have gone through before she rescued him! (*Presses the kitten to her cheek.*) There are dogs in all the other houses: Jack here, Kuzya next door.

FYODOROVNA. Oooh, it doesn't bear thinking about. I'll get the princess herself. (*Goes off, calling out in a high-pitched voice*). Elka, Elka . . . here puss, puss, puss . . . Elka, Elka . . . Where's she got to . . ? Where are you, Elka . . . (*Exit.*)

IRA (*in the same buoyant happy tone*). Oh and my mother was taken off to hospital. She went straight into theatre. It turns out to be a strangulated hernia. If she'd gone in the least bit later, it could've done for her. I'd taken myself off for a couple of days and knew nothing about it, so Pavlik was left on his own for a whole day. And part of the night. I couldn't get a seat on the plane to come back. There were simply no tickets, but I screamed at the booking clerk: 'For God's sake help me, my boy's on his own, his grandmother's left him locked in the flat! His grandmother's gone to hospital and the boy's ill.' He said: 'Just settle for one story at a time – either the boy's ill or the grandmother's ill, then you can go down on your knees and beg.' So I did. It was hysterical. (*Laughs joyously.*)

TATYANA *nudges* SVETLANA, *meaning 'Look, she's laughing'.*

IRA. Then a man from Moscow said to him: 'Captain, I have a container-full of urgent freight that must leave today.' And the booking-clerk was already writing out my ticket.

SVETLANA. I'd never go down on my knees, not even to a
captain.

IRA. But it gets even better: I had a ticket, but Moscow wouldn't
accept a passenger flying in a cargo plane. (*Laughs.*) So I went
to the pilots, and they got me on to the first outgoing aircraft.
I said: 'No plane that I fly with is going to have an accident,
because if it did my little boy would die!' And they roared
with laughter! Then when I got home I couldn't open the
front door! (*Laughs.*) Pavlik, it turned out, had fallen asleep on
the doormat in the hall! And my God, the rain in Moscow. I
had no raincoat – *of course!* (*Laughs.*) I sold it to a gypsy
woman.

SVETLANA. The sky's been looking grim here too . . . Oh look,
it's started to rain again. (*Gets up, goes to the door and looks out.*)
This weather is crazy.

TATYANA. There's mushrooms growing on the walls in the other
half of the house.

IRA. I'm so glad to be back here. (*To the kitten.*) Are you glad too?
His little heart's pounding. Look at his face – it used to be so
vacant, like a baby's, and now it shows traces of suffering.
(*Hugs the kitten.*) His tiny little heart's pounding like a
sledgehammer.

Enter FYODOROVNA, *carrying the cat. The cat, as usual, struggles
and jumps out of her arms.*

FYODOROVNA. She lost it, now she can find it for herself. She's
already been out on the tiles with those toms again. Have
you forgotten your little baby, eh? Have you . . ? Yes, she
has. Expect her milk's dried up too. We'll take 'em both up
to the loft. Can't leave a kitten loose out of doors here – that
Jack'll gobble him up in no time.

ANTON, MAXIM, FYODOROVNA *and* IRA *go off in a
procession, running through the rain clutching cat and kitten.*

SVETLANA. I told you – she was off on the razzle with that
Nikolai. And Fyodorovna kept saying it was a 'bad omen'.
She dreamt someone was spreading something black on a
piece of bread.

TATYANA (*giggling*). Perhaps it was caviar?

SVETLANA. So what happens to us now?

TATYANA. I thought we'd decided. We're not budging.

Enter IRA *and* FYODOROVNA.

IRA (*joyously*). They recognised each other! Fyodorovna was holding Elka and I showed her the kitten, who started to suckle. Elka jumped as though she'd been scalded.

FYODOROVNA. Outgrown it, you see.

IRA. But the moment the kitten started to mew, Elka lay down again and let him have it.

FYODOROVNA. Well, I'm fed up with those cats prancing about over my head at night when I want to sleep.

IRA. Fyodorovna let Pavlik, Maxim and Anton sit up in the attic with the cats. The three boys are being so quiet and good together.

FYODOROVNA. They're brothers.

TATYANA. Third cousins twice removed – hardly brothers.

FYODOROVNA. All men are brothers!

IRA (*cheerfully*). Not all – some are sisters.

SVETLANA (*sighs*). Look, Ira – I'm sorry, but we're not moving out of here. We've all had enough of this traipsing backwards and forwards.

TATYANA *bursts into giggles.*

IRA. Stay, for heaven's sake. It suits me fine. I'll be having to drag myself off to see my mother in hospital every day. She's in intensive care at the moment, so she can't see anyone, but from tomorrow she'll be moved into a general ward. That means I can leave Pavlik with you – what a relief.

SVETLANA. With *me*, you mean.

IRA (*smiling*). There's no one else I can rely on.

SVETLANA. You should learn to rely on yourself.

TATYANA (*giggling*). Now that you've got that lovely, smart new bog.

IRA. Are you suggesting Pavlik and I should move? Where to?

SVETLANA. We haven't touched your beds in that room. We're

not savages, you know . . . Now look, Fyodorovna: now that Ira's here, the rent stays the same – two hundred and forty. Split three ways, that's eighty each.

TATYANA. There's three of you, Svetlana.

SVETLANA *(firmly)*. Eighty each. And if anyone doesn't like it they can clear off.

TATYANA. But I only sleep here.

IRA. I shall only be sleeping here, too, for the time being. Thank God I've already paid Fyodorovna a hundred in advance.

TATYANA. And we do the shopping and cooking on a rota. And Maxim has got to stop bullying the others. OK? Bully boys end up in the yard. And just you remember that, Svetlana, if one of the other boys gets beaten up. There are two of us now!

FYODOROVNA. Ira, you should bring your mum down here to recuperate. She can sleep in my room. We two old people will get along fine together. It's so boring, being old!

IRA *(smiling weakly)*. I'd rather go and visit her there.

FYODOROVNA *(not listening)*. I won't charge her much. Let's say seventy on top of your twenty. You can't say fairer than that, can you?

SVETLANA. Just look at that rain.

LEOKADIA *appears in the doorway of the adjoining room, holding an open umbrella.*

LEOKADIA *(in an unexpectedly loud, clear voice:)*. The roof is leaking in that room.

Tableau

Curtain